Welcome

When Rome fell to the sword, its death throes affected more than just the city and its immediate vicinity. For centuries the Roman Empire had commanded great tranches of Europe, and with its light snuffed out, an age of darkness fell on the lands that had once basked in the Roman sun. Yet though the period between Rome's fall and the Norman conquest of Britain was riven with conflict, it was not as dark an age as you might at first suppose. Turn the page to begin a journey into an age of drama, adventure, and exploration…

Contents

- **6** — **Darkness to light**
  Are the stereotypes about the Early Middle Ages true?

- **8** — **Everything you wanted to know about the Dark Ages but were too afraid to ask**
  Debunking misconceptions about the Dark Ages

- **14** — **Last days of the West**
  The earth-shattering collapse of the Roman Empire and its implications for the territories it controlled

- **20** — **The Byzantine Empire**
  The Eastern Roman Empire

- **26** — **Rise of the holy empire**
  The role of the Church

- **30** — **The Seven Kingdoms**
  The Heptarchy of Anglo-Saxon England

- **38** — **Blood and sea**
  A timeline of the Viking Age

- **42** — **Early Viking raids on Britain**
  From Lindisfarne to full invasion

- **46** — **When Vikings ruled the waves**
  The terror of the Dark Age seas

- **54** — **Lost kingdoms of the Vikings**
  The story of Viking expansion

- **64** — **Charlemagne**
  A powerful ruler emerges

- **68** — **Kingdom of the Northmen**
  How Normandy became a formidable power across Europe

- **72** — **Alfred versus the Vikings**
  The war for England

Contents

78 The Danelaw
What happened when the Vikings settled in England?

82 Emperor of the North
How King Cnut built a North Sea empire

90 The queen who ruled kings
How Emma of Normandy changed England's fate

94 The pious king with no heir
Why Edward the Confessor threw England into chaos

98 The last Anglo-Saxon king
Harold Godwinson's short but eventful reign

102 The last Viking king
Harald Hardrada bids to seize the English throne

108 William the Conqueror
How and why the duke of Normandy became king

116 Clash of crowns 1066
The complex and brutal conflict that shaped the rest of British history

126 The Norman conquests
How the ex-Vikings of Normandy carved out kingdoms across Europe and beyond

Darkness to Light

Are the stereotypes about the Early Middle Ages really true, or a Renaissance-era fiction?

The Dark Ages. The name alone conjures an image of a bloody, brutal world; one where crude peasants dwell miserably in fetid huts until they're burnt out of their rough villages by a cruel overlord or invading horde. The Church looks on serenely, interested in nothing more than keeping its flock uneducated enough to lap up its doctrine – so different to the tenets of early Christianity – and keep paying their tithes. But was this really the case?

The term 'Dark Ages' is an invention of the 14th century Italian writer Petrarch, who saw in the art and culture of ancient Rome a time of greatness, while his own was an era of "varied and confusing storms". Subsequent historians took his idea and ran with it. 'The Dark Ages' came to signify the entire medieval era, between the end of classical antiquity and its rebirth in the 15th century with the Renaissance.

And yet the Middle Ages wasn't 'dark' at all, just different from the classical era, and today historians try to avoid using the term wherever possible. When the term is used, it's to describe a very particular era – from the fall of the Western Roman Empire in 476 to the Norman Conquest of Britain in 1066 – in a very particular place: Western Europe. This encompasses Britain, Ireland, modern-day France, modern-day Germany, and parts of Scandinavia. These regions were the western edgelands of the Roman Empire, and when the Great Peace of Rome (the Pax Romana) was withdrawn from these lands they returned to their long history of northwestern cultures moving around and jockeying violently for supremacy. It's the Romans who told history that the Britons, the Celts, the Saxons, the Franks, the Gauls, the Picts and the Norse were savages, and it's this Roman-centric idea that informs the concept of a Dark Age, 'dark' here being a cipher for 'not classical'. The cultures of these northwestern Europeans were in fact rich and vibrant and gave us many of the things we associate with the flowering of the High Middle Ages: Epic poetry, jurisprudence, parliamentary debate, stylised art, exceptional craftsmanship, knightly virtue, courtly love. It was during the Dark Ages – also known as the Migration Period – that Europeans first visited the shores of North America.

A key force in early medieval western Europe were the originally-Scandinavian Vikings. Their quest for wealth, for farmland, and for adventure, saw them traverse the remains of ancient Rome and reshape its northwestern remnants, along with themselves. They went into the Dark Ages as one of the savage hordes of classical nightmare, forged a North Sea empire, expanded its boundaries south and east, and ended this eventful era in the pan-European light of Norman civilisation.

LEFT
Western Europe was more volatile after the end of the Pax Romana due to territorial disputes

ABOVE
In western Europe during the Early Middle Ages more people lived and worked in the countryside than in towns and cities

RIGHT
The Early Middle Ages is stereotyped as a time of despair and darkness

Darkness to light

"It's the Romans who told history that the Britons, the Celts, the Saxons, the Franks, the Gauls, the Picts and the Norse were savages"

The so-called Dark Ages were local to western Europe. At the same time elsewhere in the world, the Middle East and southern Spain were experiencing the scientific revolution of the Islamic Golden Age, Japan and China were enjoying the cultural flowering of the Heian period and the Tang dynasty, the wealthy African empires of Mali, Ghana and Songhay were flourishing, and the Byzantines were stealing the secrets of silk from the Far East.

ANO · DNI M CCC XX VIII

Everything you wanted to know about

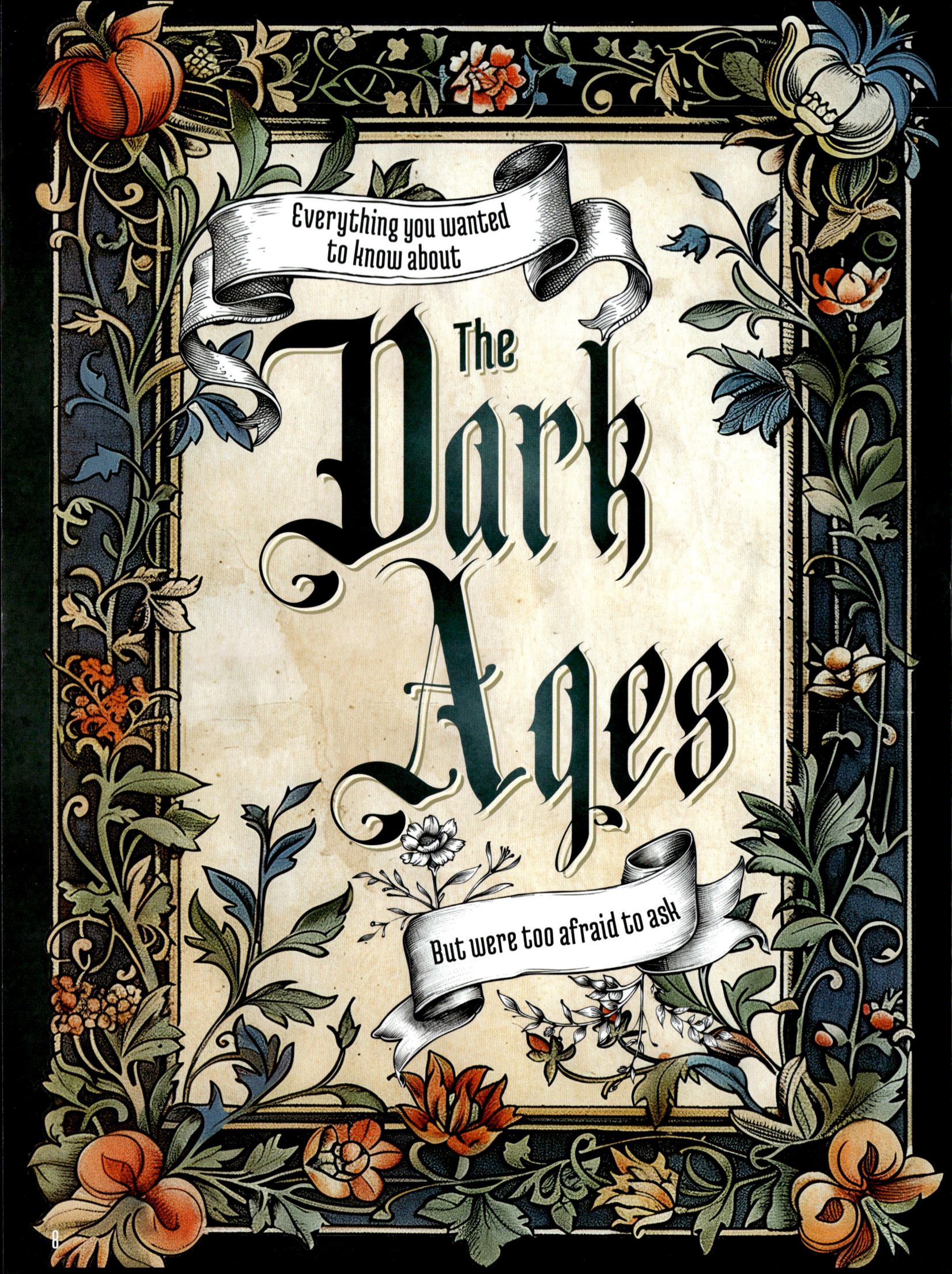

The Dark Ages

But were too afraid to ask

Everything you wanted to know about the Dark Ages

What were the Dark Ages exactly?

The 'Dark Ages' is a term that is now widely considered to be archaic and inaccurate. It has long been believed that Europe went backwards technologically, culturally and socially after the fall of the Western Roman Empire in the 5th century, hence why this era has been labelled 'dark'. Another reason for this unflattering nickname is because of the lack of documentation from this time. However, new research has exposed this interpretation of the era as barbaric and uncivilised as being entirely unfair. Historians now prefer to label it the Early Middle Ages or Early Medieval era, leaving behind the incorrect connotations of darkness. Some see the Dark Ages as ending with the advent of the Medieval Warm Period in the year 900, but others see it as having lasted until the Norman Conquest of Britain in 1066 as we have done here.

The known world didn't just fall to its knees immediately after the fall of the Roman Empire. Here's what really happened in the Dark Ages

How quickly did the Roman Empire crumble?

The saying goes that Rome wasn't built in a day, and it definitely didn't fall in a day either. The one-time capital of the Roman Empire was assaulted numerous times and its fall was a gradual economic and social degradation of a once all-conquering force, not a single one-off catastrophic event. The closest there is to one single key moment is the sacking of Rome in 410 by the Visigoths, when the Eternal City was plundered by the foreign invaders. At this time, the empire had already been split into two and Constantinople was now the most prosperous of the Roman cities. The Western Roman Empire limped on until 476 when the final emperor, Romulus Augustus, was forced to abdicate by Odoacer, who would become the first Gothic king of Italy. Meanwhile, the Eastern Roman Empire, or Byzantine Empire, flourished until 1453 but did not make many significant territorial gains in Europe and instead branched out into Asia Minor and North Africa. Meanwhile, western and central Europe were now divided and dominated by warring factions such as the Visigoths, Slavs, Ostrogoths, Vandals, Angles and Saxons. To many historians, this signalled the beginning of the Dark Ages, but was it as 'dark' as we've been led to believe?

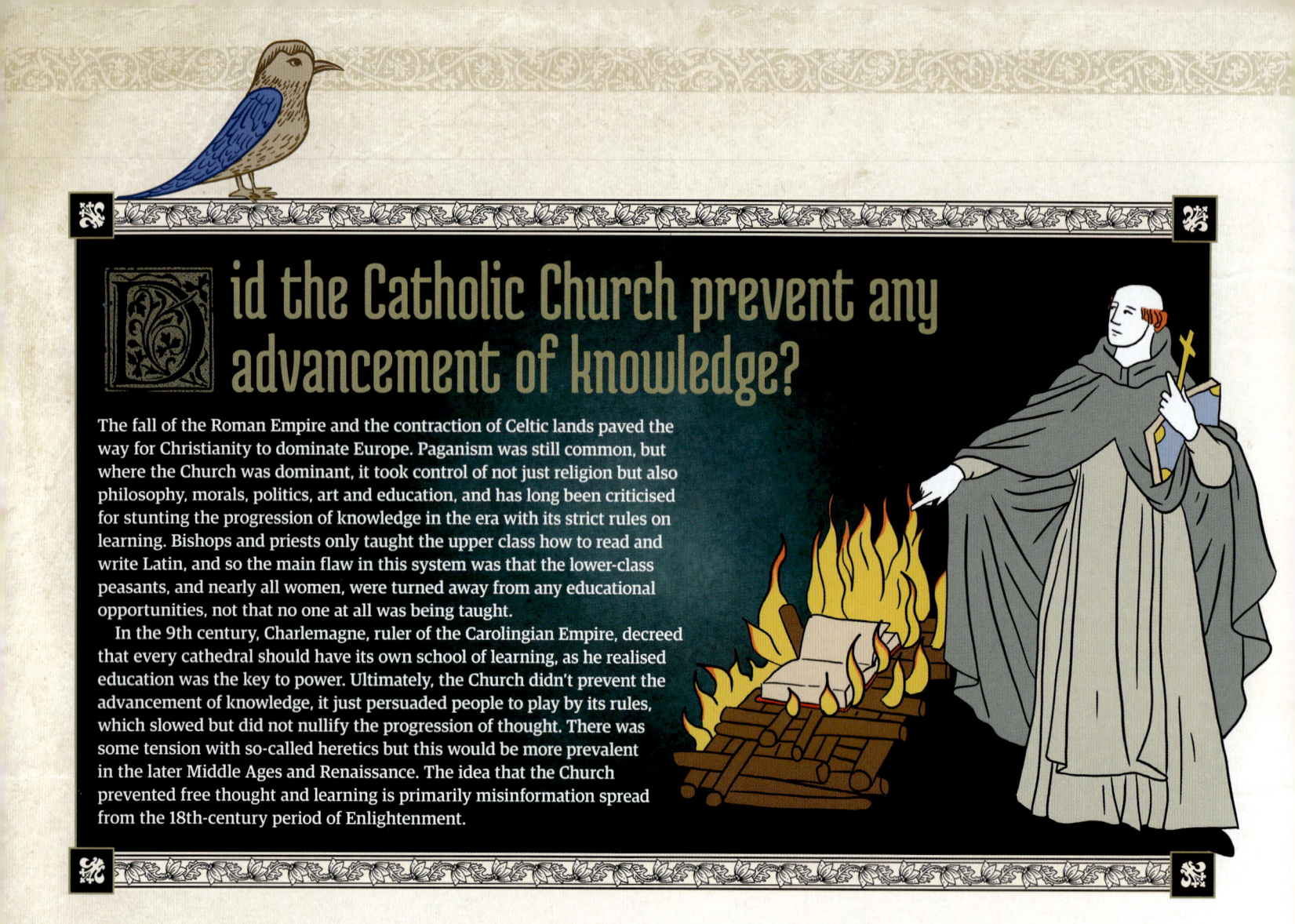

Did the Catholic Church prevent any advancement of knowledge?

The fall of the Roman Empire and the contraction of Celtic lands paved the way for Christianity to dominate Europe. Paganism was still common, but where the Church was dominant, it took control of not just religion but also philosophy, morals, politics, art and education, and has long been criticised for stunting the progression of knowledge in the era with its strict rules on learning. Bishops and priests only taught the upper class how to read and write Latin, and so the main flaw in this system was that the lower-class peasants, and nearly all women, were turned away from any educational opportunities, not that no one at all was being taught.

In the 9th century, Charlemagne, ruler of the Carolingian Empire, decreed that every cathedral should have its own school of learning, as he realised education was the key to power. Ultimately, the Church didn't prevent the advancement of knowledge, it just persuaded people to play by its rules, which slowed but did not nullify the progression of thought. There was some tension with so-called heretics but this would be more prevalent in the later Middle Ages and Renaissance. The idea that the Church prevented free thought and learning is primarily misinformation spread from the 18th-century period of Enlightenment.

> "Charlemagne decreed that every cathedral should have its own school of learning, as education was key to power"

Is it true that no one lived in cities?

With hindsight, it's easy to believe that the fall of Rome signalled the end of civilised urban centres and the beginning of a war-torn, barbaric Europe. The city of Rome was a shadow of its former self and had not been the capital since the empire split. Despite this move away from the historic centre of the Roman Empire, cities like Ravenna and Florence still functioned and maintained at least part of the splendour they had during the days of empire. It's true though that many did embrace a more nomadic lifestyle – the Huns being an obvious example, sweeping in from Asia in 445. Led by their infamous leader Attila, their vicious attacks prevented significant settlements arising in eastern Europe for centuries. Their tactic of destroying everything in their path rather than constructing settlements was a key reason for the lack of cities in central and eastern Europe. The same could be said for the Vikings in northern Europe, but despite their penchant for pillaging, they did construct long-term sites. Back on the continent, the majority of the Germanic hordes had a habit of only sticking around to build forts, not towns for trade and commerce. With all the fighting going on, it did take time for cities to be built up. By the 13th century, cities such as London, Paris and Cologne had all become important centres for trade and commerce, making them thriving residential areas.

Everything you wanted to know about the Dark Ages

Did people really only eat bread and gruel?

Dark Age cuisine gets a bit of a bad reputation, especially when compared to the glorious banquets put on by the Romans, but it wasn't all just stale bread and gruel. The access to food all depended on wealth, but for the most part even the poor had at least some access to meat including cows, horses, goats and pigs, as well as being able to fish for cod, haddock, pike and perch. The staple foods in Britain were eggs, bread, porridge, cabbage, turnips and cheese, so the cuisine was by no means completely bland or diseased; it just depended on how good the harvest was that year.

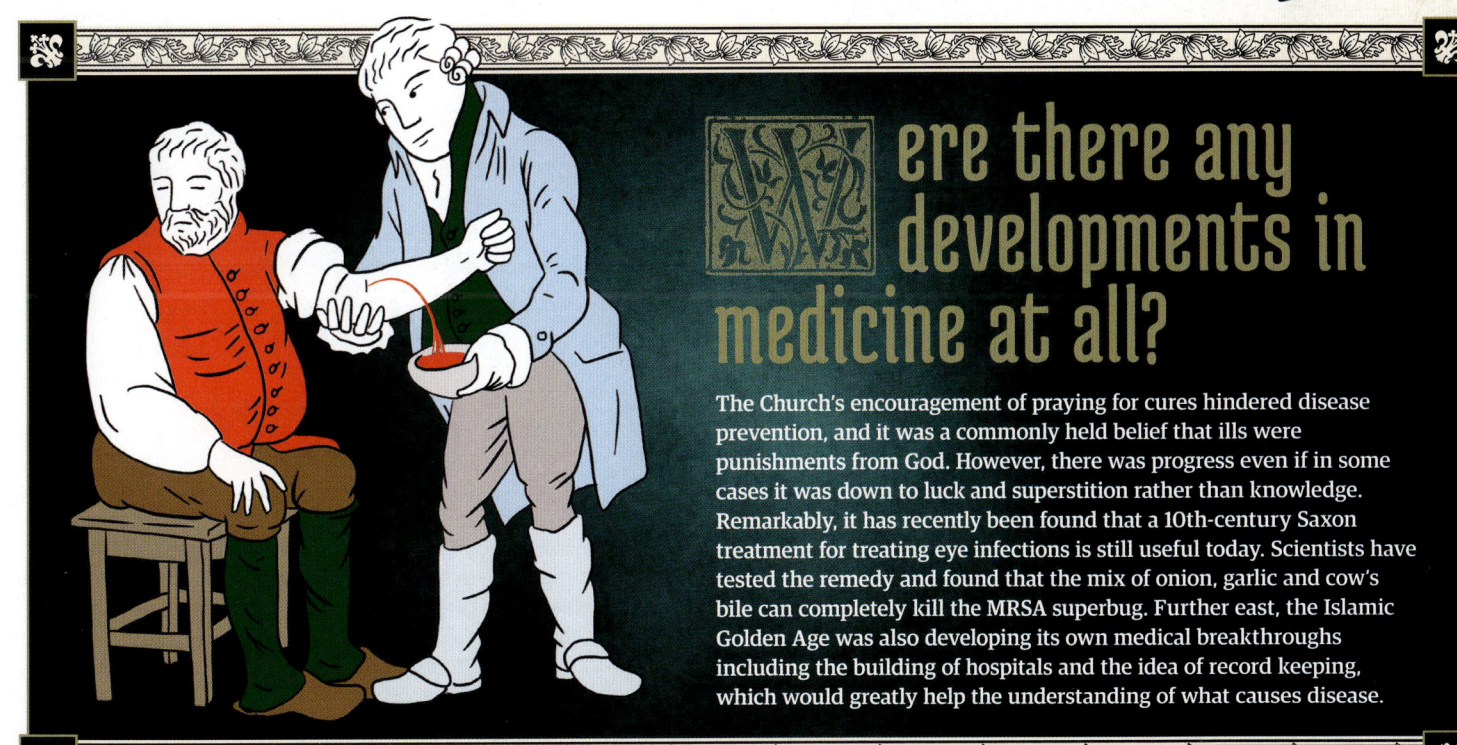

Did everybody believe that the Earth was flat?

Let's debunk a myth: the Catholic Church never taught the idea that the Earth was flat. In fact, there is no evidence at all to suggest that people in the Dark Ages ever believed that this was true.

Were there any developments in medicine at all?

The Church's encouragement of praying for cures hindered disease prevention, and it was a commonly held belief that ills were punishments from God. However, there was progress even if in some cases it was down to luck and superstition rather than knowledge. Remarkably, it has recently been found that a 10th-century Saxon treatment for treating eye infections is still useful today. Scientists have tested the remedy and found that the mix of onion, garlic and cow's bile can completely kill the MRSA superbug. Further east, the Islamic Golden Age was also developing its own medical breakthroughs including the building of hospitals and the idea of record keeping, which would greatly help the understanding of what causes disease.

Were thousands of women burned for witchcraft?

Many believe that the barmy idea of witchcraft was a phenomenon that dominated the Dark Ages and the Late Middle Ages that followed. However, the mass hysteria actually came much later in the Renaissance and Enlightenment eras, with the 1692-93 Salem Witch Trials the most well known. There were burnings, but these would have been concentrated on those the Church believed to be heretics and, on occasion, military enemies. Witch trials in fact dominated Early Modern Europe and America.

Is it true that no one took baths?

Well, no. Soap may have been a luxury that was only used sparingly even by the upper classes – who preferred to mask their body odour with strong perfumes – but this did not stop people bathing. There are conflicting accounts on how clean people were, with some sources stating personal hygiene simply didn't exist while others say the Anglo-Saxons scoffed at the Viking idea of bathing once a week. More recent research has shed light on the notion that the population knew of the importance of washing and that dirt was generally a bad thing. King John is even known for taking a bathtub when he toured England. While most Roman baths across Europe fell into disrepair, replacements were eventually constructed, with Paris having 32 by the 13th century. This made Europe more hygienic than you'd probably think.

What fun could you have?

Study on the period nearly always focuses on war, conflict and invasion, but people still knew how to have fun. Music was a popular past time and the scholar Bede tells of an event at Whitby Abbey where entertainment was provided by the playing of a harp. Literature was also popular and, as well as Bede's many writings, the epic poem *Beowulf* was written at some point between the 8th and 11th centuries. Much of the poetry from the era wasn't noted down but memorised and then recited. Riddles were also popular, as were board games and simple activities like hide-and-seek. In the Byzantine Empire many Roman amenities were maintained, so races and theatres stayed open to entertain the masses.

Everything you wanted to know about the Dark Ages

Did people only drink beer?

Water would be drunk from shared wells or straight from a river. With no real idea of how germs spread, these sources could often be contaminated and would cause illness. This was primarily down to the poor public health in communities where people would bathe in the same water they drank and would simply tip waste into the streets. Because of this, it was sometimes (but not always) safer to drink alcohol. This apart, it is a myth that people in the Dark Ages didn't drink water at all. In fact, it's quite the opposite, and we know this from the writings of Byzantine physician Paul of Aegina, who wrote about the benefits of drinking good ol' H2O. Also, the 'beer' wasn't high-percentage booze. The most common drink was low-alcohol 'small beer', which was the middle ground between polluted water and getting sozzled on strong brew.

Was the world beyond Europe a wasteland?

As the West was experiencing the Dark Ages, the Islamic world was going through its Golden Age. Islam was spreading out in the Middle East, North Africa and Asia and even Spain, and bringing with it a rich culture of learning. Dominated by the Umayyad (661-750) and Abbasid (750-1258) caliphates, Baghdad became one of the greatest cities on Earth. The Islamic caliphates were the largest economic powers of the era and would be the pinnacle of society, technology and industry, with Europe playing catch-up.

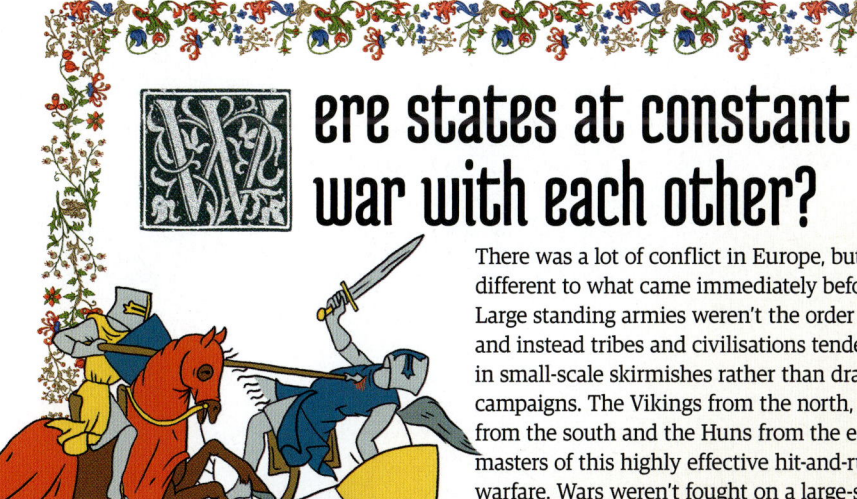

Were states at constant war with each other?

There was a lot of conflict in Europe, but it was very different to what came immediately before and after. Large standing armies weren't the order of the day and instead tribes and civilisations tended to fight in small-scale skirmishes rather than drawn-out campaigns. The Vikings from the north, the Saracens from the south and the Huns from the east were the masters of this highly effective hit-and-run tactic of warfare. Wars weren't fought on a large-scale again until the First Crusade in 1095.

An unusual alliance at the Battle of Chalons

Even after the Sack of Rome and the advent of the Dark Ages, the Roman Legion wasn't quite finished

41 years after the first king of the Visigoths, Alaric, had overseen the destruction of Rome, what remained of the Western Roman Empire joined with the Visigoths to help extinguish a new threat, the Huns. Attila the Hun and his hordes of mounted warriors had ravaged central and eastern Europe and driven the Visigoths westwards into Europe. By the summer of 451, the Huns were on the march and had already sacked major towns like Cologne, Strasbourg and Reims. Roman military commander Flavius Aetis called to Theodoric I the Visigoth king for aid and, after initially being rebuffed, was promised support and the unusual alliance met on the Catalaunian Fields in the modern day Champagne-Ardenne region of France.

The battle began with the Hunnic-Ostrogoth coalition pressing forward against Aetis's men, who managed to repulse the attack. As the Huns reeled backwards, the Visigoths entered the fray and forced the enemy back further. Attila and his army were forced to go back, and although they weren't totally driven from the battlefield, they would effectively concede defeat. The victory was one of the last for the Western Roman Empire and the Huns would be back, but Attila's aura of invincibility had been shattered for now.

The Last Days of the West

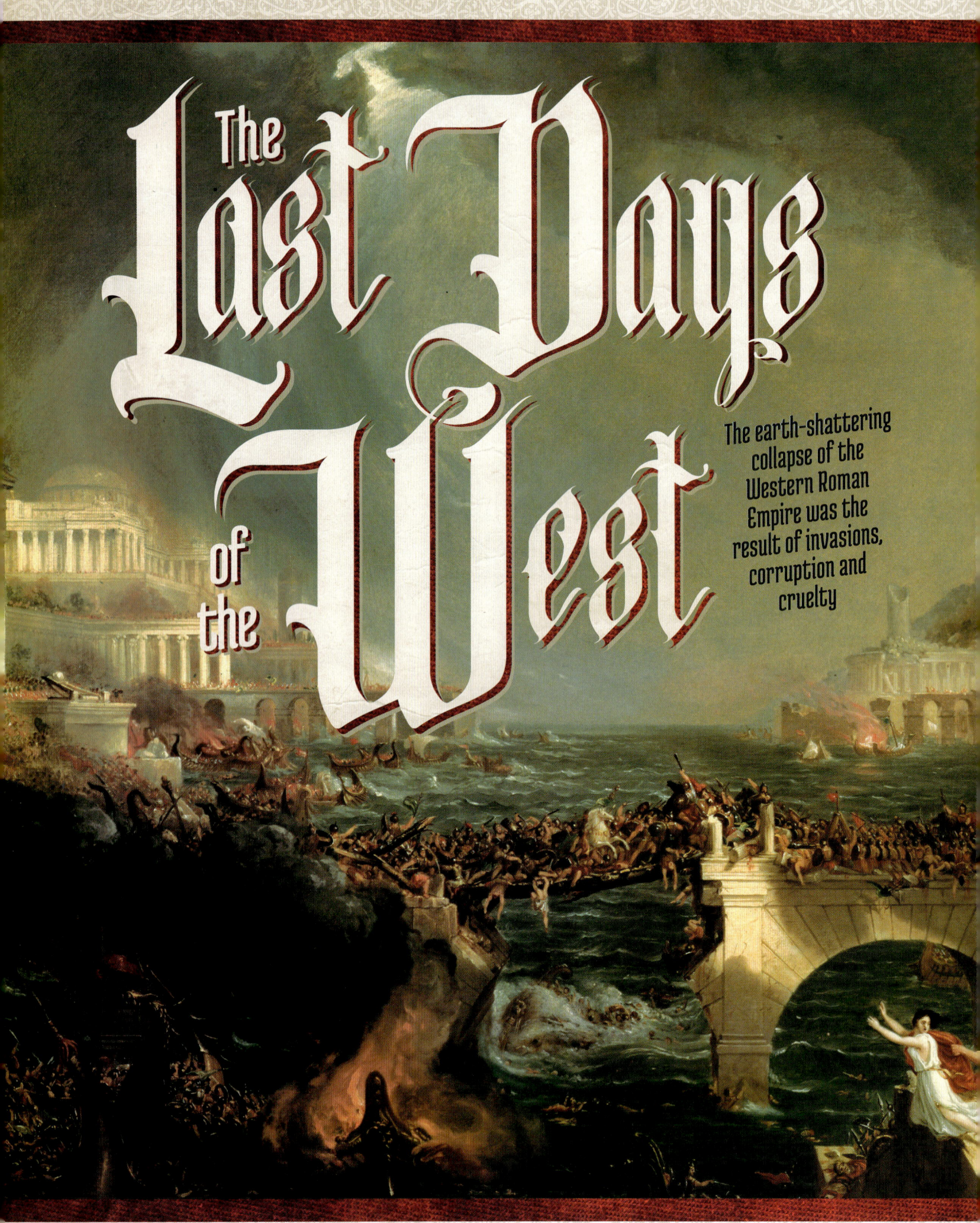

The earth-shattering collapse of the Western Roman Empire was the result of invasions, corruption and cruelty

The Last Days of the West

Throughout history, the fall of mighty empires has rarely played out as an instantaneous and devastating collapse, and the demise of the Western Roman Empire was certainly no different. Pinpointing a precise start date for the empire's decline has proven to be a difficult and contentious task, with many historians pointing the finger of blame at Emperor Caracalla's decision to grant all free men within the empire citizenship in 212 CE, thereby removing the main incentive to join the Roman legions and consequently starting a downward spiral that would see Rome forevermore struggling to field adequate armies.

Of course, it is too simplistic to apportion the responsibility for the fall of the Western Empire to one single factor, for there were many reasons for its gradual disintegration. By the time of Emperor Avitus' ascension to power in 455 CE, Rome had been sacked twice, once by the Visigoths in 410 CE and then again in the year of Avitus' coronation by a rampant horde of Vandals.

MAIN
In 410 CE, the Visigoths succeeded in sacking Rome, becoming the first army to do so in eight centuries

BELOW
Recalled as the only able Western emperor of the 5th century, Majorian sought to defend the rights of his provincial subjects

15

Conscious of his somewhat tenuous grip on power, the newly appointed Avitus moved quickly to appoint a comes (count of the empire) by the name of Ricimer, a general of Germanic descent who would play a major role in the rise and fall of several emperors. Yet the title bestowed upon him by Avitus was not as glamorous as it had previously been, for by 455 CE the once enormous sphere of Roman influence had deflated to such an extent that it now only encompassed a scattering of regions in southern Gaul and the Italian Peninsula itself. It was an empire that Avitus would not rule for very long.

Despite managing to secure an - admittedly doomed - truce with the Vandals during his first winter at the helm, the strength of this agreement was found wanting in Marc 456 CE as the Germanic 'barbarians' resumed hostilities in the south of Italy. Avitus' failure to completely stem the Vandals' incursions was compounded by the Visigoths' progress in Hispania. The Gaulish ruler of Rome was struggling abroad, and it wasn't long before his domestic unpopularity finally made his position untenable.

Never slow in seizing an opportunity, Ricimer moved quickly to topple Avitus, who was roundly loathed by Rome's hungry population (a combination of the Vandals choking off Rome's imports and the foreign troops that had accompanied Avitus resulted in food shortages in the wake of the city's destruction). The general's machinations inevitably spurred Avitus to retaliate, but his hopes were to be dashed. Heading an enormous force, Avitus marched to confront Ricimer's own army near Piacenza in northern Italy, only to witness the destruction of his host. With no option but to flee, Avitus is thought to have died during the first month of 457 CE while en route to the safety of Gaul, possibly on the orders of the man who would succeed him, an ally of Ricimer's in the rebellion called Majorian.

By the time of Majorian's coronation in December 457, the Roman Empire was spiralling terminally towards its demise, a monumental yet gradual collapse resulting from numerous overlapping factors, a primary one being continuous barbarian invasions.

In its prime, the empire had often crushed such uprisings with relative ease, but conquest and consolidation cost the empire vast sums of

> "By 455 CE the sphere of Roman influence had deflated, only encompassing a scattering of regions"

money - funds that, as time went by, could no longer be supplied in the form of war booty. Instead Rome's leaders had to look closer to home, taxing the wealthiest of its citizens in a desperate bid to support and shore up a failing military machine.

This necessary measure inevitably alienated the city's monied inhabitants, many of whom resorted to leaving Rome in order to keep hold of their wealth. When coupled with rampant corruption within the Senate and the inevitable decline in slave labour that accompanied the empire's halting expansion, this widespread avoidance of tax only served to weaken an already financially shaky empire at a time when enemies such as the Huns, Goths and Vandals were strengthening, the latter of which had inflicted a chastening lesson on Rome in 435 CE when they began to settle across North Africa, a development the Romans were powerless to stop. If the empire was going to survive, this vital region would have to be reclaimed, a goal that Majorian quickly set his sights on.

A leader who sought to curtail the financial deviance so damaging to his beleaguered realm, Majorian took his administrative obligations as seriously as his military ones, yet he is best remembered for his martial efforts. Intent on

LEFT
The disastrous Battle of Adrianople dealt the Romans a blow they would never truly recover from, culminating in the death of Emperor Valens

FAR LEFT
The Western Roman Empire as its greatest extent

The Last Days of the West

King Geiseric led his Vandal hordes into Rome in 455 and laid waste to the city for a fortnight

Rome's kingmaker

Born in 405 CE to Rechila, a member of the Germanic Suebi tribe and king of Galicia, a region in what is today northern Spain, and his wife, a daughter of the king of the Visigoths, Flavius Ricimer would grow into a ferociously ambitious young man who refused to allow his barbarian lineage to hold him back.

It is estimated that Ricimer began his service to the Roman military in the early 420s. He would rise rapidly through the ranks, befriending a future emperor in a man called Majorian and raising his own forces in the mid 450s with which to crush the Vandals in two key engagements. Both of these victories came in 456 at the battles of Agrigentum and Corsica – achievements that gained him heroic status back in Rome.

With glory on the field secured, Ricimer turned his attention back to Rome's political scene, aiding his former comrade Majorian in toppling Avitus and stealing the throne. Unable to rule due to his background and Christian faith, Ricimer determined to take a slightly subtler route to power, controlling a number of Western Roman emperors for almost 20 years, during which time any incumbent ruler who displeased him quickly found themselves removed from power – violently.

---

resurrecting Rome's crumbling empire, Majorian swiftly smashed an Alemmanic (German tribe) invasion before storming into Gaul in 458 and putting King Theodoric II's Visigoth force to the sword at the Battle of Arelate. Success in Hispania would follow for an emperor described by many scholars as brilliant in every respect. However, glory in the field of battle would prove elusive just when Majorian needed it most.

Hungry to reclaim the precious resources of North Africa, Majorian had wisely accrued a fleet of 300 vessels with which to transport an invasion force across the Mediterranean and onto the shores of the former Carthaginian Empire. Sadly for the ambitious emperor, he would never even get the chance to attempt a crossing, for his entire fleet was destroyed while anchored off the coast of Hispania by men in his own ranks who had treacherously accepted payment from the Vandals to betray Rome.

Crushed by this astounding reversal, Majorian soon made for Rome. Upon reaching the city he must have been startled to be arrested by none other than his old ally Ricimer. His incarceration was tortuous but brief, for five days later Majorian was beheaded on 7 August 461 CE. Yet again, the empire was in need of an leader.

A brief jostle for power ensued as Emperor Leo I of the Eastern Empire sought to promote a candidate of his choosing, but Ricimer would triumph in the end with the eventual appointment of Libius Severus, a man who would rule (under the watchful gaze of Ricimer) for four years before he died of natural causes.

Thankfully for the Western Empire's cause, this period of unrest between both halves of the empire wouldn't last, with the ascension of Anthemius as emperor in 467 CE, an elevation that pleased both Ricimer and Leo I. However, while the two realms worked to come together again, the differences between them were many and stark.

While its sibling struggled with numerous issues, the Eastern Roman Empire went from strength to strength as the 5th century wore on. Blessed with greater financial resources than the West, the East was better placed to bribe ambitious barbarian leaders, which it did successfully when it came to keeping the ruthless Attila the Hun at bay. By contrast, the West suffered greatly at the hands of Attila prior to his death in 453 CE, both indirectly due to the sudden influx of refugees that poured across the Roman borders as the Huns rampaged across Europe, and as a direct result of his invasion of northern Italy.

If gold didn't prove sufficiently enticing to ward off an invasion, the East - again, thanks to its wealth - could rely on a stable standing army to defend it (not to mention the imposing walls erected to protect Constantinople, a fixture that thwarted Attila's efforts to take the city),

17

ABOVE
Odoacer triumphantly rides into a humbled Ravenna (by then capital of the Western Empire) as Romulus bows to Italy's conqueror

BELOW RIGHT
Majorian lost 300 ships at the Battle of Cartagena in 461, an act of betrayal that prevented Rome from retaking North Africa

something that only served to encourage invading tribes to turn their attentions to the weaker West. Of these tribes, the Vandals proved to be a thorn in Roman sides, and the situation was no different for Anthemius.

By 468 CE, Anthemius was a year into what was turning into a promising reign. Supported by both the ever-present Ricimer and his counterpart in the East, Leo I, Anthemius enjoyed cordial relations with the other half of the empire, a unity that resulted in both sides determining to work as one to finally put an end to the Vandal presence in North Africa.

Led by Basiliscus (Leo I's brother-in-law), an armada of about 1,000 ships set sail for what is today the coast of Tunisia with a vast army of both Western and Eastern Roman troops on board. Yet while this new invasion force would better Majorian's in actually making landfall, their hopes of victory were dashed just as brutally at the Battle of Cape Bon.

Alert to the real and pressing threat to his empire, King Geiseric sent forth a wave of fireships into the Roman ranks before unleashing his own fleet, causing truly catastrophic losses of 10,000 men and 100 vessels. In one fell swoop, the Germanic ruler and one-time sacker of Rome extinguished the last remaining hope of survival for the Western Roman Empire.

Bereft of the resources offered by its former African territory, the beleaguered empire soon found maintaining its armed forces a far heavier burden, one made no easier to bear in 470 CE when a force commanded by Anthemius' son failed to make any headway against the Visigoths in Gaul. With the south lost and Rome's grip on the western provinces loosening, Anthemius' reign appeared doomed, and it was little helped by the Senate's suspicions of a ruler of Greek birth. Even

the once-guaranteed support of Ricimer could no longer be relied on.

In 472 CE the opportunistic general moved against his former friend by declaring Olybrius (a man close to Leo I) as the new emperor of the West following tensions with Anthemius. This inevitably sparked open war between forces loyal to the emperor and those beholden to Ricimer. The conflict culminated in a savage engagement in Rome in which Anthemius' troops were scythed down en masse by a barbarian army that showed no mercy. Clemency was not even afforded to Anthemius, who, having scrambled to the 'safety'

Odoacer: First king of Italy

Believed to have hailed from the eastern-Germanic Scirii tribe, Odoacer was born in 435 CE. It was by this time Roman custom to provide foederati (barbarian regions loyal to Rome) with various benefits in return for their military aid, evidence of how weak the empire had become. As such, Odoacer journeyed to Italy in around 470 to serve in the Roman army.

His career fighting for the failing empire, which began during the rule of Anthemius, lasted for around six years; sufficient time to rise to a position of command. By 476, Odoacer clearly felt he and his troops were due some reward for their efforts on Rome's behalf, and initially Orestes, who had recently installed his son Romulus, promised to grant the barbarians under Odoacer the territory they demanded. However, he unwisely chose to renege on this deal, unleashing an uprising that would prove the death of the Western Roman Empire.

During his reign as king of Italy, Odoacer enjoyed martial success, conquering the independent region of Dalmatia after a two-year campaign. He would rule until 493, when he fatefully accepted an invitation to a banquet held by King Theodoric, who had been nominated as king of Italy in 488 by the Eastern Roman emperor Zeno in a bid to depose Odoacer. Ignoring all the rules of hospitality, Theodoric broke bread with his rival before killing him with his own hands by cleaving his enemy in two.

The Last Days of the West

of a church, was arrested and executed. No doubt pleased to have yet again bested a political rival and secured power for his chosen candidate, for once Ricimer had played the wrong hand. Olybrius (who was deemed an illegitimate ruler by an outraged Eastern Empire) would only last for seven months before he passed away from dropsy. He was soon followed into the afterlife by Ricimer, the indomitable military powerhouse eventually laid low by a haemorrhage in 472.

Olybrius was succeeded four months after his death by a Dalmatian called Glycerius at the behest of Gundobad, king of the Burgundians and nephew of Ricimer – a second affront to the East. Without the backing of Ricimer and aware of the East's refusal to accept him, Glycerius made overtures to Leo I in a bid to heal the rift between the empires. His olive branch was snapped and thrown back in his face with force as Leo, by now hugely unpopular due to his banning of non-religious festivals in the East, not only nominated Julius Nepos as emperor of the West, but then proceeded to send a fleet to invade Italy and claim the throne. This was one of the last acts of Leo's reign, as dysentery claimed him that year, putting an end to a reign that had begun in 457 CE.

As the husband to Leo I's niece, Nepos had extremely close ties to the Eastern emperor's court, which explains why he was Leo's preferred choice to replace Glycerius in the summer of 474. Nepos' fleet duly made for Ostia (near to the port of Rome) in June, landing on Italian soil at a time when Glycerius was hopelessly exposed (his master, Gundobad, had returned to Gaul to rule his kingdom in Burgundy). The hapless usurper had little choice but to quit the city, but he was soon unearthed. Nepos displayed remarkable restraint upon his rise to power, choosing to nominate his predecessor as a bishop instead of having him put to death, an act of kindness that he would one day come to regret.

Nepos' reign would prove to be as short-lived as his new bishop's, but before he was toppled by his own magister militum (a senior commanding officer in the Roman military), Orestes, he first had to suffer the ignominy of acknowledging the Gothic kingdom that had been established in Gaul. The fact that he had no alternative but to do so is testament to how feeble the empire had become by 475 CE.

Having been ejected from office in August by Orestes, Nepos escaped to his native Dalmatia to 'rule' at a distance. In truth he was emperor in name alone – as was ever the case in Ancient Rome, he who controlled the military also held the empire. In this case it was Orestes, a former servant of none other than Attila the Hun.

Despite his sudden and public deposition at the hands of an adviser he should have been able to trust, Nepos would survive until 480 CE. Sources suggest that he was stabbed to death in his own villa, either by friends of a vengeful Glycerius (to whom Nepos owed his life) or on the direct orders of Odoacer, the man who would finally end Rome's rule of Italy.

Unusually for the age, Orestes decided not to rule himself, instead opting to crown his 15-year-old son Romulus Augustus as the new leader of a rapidly disintegrating Western Roman Empire in October 475 CE. His public reluctance to claim the throne for himself was merely an act; as father to the emperor and head of the military, he reigned from the shadows. His lust for power fdoomed his son to an ill-fated reign set to end in disaster.

Mocked as 'Augustulus' (Little Augustus), history has often judged Rome's last Western emperor harshly, forgetting that he was a teenager forced into office by a father hungry to rule a shattered empire at a time when the formerly stable East was tearing itself apart in a power struggle.

Crowned in February 474 CE by his seven-year-old son as co-emperor, Zeno ruled as emperor of the Eastern Roman Empire until he was betrayed by a close advisor and Basiliscus (the same man who was so roundly beaten at the Battle of Cape Bon). At the time of Romulus' rise to power, Zeno – who, along with his bitter rival for the throne, refused to accept Romulus as emperor in the West – was plotting what would turn out to be a successful return to Constantinople.

The extent to which Romulus was aware of the troubles in the Eastern Roman Empire is unclear, but he had little time to consider its ramifications – rebellion was well and truly afoot in his empire. Emboldened by the knowledge that the West was ailing, a confederation of Germanic tribes led by a formidable warrior named Odoacer decided to test the strength of Orestes' resilience by demanding that one-third of Italy should now be handed over to them.

When Orestes promptly rebuffed their 'offer', Odoacer ignited a vicious uprising during which a rag-tag army led by Orestes was slaughtered outside the city of Placentia (modern-day Piacenza) before their leader was executed. With the empire decapitated by Orestes' death, Odoacer was free to march on Ravenna in northern Italy, where on 2 September 476 CE his mercenary hordes once again capably set about annihilating a weakened Roman army.

With nothing left standing between him and Odoacer's rampant army, young Romulus had no choice but to bend the knee to Italy's new conqueror and surrender the throne. In a matter of weeks, Odoacer had violently ended 1,200 years of Roman mastery of Italy, and in doing so he struck a final, fatal blow from which the Western Roman Empire would never manage to recover. The once-great empire was at an end.

ABOVE Anthemius was appointed as emperor by Leo I in a move that removed him as a candidate for the throne of the Eastern Empire

RIGHT Prior to his death in 473, Leo I appointed his seven-year-old grandson Leo II as his heir

In spite of how he came to power, sources suggest that Odoacer enjoyed the full support of the Roman Senate

The Byzantine Empire

The dramas of the Eastern Empire were a match for anything that the West had been able to offer

In 968 CE, Liutprand, bishop of Cremona, undertook a challenging diplomatic mission to Constantinople. He was far from impressed by the treatment he received and the people with whom he had to deal. He complained that the local wine was undrinkable and that his lodgings lacked both fresh water and a roof. As for the Byzantine emperor, well, he was a brute.

Nicephorus II, according to Liutprand, was a "monstrosity of man", full of ignorant opinions and as ugly as sin. He was "fat-headed and like a mole as to the smallness of his eyes… one whom it would not be pleasant to meet in the middle of the night." The people, in contrast, seemed to adore their emperor, though they were really just a "plebian, barefooted multitude". When Nicephorus paraded through the city, the crowds would shout out in adoration. What they really should have been saying, Liutprand suggested, was "you burnt-out old coal, you fool… you goat foot".

Liutprand claims to have found none of the glamour that was supposed to define the Byzantine court. The food was lousy, the clothes were third-rate, and the hospitality extended to visiting dignitaries was atrocious. This, it is fair to say, was an unusual response. Visitors usually raved about how beautiful and civilised Constantinople was, about the cultural riches and the elaborate ceremonies of the city.

Perhaps Liutprand was simply in a bad mood. Or perhaps Constantinople was just going through a bad patch since, just a few decades earlier, Liutprand had been involved in another mission to the Byzantine court and appears to have had rather a jolly time. Constantine VII had been a much better host and Liutprand wrote of the "marvellous and unheard of manner of our reception". The place was filled with gorgeous thrones, bronze lions and mechanical animals. Dinner was served in huge golden bowls covered with purple cloth, and when being introduced, Liutprand was carried into the emperor's presence with great solemnity on the shoulders of eunuchs. The empire, as always, had its ups and downs: a defining characteristic of Byzantine history.

The phrase 'Byzantine' only began to be commonly applied to this mighty civilisation

The Byzantine Empire

Picturing Jesus

Concern about the portrayal of holy subjects was particularly keen in the Eastern Christian churches. Matters came to a head in the 8th century when Emperor Leo III ordered a wide-scale destruction of religious images. Riots ensued and many of the protestors were whipped, exiled or mutilated. Art was burned and, as one contemporary lamented, churches were "scraped down and smeared with ashes".

These events provoked uproar in the Western Church, and many angry letters were passed between popes and emperors. Images, as Pope Gregory II explained, were of great value because they could instruct the illiterate. Empress Irene approved the use of images in 787. Emperor Theophilus reversed her decision early in the next century, ordering artists to destroy or spit (quite literally) upon their works, inflicting harsh punishments on those who would not comply. An artist named Lazarus was subjected to "such severe tortures that his flesh melted away" and when he stubbornly began work again, following his recovery, red hot irons were pressed into his hands, maiming him. Happily, by the mid 9th century, the turmoil came to an end and religious art was once again sanctioned in Eastern churches.

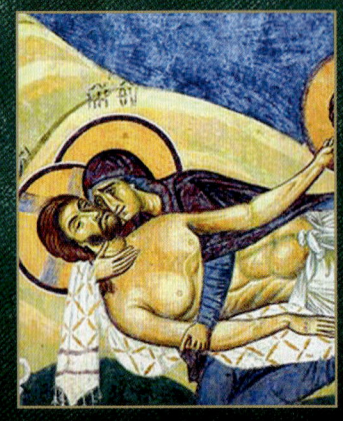

RIGHT
The mighty walls of Constantinople that repelled many a would-be invader through the centuries

BELOW LEFT
The Lamentation; just the sort of image that infuriated the iconoclasts

BELOW RIGHT
Michael VIII Palaiologus managed to retake Constantinople in 1261 following the sack of the city in 1204

during the 16th century, but it represents a very different, but no less colourful, period in the history of the Roman Empire. And make no mistake, while the empire in the East had its share of unique characteristics - the use of the Greek language and the forms of religious devotion, for example - the emperors were always adamant that they, and they alone, were the true successors of earlier rulers in the West.

Though Constantinople had been an important city since the 4th century, it entered its heyday following the fall of the Western Roman Empire in 476 CE. The territories over which it ruled came and went with alarming frequency - indeed, the extent of those territories was something of a geopolitical seesaw - and there would be both gifted and atrocious rulers. But Constantinople was mighty. It was blessed by its location on vital trade routes and, however hard Byzantium's enemies tried, the city's famously robust walls rarely succumbed to their onslaughts. As one historian put it: "You can't have a century without a couple of sieges of Constantinople."

But it was only with the advance of the Ottomans in the mid 15th century that the empire finally came to an end. By then, 1,000 years of triumphs and tribulations had passed. Along the way, the empire had fostered some of the most spectacular artistic and cultural achievements the world had ever seen.

The story began well, under rulers such as the hard-working Anastasius I (r.491-516 CE), an able administrator, but grander dreams had not evaporated. Could the Western Empire, or at least some of it, be reclaimed? Enter one of Constantinople's most famous rulers, Justinian, during whose reign (527-565) the great military leader Belisarius and his colleagues managed to seize parts of Italy, North Africa and southern Spain. The financial cost was exorbitant, but the boost to morale was perhaps a price worth paying.

Less satisfactory were the attempts to battle Persia, Byzantium's traditional enemy, and, distracted by adventures in the West, the empire failed to rebuff encroachments by the Slavic peoples. Justinian also found time to codify law to reduce the risks of arbitrary justice; his efforts would be reflected in the legal systems of dozens of countries for centuries. He even found time to

The Byzantine Empire

This almost got Justinian deposed, but he weathered the storm and set about rebuilding the city. Unfortunately, almost all the territorial gains he had made in the West were lost under his successors and the Byzantines' central dilemma had come into sharp focus. It was surrounded on all sides by enemies and for the next millennium, a ludicrous number of conflicts would have to be fought. The Sassanid War in the early 7th century drained the imperial coffers, with the Persians keeping up the pressure and deploying the sneakiest of tactics.

Emperor Maurice (reigned 582-602) had been an ally of the Persian ruler and when Maurice was killed by the ambitious military leader Phocas, Persia swore to avenge his death. But this was merely an excuse for intervening in the Byzantine Empire's politics. A decades-long war ensued, with the Persians managing to reach the gates of Constantinople. The pretense of good intentions soon evaporated and before long, the Persian ruler was describing the Byzantine emperor as his "vile and insensate slave".

Matters improved greatly under Heraclius (r.610-641 CE), who secured a famous victory over the Persians at the Battle of Nineveh in 627. Even his enemies had to concede that he was a ferocious warrior. As a Persian ruler once put it: "He fears these arrows and spears no more than would an anvil." At this very moment, however, the rise of Islamic power in the Near East was in full flow and, due to their financial weakness, both the Persian and Byzantine Empires were vulnerable. During the 7th and 8th centuries, Byzantium would lose Armenia, Syria, North Africa and, most devastatingly, the economically crucial Egypt. Affairs at home were hardly any rosier, with the disruptive quarrel over religious icons creating havoc from the reign of Leo III (r.717-41 CE) through much of the 8th and 9th centuries.

The arrival of the Macedonian dynasty (867-1056) represented another turning point, at least at first. Its founder, Basil I (r.867-886), managed to regain substantial territories but, as so often, his immediate successors squandered his legacy. Lands were lost and, throughout the period, Egypt was never reconquered. It also proved difficult to retake Jerusalem, which provoked a rather famous series of events known as the Crusades - though all the troops that flooded in from the West over the next few centuries were chiefly concerned with asserting their own interests and had no great desire to see the city being placed back in Byzantine hands.

The Macedonian period - particularly during the 10th century under the rule of Constantine VII (r.913-959) - did, however, represent one of the high watermarks in Byzantine cultural achievement: the Macedonian Renaissance.

> "Losing control in such a way almost got Justinian deposed, but he weathered the storm"

Perhaps no artefact better encapsulates this era's artistic achievements than the so-called Joshua Roll, which depicted the biblical tale in an exquisite 11-foot parchment roll that demonstrates a spare but intoxicating use of colour.

One military superstar also emerged in this period: Basil II (r.976-1025), who managed to claw back Greece, the Balkans, Syria and Georgia. But as sure as eggs is eggs, new foes emerged. The Normans assaulted the empire's Sicilian outposts and, during the reign of Romanos IV Diogenes (r.1068-71), the Seljuk Turks inflicted a devastating defeat on the empire at the 1071 Battle of Manzikert. The whole of Anatolia would be lost in the wake of this crushing blow.

Yet again, however, Byzantine fortunes were rekindled with the arrival of a new dynasty: the Comnenid. Its greatest glories, under rulers such as Alexios I (r.1081-1118) and the unusually charitable and lenient John II (r.1118-43) lay in the realm of culture and the arts, but some progress was made on the territorial and military fronts. But, of course, they were followed by a run of some spectacularly incompetent emperors.

By now, the West had lost much of its respect for Byzantium: indeed, ever since the Frankish ruler Charlemagne had been declared as the Holy Roman Emperor and the true successor to Rome in the 9th century, that respect had been steadily fading away. Nor did the great schism between the Eastern and Western Churches in 1054 - stemming from a confusing blend of theological differences - do much to improve relations. The spectacle

transform the empire's financial fortunes by introducing the production of silk. Indian monks smuggled in the eggs of silkworms and an irksome dependency on bought-in silk was cast off.

Less happily, Justinian's reign also witnessed an early example of just how febrile Byzantine politics could become. The Nika Insurrection of 532 CE was one of the bloodiest events in the empire's history. Chariot racing was a favourite pastime in Constantinople, with four leading teams and their supporters each sporting a particular colour: the blues and the greens were top of the tree. More was at stake than exciting recreation. The different groups would attempt to influence religious and political affairs and had a bad habit of engaging in street violence. In 532, Justinian's refusal to extend a full pardon to two of the leaders of the blues and greens led to a week-long orgy of riots, house-razing and arson. Thousands were killed and as much as half of the city lay in ruins and rubble.

ABOVE LEFT
Belisarius, Justinian's bold general, would remain a favourite figure in art through the centuries

RIGHT
John II Comnenos, known as John the Good, was an unusually kindly emperor

The Slayer of the Bulgars

The Byzantine Empire produced many military giants, but few could match Emperor Basil II

Basil II was only five when he came to the throne in 976 CE, with his mother acting as regent. He was soon asserting himself, however, and his eventful reign witnessed its share of pretenders and coup attempts. He survived them all.

Basil was not a particularly friendly man and was known for his gruffness and ascetical temperament. But while he was not especially likeable, he garnered a good deal of respect. His military successes were largely to thank for this.

His campaigning began badly when his armies were thrashed by the Bulgars at a mountain pass, but things soon looked up. From 997 CE he embarked on a series of epic conquests in Greece, the Balkans and Syria, and eventually served up revenge to the Bulgars at Kleidion in 1014. Following the battle, thousands of enemy captives were blinded or mutilated; within four years, Basil had secured complete control of Bulgar territory. Further successes followed in Armenia, and Basil's tomb said it all: "No one saw my spear lie idle."

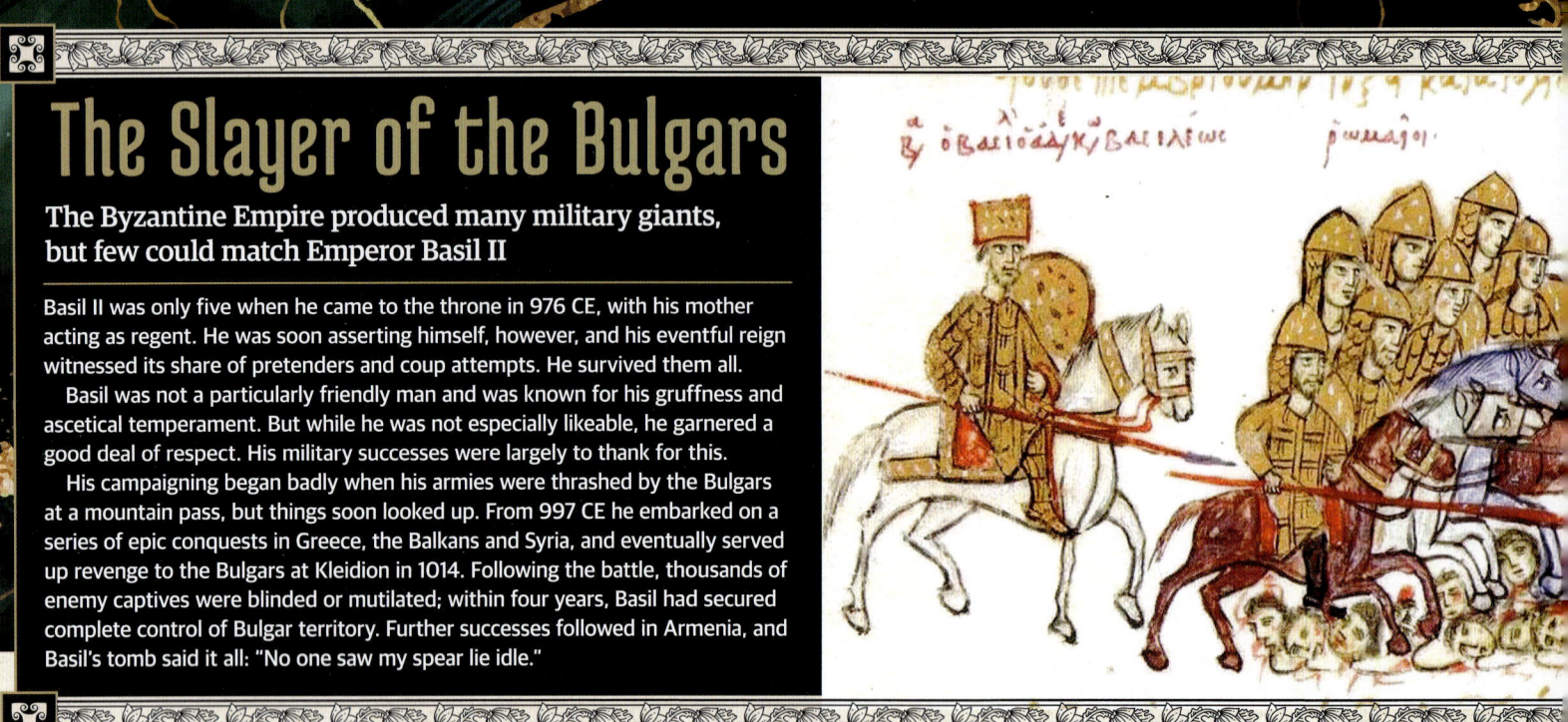

---

of a pope and a patriarch of Constantinople mutually excommunicating one another would leave religious scars that endured for centuries. A republic such as Venice was simply waiting for an opportunity to enter the Byzantine sphere of influence and it came, perhaps rather surprisingly, courtesy of the Crusades.

Faced with threats from the east, the Byzantines were always hopeful of support from the West, but things went horribly wrong in 1204. A fourth Crusade was launched at the beginning of the 13th century and the original plan was for the crusaders to stop off at Constantinople en route, help restore an emperor, and receive financial and military support in return. Everything went swimmingly for a while, but when the restored emperor Alexios IV (r.1203-04) was killed, the empire was unable to honour its commitments and the enraged crusaders launched an assault on the city.

Following a siege, the city was sacked and, as once contemporary put it, the "tumult and noise were so great that it seemed as if the very earth and sea were melting together". Western control of Constantinople was established, the

LEFT The preaching of the Fourth Crusade, which would unexpectedly bring disaster to Constantinople

> "The rich millennium-long drama that was the fabled Byzantine Empire had all but come to an end"

The Byzantine Empire

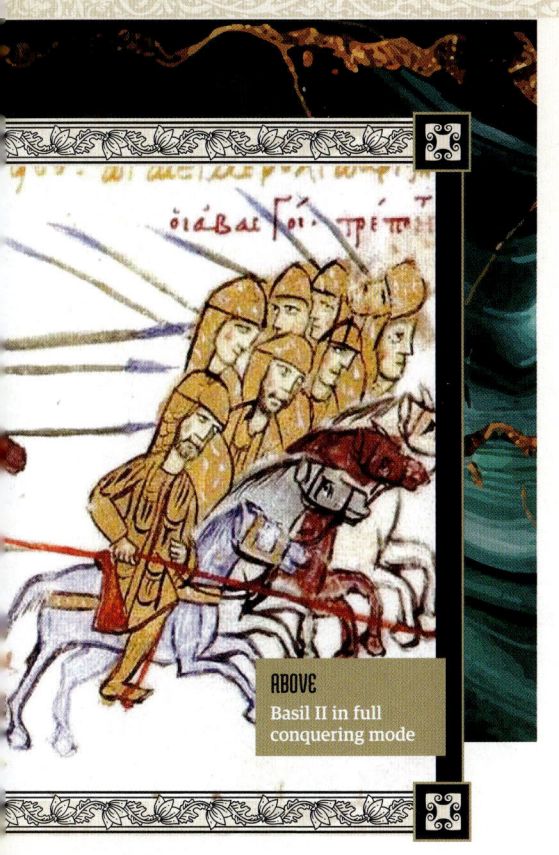

Andronicus I, or the sons of Romanos I Lecapenos deposing their father and shipping him off to a monastery to live out his days.

Restraint was rarely shown by the warring factions that jockeyed for power. Following the death of Heraclius, Constans I emerged victorious from the power struggle in 641 CE and behaved as any self-respecting Byzantine would when it came to his rivals for the throne. Heraclius' widow, Martina, had her tongue cut out, and his son, Heraclonas, had his nose chopped off. Both were then banished to the island of Rhodes.

The uncertainty of succession in the empire created many difficulties. It was not a simple father-to-son affair. An ambitious soldier could easily seize power and even those of the humblest origins had a shot at the top job. This, in a way, was meritocratic, but if an emperor failed to live up to expectations, his days were always numbered.

The wonder, though, is that through all this, the Eastern Empire usually retained its prestige and its economic power. The borders might shift, but a Byzantine solidus was a coin accepted across Europe and beyond. And let's not forget the astonishing cultural and artistic legacy – from art and literature to science and philosophy.

Nothing sums this up more elegantly than Hagia Sophia, the church that Justinian built and then rebuilt. As the ancient scholar Procopius explained, the emperor brought in "workmen from every land" and the results were "distinguished by indescribable beauty, excelling both in size and in the harmony of its measures". "No one," Procopius announced, "ever became weary of the spectacle."

Edward Gibbon, the great 18th-century historian, famously denounced the Byzantine Empire as a place of over-indulgence and petty infighting. It was, he wrote, a Roman Empire "contracted and darkened", akin to the mighty Rhine ending in a trickle, losing itself in the sands before reaching the ocean. But there was a good deal more to the story than that.

ABOVE
Basil II in full conquering mode

empire's territories were divided up between the Western powers and, over the following decades, Byzantine emperors suffered the indignity of ruling in little more than name from exile. Three so-called successor states, all claiming to continue the authentic Byzantine tradition, fell into competition.

The tables turned under Michael VIII Palaiologos (r.1259-82), who retook Constantinople in 1261. But, as ever, new threats and challenges were on the horizon. The 14th century proved to be one of the worst in Byzantine history, with an absurd number of imperial depositions and civil wars. Into the bargain, the rise of the Ottoman Turks placed the empire in great jeopardy: for periods it was forced to become a vassal state of the Ottomans. Truly embarrassing incidents came thick and fast – the need to pawn the imperial crown jewels in 1343, or John V (r.1341-76) being detained for a spell as a debtor on a trip to Venice. Ultimately, in 1453, the death knell sounded.

Under Mehmed II, the Ottomans captured the city of Constantinople itself. The rich millennium-long drama that was the fabled Byzantine Empire had all but come to an end. Only the Trebizond Empire, based around northern Anatolia and the Crimea, remained. It had always claimed to be the heart of the true Roman Empire, denouncing Byzantium's audacity, but it, too, was snuffed out by the Ottomans in 1461.

It's impossible to deny just how muddled and horrific Byzantine history could sometimes become: a tale of coups, pretenders and internecine strife. The list of usurpations and vengeful treatment of political rivals is almost absurd – Constantine III being poisoned, Justin II going mad, Constantine VI being blinded. Not to mention Michael V's castration, the lynching of

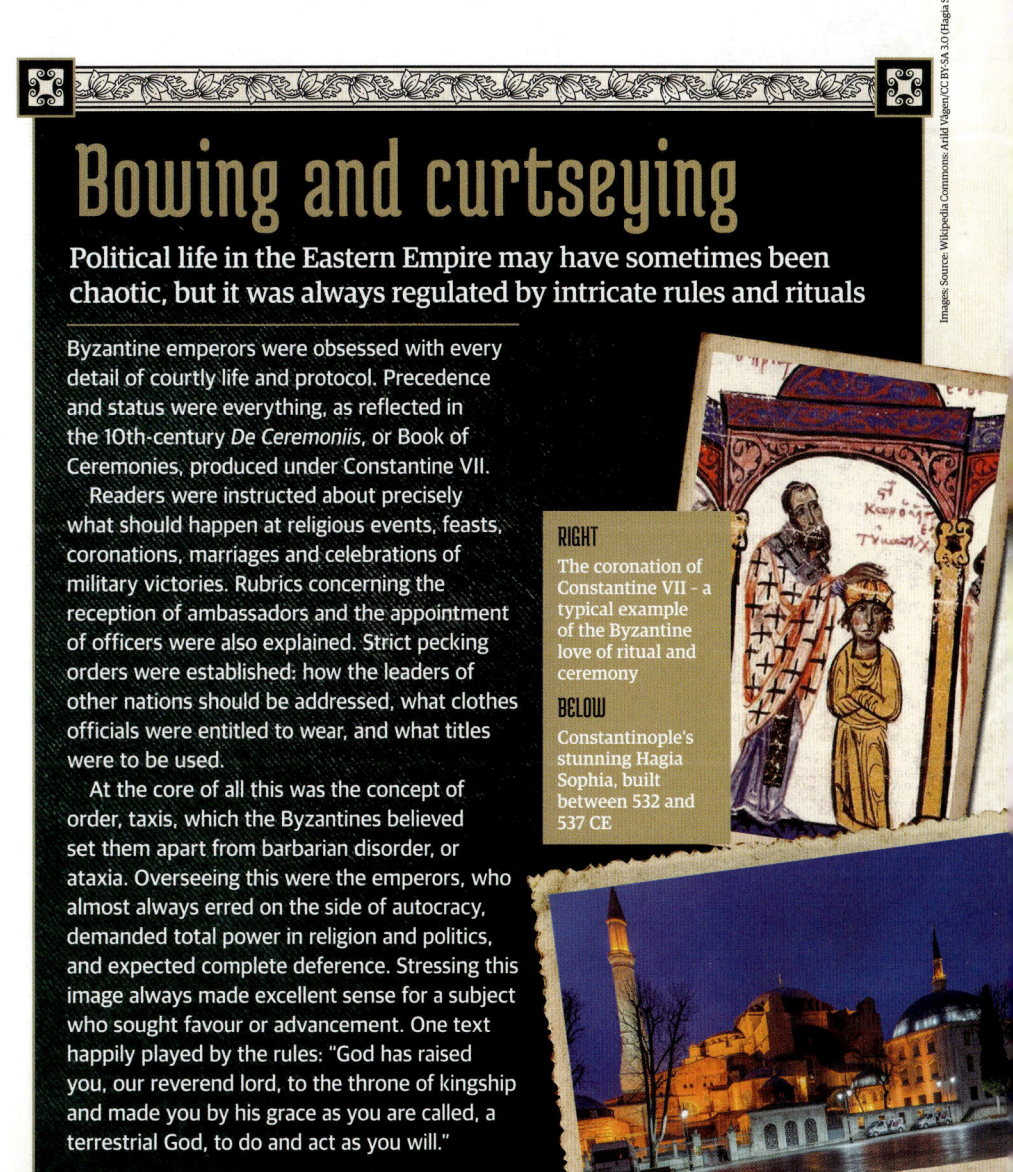

Bowing and curtseying

Political life in the Eastern Empire may have sometimes been chaotic, but it was always regulated by intricate rules and rituals

Byzantine emperors were obsessed with every detail of courtly life and protocol. Precedence and status were everything, as reflected in the 10th-century *De Ceremoniis*, or Book of Ceremonies, produced under Constantine VII.

Readers were instructed about precisely what should happen at religious events, feasts, coronations, marriages and celebrations of military victories. Rubrics concerning the reception of ambassadors and the appointment of officers were also explained. Strict pecking orders were established: how the leaders of other nations should be addressed, what clothes officials were entitled to wear, and what titles were to be used.

At the core of all this was the concept of order, taxis, which the Byzantines believed set them apart from barbarian disorder, or ataxia. Overseeing this were the emperors, who almost always erred on the side of autocracy, demanded total power in religion and politics, and expected complete deference. Stressing this image always made excellent sense for a subject who sought favour or advancement. One text happily played by the rules: "God has raised you, our reverend lord, to the throne of kingship and made you by his grace as you are called, a terrestrial God, to do and act as you will."

RIGHT
The coronation of Constantine VII – a typical example of the Byzantine love of ritual and ceremony

BELOW
Constantinople's stunning Hagia Sophia, built between 532 and 537 CE

25

Rise of the Holy Empire

The dominant institution in the lives of kings and peasants alike, the Church promised heavenly salvation to all yet frequently delivered earthly schism

For the majority of the population in western Europe, life in medieval times was unremittingly grim and frequently short. Death was a constant shadow; if poverty, famine or pestilence didn't carry you off, there were plenty of warmongering emperors and kings looking for battlefield expendables. Yet one organisation offered some semblance of reassurance that everything was not forlorn or futile – the Church.

Its message was simple: no matter how horrible a life was on Earth, if the person living it followed the teachings of Christ, a heavenly reward was assured. Conversely, living a sinful, wicked life meant being cast down into hell for eternity. The hope of salvation or the expectation of damnation gave the Church considerable power over the hearts and minds of people. It dominated the lives of rich and poor alike, essentially from cradle to grave, in that baptism, worship, marriage, and burial after death most usually took place either in holy establishments or on hallowed grounds.

The Church was one of the few outlets for education too. There weren't many people in the Middle Ages who were able to read and write. Those that could were often priests, monks in monasteries or nuns in convents, who naturally taught from their own religious texts, perpetuating those beliefs.

To be a Christian in western Europe in those times was to be a Catholic as, unlike today, it was the only religion of the period that believed in the risen Christ. As the conversion of pagans to Christianity spread across Europe through the early centuries, so the Church grew in numbers and influence. It acquired lands, developed its own laws and collected taxes. Its centre was Rome at the heart of the Western Roman Empire, while at its head was the pope, believed to be a successor of Saint Peter, the founder of the Catholic Church.

Other important early outposts were at Constantinople, Jerusalem, Antioch and Alexandria, all in the Eastern Roman Empire, which was also known as the Byzantine Empire. While this contracted or expanded over the centuries, remaining relatively intact until 1453, Rome stayed the primary centre of the Catholic Church despite the collapse of the Western Roman Empire in 476. The spread of Christianity continued apace after this date, however, even into areas that had been beyond Roman control previously. Key groups of pagans, such as the Franks in Germany who converted en masse in

> Roman-style churches of the Early Middle Ages were dark and gloomy. Thick, small-windowed walls were needed for roof support

Rise of the holy empire

The Crusades

Despite the recent East-West schism in Christianity, the leader of the Byzantine Empire, Alexius I, requested help from Pope Urban II in resisting Muslim incursions into his territory. Urban decided to do more than 'help'; in 1095, he ordered a large invasion force to not simply defend the Byzantine Empire, but to recapture Jerusalem and the Holy Lands from what he saw as Muslim occupiers. The Crusades had begun.

Definitions vary, but generally there are considered to have been nine major Crusades fought between 1096 and 1291, in addition to an unnumbered series of smaller ones. Ultimately, they all failed. The first, instigated as a Christian war by Urban, who proclaimed it offered full penance for those taking part, may also have been an attempt by him to heal the divisions of the recent schism. However, subsequent crusades aggressively attacked other religions besides Muslims. Even fellow Christians fell to Crusader swords when Constantinople was attacked in the fourth endeavour. As they descended further into indiscriminate slaughter of innocents, the papacy lost moral authority and European Christendom unity suffered.

Nevertheless, contact with the advanced Muslim culture of the time delivered advances in science, mathematics, medicine, philosophy and art to the West.

LEFT
Charlemagne And The Pope, by Antoine Verard

496, regularly turned to Catholicism. Some time in the second half of the 5th century, Saint Patrick landed in Ireland to introduce Christianity there. In 596, Pope Gregory I, often known as Saint Gregory the Great, sent a mission to Britain to convert the Anglo-Saxons – pagan tribes who had invaded and settled after the Romans had left – with great success.

Yet as the area of Catholic influence and power in western Europe grew, to the extent that no king or emperor could ignore it, invasions into its sphere from hostile tribes nevertheless took place. In 772, for example, the pagan Lombards marched deep into papal territory, threatening Rome. The pope at the time, Adrian I, called for help from the king of the Franks, Charlemagne. By that time, he had expanded his territory to include modern-day France, Germany, Northern Italy and beyond. Charlemagne's army swiftly defeated the Lombards, underlining the role of the Franks as papal protectors.

Under Charlemagne, the Catholics were also ruthless in forcing conquered tribes to embrace Christianity or be put to death. At Verden, Saxons who had previously submitted to Charlemagne attempted to rebel. This act incurred biblical-level wrath from the Frankish king when he had 4,500 of them to be beheaded as a consequence.

In 800, a subsequent pope, Leo III, called for Charlemagne's support when he was accused of being unfit for papal office. Entering Rome in December, Charlemagne backed Leo, and the plotters were exiled. In gratitude, and in acknowledgment of the leader's importance, on Christmas Day at Saint Peter's Basilica, Leo crowned Charlemagne emperor of what would later be known as the Holy Roman Empire.

At the time, this caused no small amount of resentment in the Eastern Roman Empire. There, Irene of Athens, the de facto empress of the Byzantine Empire, already had claim to that title. Yet this was just one of a number of contentious issues between the two regions. Matters really came to a head some 200 years later. By then, the Latin-speaking West and the Greek-speaking East contained very few individuals who could speak and write both languages. As basic communication became more difficult, cultural unity suffered too, giving rise to different approaches to religious doctrines. One such doctrine concerned the filioque clause in the Nicene Creed, and that, along with a dispute over the extent of papal authority, were the two principle reasons for the event known as the Great Schism of 1054.

The Nicene Creed is the statement of faith made by Roman Catholic, Eastern Orthodox and other Christian churches. It was named after the First Council of Nicaea, held in 325, when the statement was formulated. Its wording was revised after the First Council of Constantinople in 381. The third Ecumenical Council in Ephesus in 431 reaffirmed the Creed in its second format, but specifically forbade making any further alterations to it.

However, after the Synod of Toledo in Spain in 589, Western churches included the filioque clause, which translated from Latin means 'and the son', to a section of the Creed. The amended section now stated, "We believe in the Holy Spirit, the Lord, the giver of life, who proceeds from the Father and the Son." Eastern churches were categorically opposed to that inclusion.

The extent of papal authority also greatly vexed the Eastern Roman Empire. They accepted that the head of the Roman Church, the pope,

Monasteries and convents – as nuns took the same vows as monks – offered health services, taking care of the sick

Defining moment
The venerable Bede 735
The death of Saint Bede brings to an end the life of an important 8th-century scholar and writer. A Benedictine monk, his works include books on science, religion and history. Bede's *Ecclesiastical History Of The English People* will become one of the foremost primary sources of English history. Chronicler monks like Bede allow monasteries in the Middle Ages to become centres of learning. There, libraries of painstakingly hand-written volumes – with book printing being more than 500 years away – are assembled. Without such endeavour by people such as Bede, we would know far less about the history of the period.

Defining moment
Murder most foul 1170
A group of knights brutally slay the archbishop of Canterbury, Thomas Becket, at the altar of Canterbury Cathedral. King Henry II is suspected of inciting the murder even though Becket was formerly his friend. The monarch had previously appointed him chancellor, and as archbishop as well; he hoped Becket would keep the church in check. Yet the 'turbulent priest' put Church before king and refused to implement Henry's religious reforms. The clash between church and state brings about Becket's death. Later, Henry is penitent, while reports of miracles at the victim's tomb are spread, and pilgrimages to it begin, leading to Becket's sainthood.

Timeline
The medieval Church

597
● **Holy mission**
Sent by Pope Gregory I, St Augustine leads a party of about 30 monks to England and becomes the first archbishop of Canterbury after founding the English Catholic Church.

● **A key conversion**
Clovis I, the first king of the Franks to unite the Frankish tribes under one ruler, converts to Christianity, allowing for widespread conversions among his people.

1008
● **Converting a continent**
Sweden's king converts to Christianity and his people follow. After Russia converts in 988, Poland in 966, Denmark in 960 and Bulgaria in 846, much of Europe is now Christian.

1054
● **Christianity torn asunder**
Leo IX's death in April doesn't stop his deposition, carrying a papal bull of excommunication, travelling to Constantinople. Meetings with patriarch Michael Cerularius fail, the bull is severed – Rome and Constantinople irrevocably divide.

1099
● **To The Holy Land**
The First Crusade captures Jerusalem. Briefly a Christian kingdom is founded upon it, but Jerusalem is retaken by Saladin in 1187 and the last Crusader stronghold, Acre, is lost in 1291.

28

Rise of the holy empire

RIGHT An anonymous depiction of Pope Martin V. His election ended the Great Papal Schism

had primacy over the other four early Church outposts in the east, but maintained this was at an honorary level only, and that he had no direct authority over them, or their congregations.

Ultimately, centuries of dispute and rancour fuelled by political jealousies and vested interests came to a head in 1054. Mutual excommunications served by the pope, Leo IX, and the head of the Church in Constantinople, Michael Cerularius, led to a formal split. The Roman Catholic Church became separate from the Eastern Orthodox Church along doctrinal, theological, linguistic, political and geographical lines.

Several attempts at reconciliation were made, but during the Fourth Crusade in 1204, Constantinople was attacked by Western Crusaders. The Church of the Holy Wisdom there was looted, while it and other churches were converted to Roman Catholic worship. The assault struck at the heart of the Byzantine Empire, deepening the rift between East and West. Each side claims to be "the One Holy Catholic and Apostolic Church," and the schism remains in place.

Another crisis, often confusingly also referred to as a Great Schism, began in 1378. More accurately it was a Great Papal Schism, and occurred after Pope Clement V moved his court to Avignon in 1309. Previous popes had clashed with Philip IV, the increasingly influential King of France, and when Clement, a Frenchman, took office, he refused to move to Rome. Subsequent popes, all French, remained in Avignon until Pope Gregory XI took the decision to return his court to Rome in 1377. However, he died barely a year later, with a number of his cardinals still resident in Avignon.

Many in Rome feared Gregory's successor would be a Frenchman who would take the papacy back to Avignon. A confused, discordant conclave finally chose an Italian, Urban VI, as the new pope. Yet he quickly lambasted the cardinals for their behaviour and attitudes to the extent that some believed, corrupted by power, he was unfit for office. With French cardinals needing little enough excuse to rebel, they declared Urban's election invalid. Instead they voted for one of their own number, Clement VII. He took up office in Avignon while Urban stayed in power in Rome. Clement naturally had the support of France, Castile in Spain, and Scotland. Predictably perhaps, France's old enemy England sided with Urban, along with much of the German empire. Christendom was divided yet again.

Upon the death of the incumbents, new popes were elected to both seats of power. The situation got messier when, in 1410, a Church Council Of Pisa, assembled to find a solution, instead elected a third line of popes beginning with Alexander V.

It was not until the Council Of Constance, from 1414-18 that a solution was finally reached. The council was summoned by Alexander's successor, John XXIII, and at it, he himself was dismissed. So was the final Avignon pope, Benedict XIII, while Rome's Gregory XII resigned. The council then elected Martin V to be the sole pope. There was to be but a short respite from schism in the Church. Barely 100 years later, the radical priest Martin Luther set in motion the Protestant Reformation.

> "The extent of papal authority greatly vexed the Eastern Roman Empire"

Defining moment
The pre-eminent pope 1198
Innocent III takes office and faces numerous crises, yet he handles each of them shrewdly, leading many to argue he is the most important pope of the Middle Ages. In his dealings with the Papal States, and with the crowned heads of Europe, he raises his position's power and authority to its height. Angered when the Fourth Crusade diverts to sack Constantinople, moving to excommunicate those responsible, he is nevertheless unable to undo the harm it causes to East-West relations. In his later years he presides over the important Fourth Lateral Council, which introduces far-reaching reforms to Church practices.

1210 — A new order
The Franciscan Friars are founded by Saint Francis, a rich man who gave his fortune away to live a holy life. The order forsakes monasteries, taking God's word out to the people.

1260 — As it was then…
Mostly constructed in the preceding 65 years, the Chartres Cathedral is consecrated. The magnificent structure, largely unchanged since consecration, is one of the finest examples of French Gothic architecture.

1309 — All roads lead to Avignon
The reign of the Avignon-based popes begins. Sometimes called the 'Babylon Captivity of Popes', it leads to the Great Papal Schism, which is not resolved until Martin V's ordination in 1417.

1455 — Spreading God's word
Employing a system of moveable metal type arranged in words and lines, Johannes Gutenberg prints copies of the Bible. Printed in Latin, it is the first book to be mass-produced in the Western world.

1498 — Upheaval ahead
Italian friar Savonarola is put to death after heavily criticising the Church for laxity and luxury, yet others, such as Martin Luther, are also set to challenge Catholicism as never before in the tumultuous times ahead.

The Seven Kingdoms

Out of the chaos of the end of an empire, seven kingdoms emerged, known as the Heptarchy

The distribution of the kingdoms of the Anglo-Saxons and the Britons

Britain was a very different place after the Roman legions left in 410 CE. With the breakdown of the centralised Roman administration, the country dissolved into petty kingdoms, many now completely lost to memory, contending with each other for short-lived dominance. Into this mix came the Anglo-Saxons, sailing over the North Sea and using the rivers and estuaries of east and south Britain as their highways into this new country where they were carving out kingdoms. Roads were few and often dangerous. The sea and rivers provided much surer and safer means of travel. These bands of warriors established new kingdoms and brought their families over the North Sea to join them, but they fought as enthusiastically among themselves as they fought with their British neighbours.

Slowly, the smallest kingdoms were swallowed up, incorporated into larger realms and as a victorious king could give more gold and glory to warriors who came to his court, this process became self-reinforcing, leading to the gradual amalgamation of all the smaller kingdoms until there were seven, and finally four, Anglo-Saxon kingdoms in England.

The Seven Kingdoms

ABOVE
Bamburgh Castle, the ancient stronghold of the Idings. St Oswald's Gate preserves some of the Anglo-Saxon defences

LEFT
The exquisite art of the *Lindisfarne Gospels* is the product of one man's labour, Eadfrith, Bishop of Lindisfarne

Northumbria
The realm of heroes and saints

The clue is in the name; Northumbria was the Anglo-Saxon kingdom north of the Humber. At its peak it was the largest and most powerful Anglo-Saxon kingdom and it is the best recorded kingdom up to the 8th century. Northumbria demonstrates in its history the consolidation of smaller kingdoms into larger polities, for it came about through the forced union of Bernicia, with its royal stronghold at Bamburgh, and Deira, centred on the old Roman city of York.

According to the surviving king lists, Bernicia was founded in 547 by Ida – hence the kings of Bernicia were called the Idings – when he captured Bamburgh. For half a century, the Idings fought to retain their precarious hold on the coast, until an alliance of Brittonic kings drove them from Bamburgh on to Lindisfarne. On the point of extinction, the Idings were saved when one of the besieging kings took the opportunity to assassinate his rival. The siege dissolved into recrimination, the Idings escaped and re-established themselves on Bamburgh.

Soon after this, circa 593, Æthelfrith took the throne and proved to be one of the most successful warrior kings of the time, dealing a number of devastating defeats to the Britons and forcibly amalgamating the kingdom of Deira into Bernicia to create Northumbria. Under his leadership, Northumbria became the most powerful kingdom in Britain and, though Æthelfrith was killed in battle in 616, Edwin, the man who succeeded Æthelfrith, consolidated the kingdom's power and expanded its territory. Edwin also became the first northern Anglo-Saxon king to convert to Christianity, but before he could cement the new religion's place in his kingdom, Edwin too was killed in battle.

After a chaotic interregnum, Æthelfrith's son, Oswald, returned from exile to claim the throne. A devout Christian, Oswald brought monks from Iona to preach the new religion, who founded a monastery on Lindisfarne. Northumbrian power continued to expand under Oswald's brother and successor, Oswiu, and also during the reign of Oswiu's son, Ecgfrith. But, in 685, the Northumbrians suffered a catastrophic defeat at the hands of the Picts. Ecgfrith was killed and much of the Northumbrian army destroyed. The battle stopped further expansion north by the Northumbrians: the birth of Scotland can be traced back to this Pictish victory.

While Northumbria declined militarily after Nechtansmere, the 8th century saw a cultural flowering that produced, among many wonders, Bede's *History* and the Lindisfarne Gospels. The Viking invasion of the 9th century divided Northumbria again, with a Viking kingdom established at York but an English earldom retaining Bamburgh and Bernicia, cut off from the rest of the Anglo-Saxon kingdoms until the unification of the country by Æthelstan the Glorious in the 10th century.

Mercia

The Mercians took their place in the heart of the country and fought to keep it

For nearly 300 years, Mercia was the most powerful of the Anglo-Saxon kingdoms. When Ecgfrith, king of the Northumbrians, was killed in 685, Mercia filled the power vacuum, coming to dominate the land south of the Humber, with only the kingdom of Wessex holding out against Mercian hegemony. But of the three major Anglo-Saxon kingdoms - Northumbria, Wessex and Mercia - the history of Mercia mostly comes from the pens of its enemies. Most notable among these is Bede, a proud Northumbrian, who despite the otherwise broad sweep of his *History*, treats the Mercians pretty well only as antagonists.

The name Mercia derives from Mierce, an Old English word meaning the 'marches' or 'border people', and that is what it was when first settled: the border kingdom between the Anglo-Saxon kingdoms of the south and east and the Britonnic kingdoms of the west and north. These people settled in the Midlands, following the river valleys into the heart of the country. The king lists of the Mercians traced their lineage back to Icel, an Anglian prince who settled in Britain, giving the ruling family the name Iclingas.

However, the first king to be reliably recorded is Penda, the great enemy of the kings of Northumbria, who killed two of them (Edwin and Oswald), as well as three kings of East Anglia. Penda was the last great pagan king of the Anglo-Saxons and when he fell in battle with Oswiu, Oswald's brother and successor as king of Northumbria, the conversion of the Anglo-Saxons to Christianity was guaranteed.

Mercia and Northumbria continued to struggle for dominance until, with the death of King Ecgfrith in 685, Mercian supremacy was assured. It reached its height during the reign of King Offa in 757-96, when Mercian power encompassed the whole country and Offa could deal, almost as an equal, with no less a king than Charlemagne. The power Offa wielded is given earthen form in the vast labour required to build Offa's Dyke.

Mercian power declined after Offa's death and was dealt a terminal blow with the arrival of the Great Heathen Army in 868. The Vikings deposed Burgred, king of the Mercians, in 874 and installed a puppet king in his place. Following the victory of Alfred of Wessex over the Vikings, Mercia was divided, its northeast half becoming part of the Danelaw and its southwest portion being ruled by an alderman owing fealty to Alfred. Even following the reconquest of the Danelaw by Alfred's children and grandson, Mercia remained part of the expanding kingdom of the men who came to see themselves as not just the kings of the West Saxons, but the kings of the English.

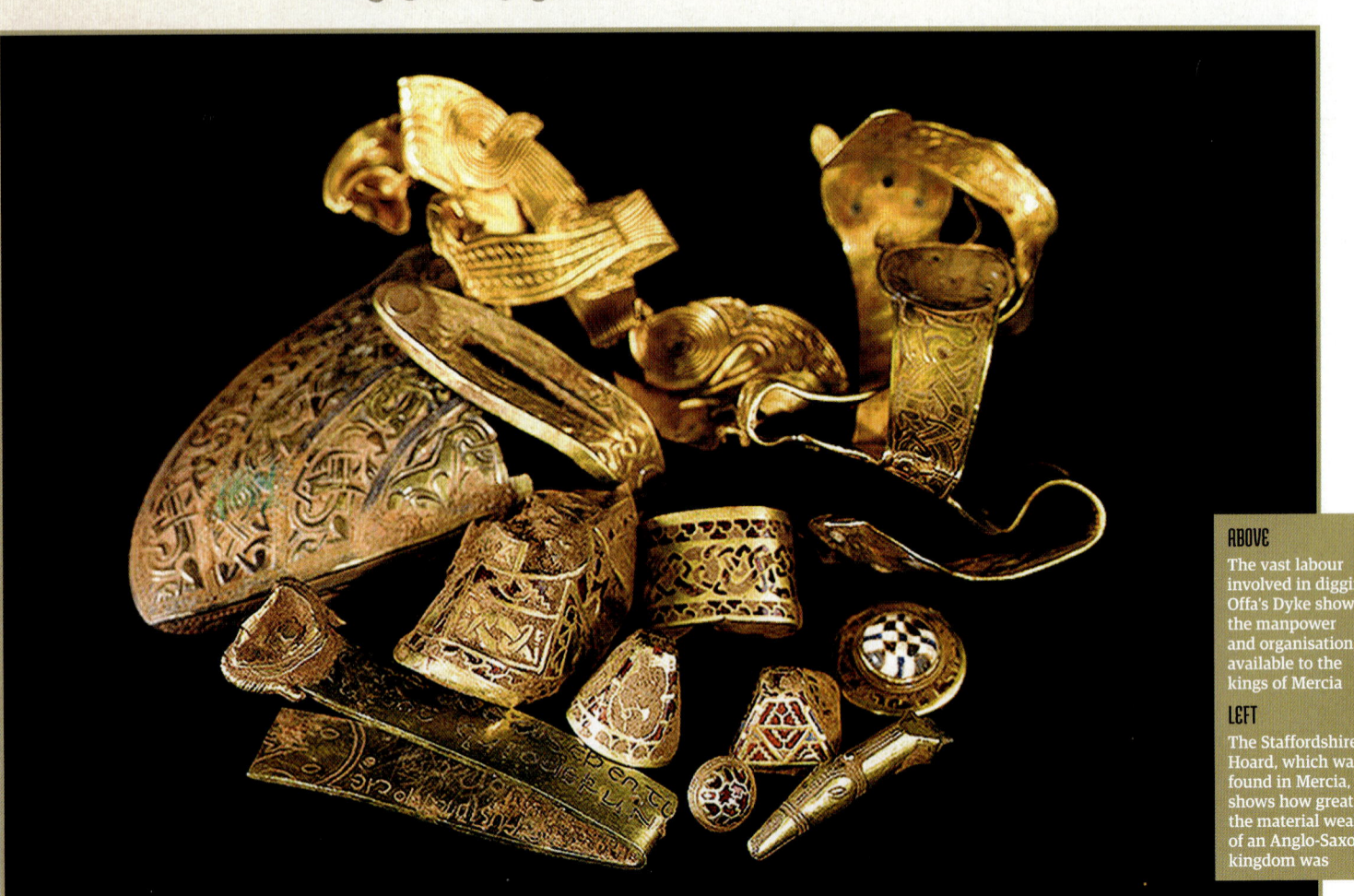

> "The Mercian king Penda was the last great pagan king of the Anglo-Saxons"

ABOVE
The vast labour involved in digging Offa's Dyke shows the manpower and organisation available to the kings of Mercia

LEFT
The Staffordshire Hoard, which was found in Mercia, shows how great the material wealth of an Anglo-Saxon kingdom was

The Seven Kingdoms

FAR LEFT
Alfred is the only king in our history to be given the appellation 'Great'. He merited it

LEFT
Æthelstan the Glorious, grandson of Alfred the Great and the first king of England

Wessex

The last Anglo-Saxon kingdom became the first Kingdom of England

Of the three major Anglo-Saxon kingdoms – Northumbria, Mercia and Wessex – the latter was the last to achieve prominence, but the kings of Wessex eventually became the rulers of a unified England. However, there was little to suggest their eventual status in the founding of Wessex.

As with the other kingdoms, the king lists go back to a founder, Cerdic, from whom the ruling dynasty drew its legitimacy, but there is little to prove that the kings who came after Cerdic, the Cerdicings, were actually related to their supposed forebear. According to the account in the *Anglo-Saxon Chronicle*, Cerdic landed on the Hampshire coast with five boatloads of men in 495 CE, establishing a kingdom on the south coast and gradually expanding inland and to the west. However, Cerdic is a Celtic name, not a Germanic one, so some scholars have speculated that the early rulers of Wessex were of Anglo/British stock.

Wessex expanded west, at the expense of the Britonnic kingdoms, while its northern expansion was checked by the increasing power of the Mercians: the River Thames marked the boundary between the two. During the 8th century, when Mercian supremacy was at its height, Wessex retained its independence to a greater degree than most other kingdoms, while its kings continued to push west, subjugating the Britonnic kingdom of Dumnonia (Devon) by early in the 9th century.

In 851, a Viking army landed in Wessex but was decisively defeated at the Battle of Aclea. So when the Vikings returned in 865, the Great Heathen Army avoided the kingdom of the West Saxons. It was only when the other three major Anglo-Saxon kingdoms had been subdued that the Great Army turned its attention to Wessex, the last kingdom. Sitting uncomfortably on its throne was a young man named Æthelred, who proved far more ready than his infamous descendant, with his younger brother, Alfred, as his chief commander. At the Battle of Ashdown in 871, Æthelred and Alfred inflicted the first significant defeat on the Great Army and the Northmen withdrew.

But Æthelred did not long survive the victory, which left his young brother, Alfred, the last king of the Anglo-Saxons. There were no other viable claimants. Remove Alfred, and the last kingdom would fall. Which was precisely what the Danes attempted to do, launching a midwinter raid into Wessex that caught Alfred completely by surprise. Fleeing into the marshes of the Somerset Levels with a handful of men, Alfred left the Vikings in control of the last kingdom.

But Alfred returned, defeated the Danes at the Battle of Edington, one of the most crucial battles in English history, and set about remaking his kingdom to reconquer the country. Under the remarkable leadership of Alfred's son and daughter, Edward and Æthelflæd, who became the effective ruler of Mercia, the Danelaw was reconquered and it was Æthelstan, Alfred's grandson, who united England under his leadership. The king of the West Saxons was now the king of England. It was an extraordinary achievement by an extraordinary family.

The Kingdom of the East Angles

The riches of Sutton Hoo show the wealth of an Anglo-Saxon kingdom

On 14 June 1939, light broke into the darkness that had shrouded the so-called Dark Ages for centuries. Archaeologist Basil Brown opened the burial chamber of the great ship burial at Sutton Hoo. Over the next weeks, archaeologists discovered the extraordinary riches that a Dark Age king could command. That king was probably Rædwald, the first king of the East Angles of whom we know anything more than a name.

The people who settled in the land almost cut off from the rest of country by the Fens were Angles, split into the North Folk and the South Folk (names that continue as Norfolk and Suffolk), and the kings of the Angles traced their lineage back to one Wuffa, making them Wuffingas ('sons of the Wolf'). Rædwald became king of the East Angles in the early 7th century as the power of Æthelfrith of Northumbria was steadily growing. However, the two kingdoms were separated by the Fens and the kingdom of Lindsey (another Anglo-Saxon kingdom roughly corresponding to Lincolnshire, that is not numbered among the Heptarchy although it probably should have been), so Rædwald was happy to give sanctuary to a fugitive Northumbrian prince, Edwin. But when Æthelfrith learned Edwin had taken shelter with Rædwald he sent a series of messengers, bearing increasingly explicit threats, demanding Edwin's head. Rædwald vacillated, then decided to fight. Together with Edwin, he defeated and killed Æthelfrith, installing Edwin on the throne of Northumbria and becoming himself Bretwalda, the pre-eminent king in Britain, until his death circa 626. His successors fought a series of campaigns to retain their independence from the rising power of Mercia, campaigns that usually ended with the East Anglians having to find a new king. The East Anglians continued to kick against Mercia throughout the 8th century and managed to regain independence in the 9th century, only to be conquered by the Great Heathen Army in 869.

The last independent king of the East Angles was Edmund the Martyr, venerated after his death by the newly Christian children of the Vikings who had killed him. These Christian Vikings, who had settled in East Anglia, created the shrine of Bury St Edmunds to commemorate an Anglo-Saxon king.

ABOVE Knowing he could not defeat the Great Heathen Army, King Edmund offered himself as a sacrifice to save his people

LEFT A reconstruction of the helmet excavated at Sutton Hoo

The Kingdom of Kent

This was where, according to tradition, the first kingdom of the Anglo-Saxons was established

The kings of Kent were not Angles or Saxons – they were actually Jutes, from the north of the Jutland Peninsula. The social organisation of Kent was significantly different from those of the other Anglo-Saxon kingdoms, with only one class of noble as opposed to the two in other kingdoms, while Kentish peasants (ceorls) were also more important than those in the other kingdoms.

According to tradition, the first kings of Kent were the brothers Hengist and Horsa, mercenaries for hire who were invited to Britain by Vortigern to fight against the Picts raiding down the east coast following the collapse of Roman power. In the declining years of the Western Roman Empire it was not at all unusual for barbarian mercenaries to be hired to fight barbarian raiders, so there's nothing intrinsically unlikely about the tale. It was, however, later embroidered to include details such as Vortigern becoming infatuated with Hengist's daughter Rowena and signing over Kent to her father in return for the daughter.

It's only with the long reign of King Æthelberht that historical evidence for the kingdom emerges. The kings of Kent maintained close relations with the Merovingian kings across the Channel, trading widely with them and, as a result, having greater wealth at their disposal than the other kings in Britain. It was this wealth that gave Æthelberht the political clout to be regarded as Bretwalda and it enabled his marriage to a Frankish princess, Bertha. Bertha was Christian, however, and the marriage was contracted on the basis that she would be allowed to remain so.

In 599, Æthelberht received a mission of Italians, coming all the way from Rome, that was led by a monk called Augustine who had been dispatched by the pope to convert the pagan Anglo-Saxons. Æthelberht accepted the new religion, and installed Augustine at Canterbury, making the church there the mother church of the country.

Kentish dominance did not survive Æthelberht, though, and while the kingdom remained rich, there was savage internecine strife in the ruling family. Thus weakened, in the latter part of the 7th century Kent came under the domination of Mercia, which continued off and on until the rise of the West Saxons in the early 9th century, when the kingdom became part of Wessex. As such, Kent played a key part in Alfred's struggle against the Vikings, coming to the fore in the Viking attacks during the 890s, the last decade of Alfred's reign, when the threat of the Northmen was broken for a century.

TOP
Æthelberht, king of Kent from c.589 to 616 CE

RIGHT
King Vortigern striking a deal with a band of Germanic mercenaries that he would come to regret

> "The first kings of Kent were the brothers Hengist and Horsa, mercenaries for hire who were invited to Britain"

Sussex

Sandwiched between Kent and Wessex, with Mercia bearing down from the north, Sussex struggled to survive

Although included among the Heptarchy, the history of the Kingdom of the South Saxons is obscure and its status more a product of being included in the list of main Anglo-Saxon kingdoms produced by the 12th-century historian Henry of Huntingdon than any real claim to eminence among the kingdoms of the Anglo-Saxons. However, despite its perilous position between Kent and Wessex, with Mercia threatening from the north, the kingdom of Sussex retained its independence longer than other similarly sized kingdoms, such as Lindsey, only finally submitting to the rule of the kings of Wessex in 827.

According to the Anglo-Saxon Chronicle, the kingdom was founded by Ælle in 477 CE when he landed with his three sons and three boatloads of warriors near Selsey. The kingdom followed the pattern of gradual expansion against Britonnic resistance, although the archaeology of the area suggests that Saxons had settled in Sussex before Ælle's arrival, possibly originally coming as paid mercenaries in the service of the Roman Empire to man the forts of the Saxon Shore. This was a series of strongholds and ports that the Romans established to guard against barbarian raiders.

The kingdom comes briefly into the light of history in the second half of the 7th century, when the baptism of its king Æthelwealh is recorded. Æthelwealh's sponsor and godfather was Wulfhere, the king of Mercia, and as a baptismal gift, Wulfhere gave Æthelwealh the Isle of Wight and the Meon Valley. Standing as godfather to another king was both an act of spiritual brotherhood and political mastery – a mastery emphasised by Wulfhere's giving of land as gift: Æthelwealh was very much the junior of the two monarchs.

However, although Æthelwealh had become a Christian, his people had not. Their conversion, the last of the major Anglo-Saxon kingdoms, waited upon the rain. Wilfrid, the most tumultuous of Northumbrian bishops, had been deposed from his throne by King Ecgfrith and exiled to Sussex. Arriving in the midst of a severe drought, Wilfrid brought the rain. The South Saxons, abandoned by their gods, accepted Wilfrid's offer of a new god, an offer Wilfrid sweetened by throwing in lessons on new methods of fishing that helped alleviate the effects of the famine the drought had brought. Sussex became a client kingdom to Mercia in the 8th century when Offa was supreme, but by 825 it had been subsumed into the kingdom of Wessex.

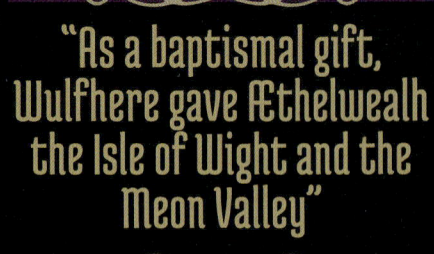

RIGHT Ælle, the semi-legendary first king of the South Saxons

BELOW Wilfrid receiving a grant of land from the king

> "As a baptismal gift, Wulfhere gave Æthelwealh the Isle of Wight and the Meon Valley"

Essex

The kingdom of the East Saxons spread through Hertfordshire and included the land of the Middle Saxons (Middlesex)

The history of the kingdom of the East Saxons is as obscure as that of the South Saxons. Its origins probably lie in the 6th century, when Saxons settled in the flat lands north of the Thames. However, even the king lists for the East Saxons are late, from the 9th century, with some disagreement about the dynasty's founder. Kings Æscwine and Sledd are separately credited as the first king in different genealogies, although the one listing Æscwine first works Sledd in as his son and successor.

The kingdom grew by agglomerating small tribal groups, eventually encompassing the modern county of Essex as well as parts of Hertfordshire and the now lost county of Middlesex. London was under the control of the kings of the East Saxons in the 7th century, when the first attested king is recorded. His name was Sæberht and in 604 he was baptised, with King Æthelberht of Kent standing as his godfather.

Pope Gregory's initial plan had been that Britain should have two metropolitan sees, in London and York, corresponding to the administrative centres of the old Roman province. However, having established his bishopric in Canterbury under the protection and sponsorship of Æthelberht of Kent, Augustine could not move to London. He did, however, send Mellitus to London as its bishop, where he founded the first St Paul's on the site of the present cathedral. However, when Sæberht died, his three sons, who had remained pagan, expelled Mellitus, apparently over his refusal to give them communion without their first being baptised, and the bishopric lapsed. The conversion of the kings of the East Saxons continued back and forth over the next generation, with another pagan succeeding the three brothers after their death in battle. Then followed King Sigeberht II, who converted to Christianity under the influence of King Oswiu of Northumbria, only to be murdered by two brothers who disapproved of the novel approach King Sigeberht was taking to rule: he was forgiving his enemies rather than going the usual route of killing them.

In the 8th century, Essex fell under the control of Mercia, then was subsumed into the kingdom of Wessex in 825, only to become part of the Danelaw as part of the treaty signed between Alfred and Guthrum. Essex was conquered by Edward the Elder, Alfred the Great's son, in 917, and duly became part of Wessex as that kingdom expanded towards becoming a newly unified country: England.

ABOVE
A stone in St Augustine's Abbey, Canterbury, marking the grave of Mellitus, first bishop of London

LEFT
The old St Paul's Cathedral, destroyed in the Great Fire of London, stood on the site of the Anglo-Saxon church first raised by Mellitus

Blood and Sea

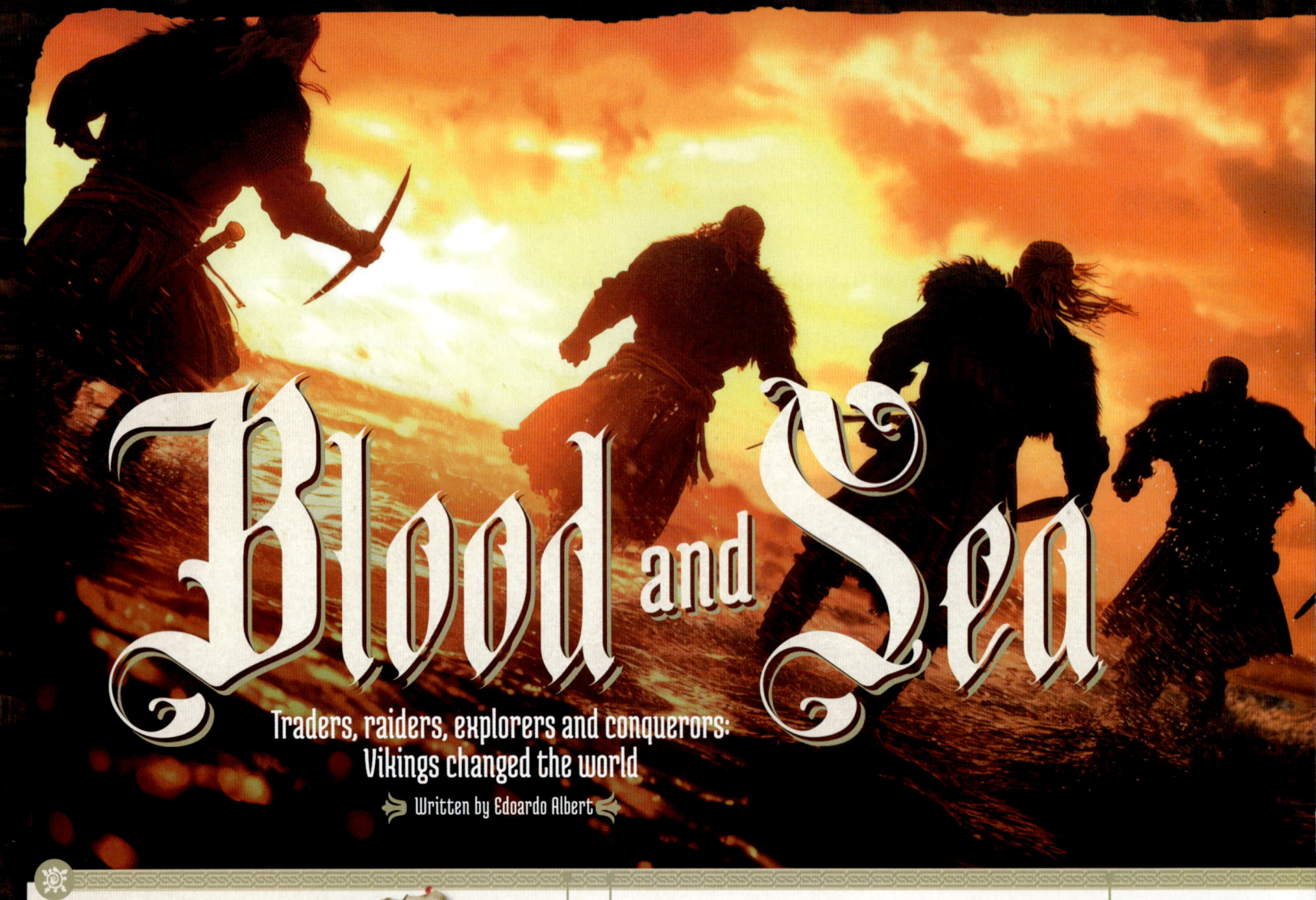

Traders, raiders, explorers and conquerors: Vikings changed the world

Written by Edoardo Albert

LEFT Ruthless Viking raiders round up terrified monks in the aftermath of their infamous attack on St Cuthbert's Church in Lindisfarne

First meetings
789

The *Anglo-Saxon Chronicle* records the first English encounter with Vikings, when the royal reeve went to meet a group of seafarers who had landed at Portland, Dorset, to ask them for the tax on their wares. They promptly killed him.

THE BLOODY DAWN OF THE VIKING AGE
8 June 793

Imagine terrorists simultaneously destroying St Paul's Cathedral and defacing the Mona Lisa. The Viking attack on the monastery at Lindisfarne evoked the same horror, for Lindisfarne was the foremost spiritual and cultural centre of northeastern Europe, the mother house to which the churchmen who had initiated the Carolingian Renaissance looked for inspiration and support. Alcuin, the English scholar headhunted by Charlemagne for his court, expressed the widespread horror at the attack: "Never before has such terror appeared in Britain. Behold the church of St Cuthbert, splattered with the blood of God's priests, robbed of its ornaments." The attack on Lindisfarne is taken as the beginning of the Viking Age (which lasted until 1066), when the Norse undertook their remarkable explorations and invasions.

Another Holy Isle sacked
806

The abbey on Iona, the mother house of the monastery on Lindisfarne, was attacked by Vikings in 795, 802, 806 and 825, with 68 monks dying during the 806 attack. After the massacre in 806, the monks established a (safer) abbey at Kells, but Iona remained the mother house until 878.

> "The royal reeve went to ask the Vikings for tax on their wares. They killed him"

IT'S COLD UP NORTH
9th century

When a Faroese mariner named Naddoðr was blown off course and landed on a desolate northern island, the island had already been discovered by Irish monks. Naddoðr called the island 'Snowland'. Cold became a theme of reports of the island, for the first Norse to set sail intentionally for the island, Flóki Vilgerðarson, named it Iceland after a particularly uncomfortable first winter. Flóki returned to Norway with reports of the island's harsh climate, but they were not enough to put off further settlers hungry for land, and in fact Flóki himself later returned to Iceland and stayed. In 874, the first permanent settlement was made by Ingólfr Arnarson and his family. They made their home at what would become Iceland's capital, Reykjavik. The Viking age of discovery had begun.

LEFT Ingólfr Arnarson making his home where the pillars of his high seat washed ashore

ACROSS OCEANS AND UP RIVERS
834

The Viking Age was a result of the perfecting of Norse ship-building technology. The longship interred in 834 in Oseberg, Norway, as the final resting place for two high-status women, is a wonderfully preserved example of such a vessel, highlighting the workmanship that allowed these clinker-built boats (made from overlapping planks) to successfully navigate rivers, coasts and seas. These supremely flexible craft allowed eastern Vikings to navigate the rivers of Europe and were light enough for portage to the headwaters of the rivers feeding into the Black Sea, opening trade routes to Byzantium and all its riches. For long-distance ocean voyages, the Vikings built deeper, broader boats that relied on sail for propulsion, with oars mainly used when the wind failed. These 'knarr' were the boats that would later cross the Atlantic.

RIGHT The elegant lines of the Oseberg ship showing its clinker-built construction

Vikings found Dublin
841

Having raided around the Irish Sea for half a century, the Vikings needed a base. They chose Duiblinn, the 'black pool', which was already an important ecclesiastical site, for its natural harbour. At first, Dublin was a winter camp, a secure base from which to sally forth on summer raids, but it became the chief city of the Norse in Ireland.

Vikings head east
862

Swedish Vikings went east and south, crossing the Baltic Sea and sailing upstream along rivers. These Vikings discovered that carrying their boats allowed them access to rivers flowing to the Black and Caspian seas. According to the *Russian Primary Chronicle*, Rurik built the first settlement near Novgorod and established a dynasty that lasted for 700 years.

VIKINGS ENTER MEDITERRANEAN AND START RAIDING
859-862

In 859, Viking chieftains Hastein and Bjorn Ironside set sail with 52 ships from their base on the Loire to raid the rich ports of the Mediterranean. The Spanish kingdoms put up stiff resistance, but the Viking fleet entered the Mediterranean and wintered at the mouth of the Rhone before raiding southern France and Italy. Trading with the Muslims of North Africa, Hastein bought slaves whom he later sold on at the Dublin slave market. All told, 20 ships made it back.

LEFT
There's only one king of England called 'Great'. Alfred deserved it

RIGHT
Part of Rollo's deal with Charles the Simple was his baptism. The Normans soon became devout Christians

THE GREAT HEATHEN ARMY
865-878

In 865 a Viking army landed on the Isle of Thanet in Kent bent on conquest, and over the next few years it destroyed the kingdoms of East Anglia and Northumbria and installed a puppet king in Mercia. Of the Anglo-Saxon kingdoms, only Wessex was left, with a young king in charge called Alfred. Despite his youth, Alfred defeated the Vikings at the Battle of Ashdown on 8 January 871. He followed this up in 878 with a crucial victory at the Battle of Edington. The resulting treaty split the country between Alfred's kingdom and the Norse Danelaw. But Alfred's son and daughter, Edward and Æthelflæd, would later begin the reconquest of England, a mission his grandson, Æhelstan, completed in 927.

NORTHMAN FOUNDS NORMANDY
911

The Carolingian Empire assembled by Charlemagne began to dissolve after his death. Among the Vikings attacking France was a Northman called Rollo. Having unsuccessfully laid siege to Paris, he set up his base on the estuary of the River Seine near Rouen, from where he raided for a decade. Unable to expel Rollo, Charles the Simple hit on the strategy of ceding the territory that Rollo had occupied to the Northman in return for Rollo swearing allegiance to him. Under the terms of the Treaty of Saint-Clair-sur-Epte, Rollo and his men converted to Christianity. The treaty did not preclude him from continuing as a Viking chieftain, and in the following decades he expanded his territory until, upon his death in 932, it included almost all the land that would become the Duchy of Normandy.

Vikings found kingdom in York
866

In 866, the Great Heathen Army conquered York, taking control of the southern half of the ancient Anglo-Saxon kingdom of Northumbria. York, or Jórvík, became the chief city of Viking England, with the Five Boroughs – Derby, Leicester, Lincoln, Nottingham and Stafford – to the south.

RIGHT
Harald Fairhair, whose strict rule in Norway possibly led to further Viking expansion

FAR RIGHT
A Christian convert, Leif Erikson introduced the new religion to Greenland as well as finding America

The last Viking king of York
954

Eric Bloodaxe, whose nickname suggests the means by which he seized and kept power, was finally deposed as king of York. With his passing ended the Viking kingdom of Jórvík.

Battle of Brunanburh
937

In 937, an alliance of Olaf Guthfrithson, King of Dublin, Constantine II of Scotland and Owain, King of Strathclyde, attempted to defeat King Æthelstan and seize England. Æthelstan's hard-won victory at the Battle of Brunanburh ensured that England remained unified.

THE FIRST KING OF NORWAY
872

According to the sagas written in Iceland in the 13th century, Harald, nicknamed Fairhair, succeeded his father, Halvdan the Black, as chieftain of the Yngling family domain in southeast Norway. Only ten at his succession, Harald clung to power with the help of his uncle. He gradually consolidated his rule, winning the Battle of Hafrsfjord somewhere between 872 and 890, whereupon he proclaimed himself King of Norway.

Blood and Sea

THE FIRST VIKING CONQUEST OF ENGLAND
1016

By 1013, the most incompetent king in English history, Æthelred, had succeeded in so enraging Sweyn Forkbeard, king of the Danes, that Sweyn personally invaded England. Sweyn's efforts were successful, but he didn't live long to enjoy them, dying on 3 February 1014. Having fled, Æthelred returned as king, forcing Sweyn's son, Cnut, to flee. In August 1015, Cnut returned at the head of another invasion fleet. Over the next 14 months he battled Æthelred's son, Edmund Ironside, eventually completing the first Viking conquest of England.

FOR THE EMPIRE
989

In 989, Basil II, ruler of the Byzantine Empire, was beset by enemies. Norsemen had been royal bodyguards for a century or more, so he turned to Vladimir I, Grand Prince of Kiev, the Norse-descended ruler of the Kievan Rus. Vladimir agreed to come to Basil's aid in return for his sister. No imperial princess had ever married a barbarian before – even Charlemagne had been rejected. But Vladimir was willing to convert to Christianity if that secured the marriage. So, in 989, a nervous Anna married Vladimir, who promptly sent 6,000 men to the emperor's aid.

Brian Boru defeats the Norse and unifies Ireland
1014

In the first millennium, Ireland had a surfeit of kings, both native and Norse: some 150 of them. Brian Boru gradually brought the other kingdoms under his control before meeting the armies of Leinster and Dublin at the Battle of Clontarf on 23 April 1014. Although Brian was killed in the battle, his army was victorious.

ABOVE LEFT
Before choosing Christianity, Vladimir sent men to report back on the religions of the peoples around him. Those faiths forbidding alcohol were quickly ruled out of the running

RIGHT
That story of Cnut and the tide? It was to show how the king was impervious to flatterers

TO GREENLAND AND BEYOND
982–c.1000

Around 982, an Icelander named Erik was exiled for murder by the island's assembly for three years. Rather than sail back to Norway, he set sail to investigate stories of a land further west. According to the sagas, he found and explored it for the term of his exile. Three years later Erik returned to Iceland with tales of this new land, which he named 'Greenland'. His son, Leif, would go even further in 1000 CE, gathering a crew to investigate reports of a land west of Greenland. Crossing 1,800 miles of sea, they eventually spotted it. They had discovered the New World 500 years before Christopher Columbus.

SECOND CONQUEST OF ENGLAND
1066

Edward the Confessor died on 5 January 1066, childless and with a history of being all too free in promising his throne to others. Through the fraught months of 1066, three claimants came forward: Harold Godwinson, Earl of Wessex; William, Duke of Normandy; and Harald Hardrada, King of Norway. Harold was crowned on 6 January, but both William and Harald set about preparing to seize the crown. After a tense summer of waiting, all these claimants came together in combat. On 25 September, Harold defeated Hardrada at the Battle of Stamford Bridge only to die at the Battle of Hastings on 14 October. The Viking Age ended with the death of Hardrada.

Paying the Dane
991–1013

Æthelred paid off raiding Viking armies from 991 until, in 1002, he ordered the massacre of all Danes in English territory. Unfortunately the sister of Sweyn Forkbeard, king of Denmark, was killed. Sweyn harried Æthelred's kingdom mercilessly: this was the start of the events that would end in the Norman conquest 50 years later.

RIGHT
Tostig Godwinson, Harold's exiled brother, inveigles Harald Hardrada to join him in an invasion of England

41

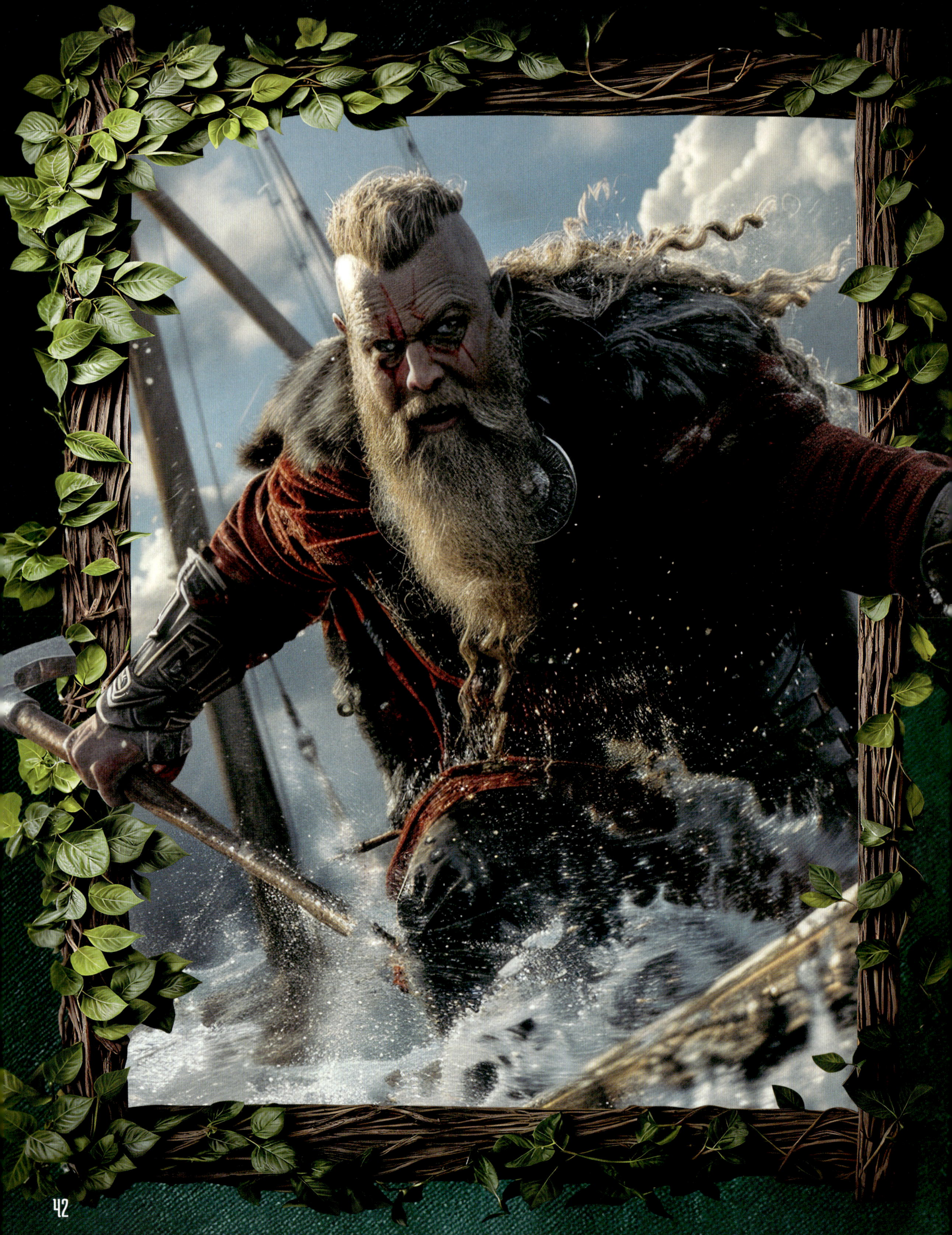

# Early Viking Raids on Britain

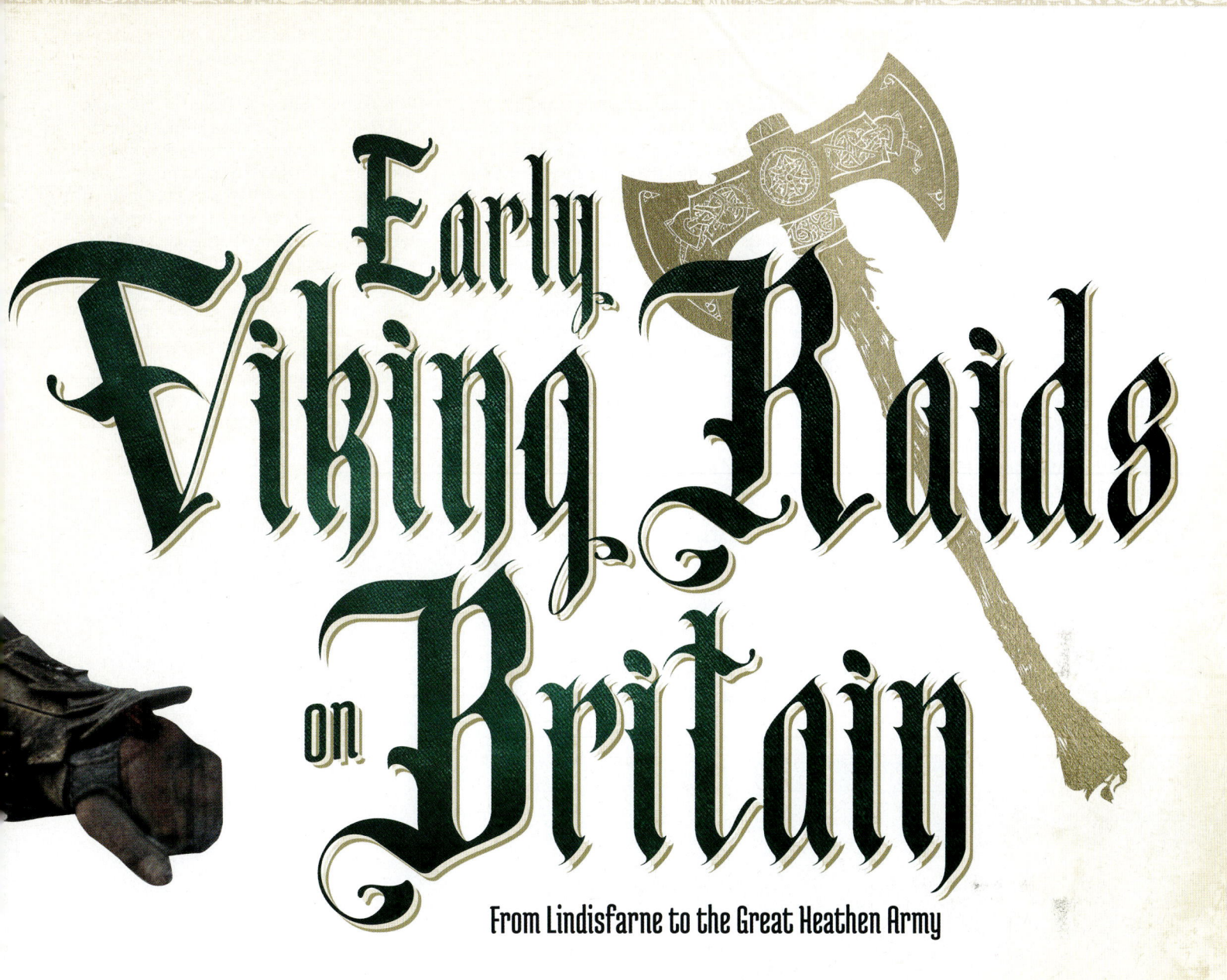

From Lindisfarne to the Great Heathen Army

The name of Beauheard is not perhaps as well-remembered these days as it should be. Beauheard was a king's reeve (or sheriff), based at Dorchester in Dorset. One day in the year 789, he received news that a group of strangers had landed on the coast at nearby Portland. Portland was probably a trading base of some local significance (certainly it would be the target for a number of Viking raids over the years) and the arrival of strangers there would need to be investigated, so Beauheard set out to do so.

The details of what happened when he arrived are unclear. Maybe there was a misunderstanding between two groups who didn't speak exactly the same language, or perhaps what occurred was quite deliberate. The end result, however, was clear enough; Beauheard lay dead, the first known victim of the Vikings in England. His killers were men from Scandinavia, probably from Hordaland in southwest Norway.

This is the first surviving reference to a Viking attack in England. That, however, does not mean there weren't any before this; it could be that earlier attacks were unrecorded or that records were subsequently lost. There are hints though that this was not an isolated incident; charters from the reign of the great Mercian king Offa (who died in 796) mention the building of coastal fortifications against "marauding heathens", which probably means Vikings, so clearly the threat from the raiders was already starting to ring alarm bells.

While the incident at Portland may have been disturbing, it was not perhaps that unusual in what were frequently violent times. The next known raid was at the opposite end of the spectrum. It was at the other end of the country, too – rather than the kingdom of Wessex suffering another attack, it was Northumbria in the northeast that fell victim to the Viking hordes.

Lindisfarne was a very sacred site at the time; the monastery there housed the relics of Saint Cuthbert, the pre-eminent Anglo-Saxon saint. Nowadays it seems a remote and distant place, but at the end of the 8th century it was a hub of spiritual and physical activity. A few miles off, well within view on most days, was the ancient Northumbrian fortress of Bamburgh, one of the oldest occupied sites of Anglo-Saxon England, keeping a distant but in this case useless watch on the monastery.

On a June day in 793, a hammer-blow fell on the monastery in the shape of a catastrophic Viking raid. The monks were caught completely unaware when the raiders came in from the sea, though it is quite probable that the raiders knew exactly where they were headed. Lindisfarne was famous and, by the standards of the day, wealthy. It is quite possible that the raiders had traded with the place before and noticed its flimsy protection. It was very common for a Viking to be a trader one day and a raider the next; whatever seemed to offer the best chance of profit in any given circumstance would dictate which one it would be.

Lindisfarne went up in flames. Its treasures were looted (to the Vikings that would mean taking gold and silver rather than the wonderful manuscripts made there – unless these happened to be in richly decorated book bindings, they were of little interest). Monks were drowned or brutally murdered where they stood. But there was another prize on offer too, one that was altogether more sinister and possibly more attractive to the raiders: slaves. The Vikings would make a very lucrative living from the buoyant slave trade and healthy young men, attractive women and children with the potential to be either were very valuable commodities. Certainly the raiders took slaves away with them from Lindisfarne, as they would on many other occasions in the future.

In Francia, the Northumbrian scholar Alcuin, who was based at the court of the great Holy Roman emperor Charlemagne, wrote back home in shock at the turn of events in Northumbria. To him, as to many subsequent commentators, the Vikings were God's avengers, a terrifying punishment for the sinful way of life lived by many Northumbrians, both secular and clerical. Loose-living, and even dressing like pagans, were quoted as some of the specific sins that had outraged God. The Northumbrians would need to mend their ways or more raids would follow.

And follow they did, for a time; other great monasteries were raided such as those at Jarrow-Monkwearmouth and Hartness (later Hartlepool). But in the first few decades of the 9th century, specific mentions of Viking raids in England dry up. This again does not necessarily mean that none took place; certainly the Vikings were known to be very active in Ireland and Scotland during this period. However, our main source for the period, the *Anglo-Saxon Chronicle*, was not written up until towards the end of the 9th century, so in the interim some records may have been lost.

Vikings were certainly active in Wessex once more in 836, when they attacked Carhampton in Somerset, an important royal estate. The West Saxon king Ecgbert was defeated when he faced them in battle. He had his revenge, though, when shortly afterwards he bested a combined Viking-Cornish army at Hingston Down near the River Tamar. Cornwall had recently been subjugated by the West Saxons and clearly some of the Cornish thought that an alliance with a Viking force was preferable to being under the control of Wessex. The Vikings were very capable of forging diplomatic alliances when it suited their purpose.

The intensity of the Viking attacks ratcheted up in the 850s and 860s. In 851 a Viking force over-wintered at Thanet in Kent rather than go home for the season. This suggested that Viking attacks were becoming more ambitious in their scope and coincided with an upsurge in activity in Ireland, too. While there was no direct political relationship between the kingdoms of England and those of Ireland, their proximity meant that Vikings were able to move and raid between the two main islands with relative impunity.

The climax of this upsurge in activity saw the arrival of what was ominously known as the Great Heathen Army (mycel hæþen here) in 865. This was allegedly led by three sons of a legendary figure, Ragnar Loðbrok, who were named Halfdan, Ubba and Ivarr (possibly another equally legendary figure known as Ivarr the Boneless). They first of all made their way to East Anglia

What's in a name?
It's time to uncover why we call them 'Vikings'

There are several theories as to how the Vikings got their name. One is that the word 'Viking' derives from the Old Norse 'vik', which means creek or bay, referring to the harbours where they moored their ships. Another theory is that the name comes from the region known as the Viken, around the Oslofjord in Norway, though this would be somewhat misleading as many Vikings came from other parts of Norway, as well as Sweden and Denmark and even further afield. In Old Norse, to go a-viking (fara i viking) was to set out on a raid, so perhaps the most likely origin of the word means some kind of raider.

They were rarely called Vikings by their victims. In the *Anglo-Saxon Chronicle* they were often referred to as Danes, while elsewhere, such as in Francia (which covered modern France, the Low Countries and much of Germany) they were called Northmen, from which the word 'Norman' derives. The suggestion of a specific national origin for the raiders is misleading: so-called Danish armies that invaded England, for example, often had warriors from Sweden and Norway among their number. There is even archaeological evidence that men might have come from as far away as Finland, Poland and Belarus on occasion.

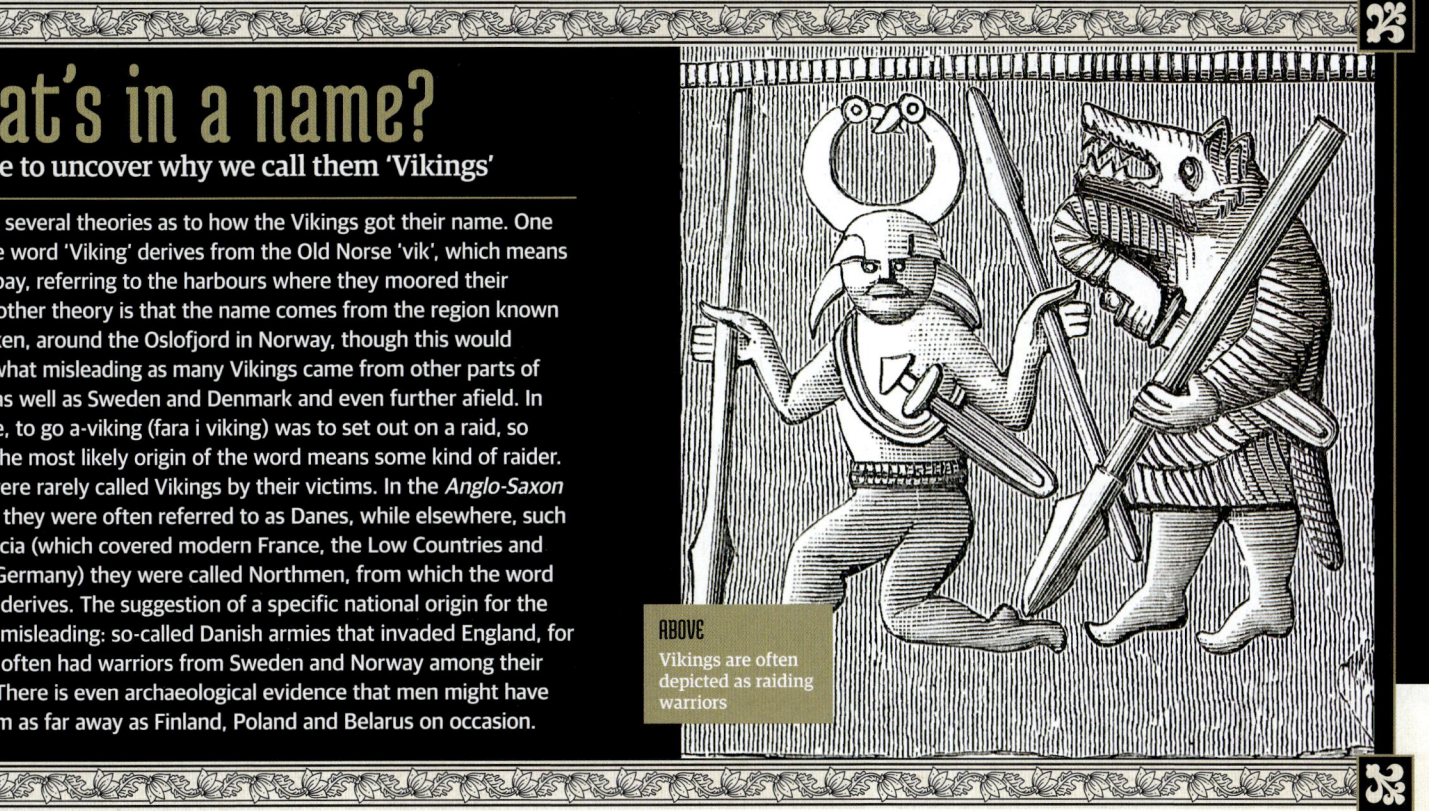

ABOVE
Vikings are often depicted as raiding warriors

ABOVE
Ivarr the Boneless and Ubba attacking England, from a 15th-century manuscript

LEFT
Lindisfarne, where the Viking attack in 793 caused widespread shock in Europe

where they forced the king, Edmund, to provide them with horses and provisions (the Vikings were outstanding horsemen as well as seafarers). This substantial force then took York (Anglo-Saxon Eoforwic), which would eventually become Jorvik, the foremost Viking settlement in England. In the process they slaughtered the incumbent king whose name was Ælle. In one lurid account, he was subjected to the brutal ritual execution known as the 'blood eagle', in which the victim's torso was cut open, his ribs hacked apart and his lungs splayed across his back like wings in a macabre imitation of an eagle. Not all historians believed that this actually happened – much of the Viking story is told by later saga-writers who clearly had an interest in embellishing their plotlines – but there are other accounts of this ritual execution being used, so we cannot be sure that the story is a complete fabrication.

The Vikings then moved on Mercia, forcing the kingdom into submission, before returning to East Anglia. This time they took the kingdom here too, in the process killing King Edmund. In some accounts (written slightly after the event) Edmund was also ritually executed, this time by being tied up and shot to death with arrows in imitation of Saint Sebastian. Certainly Edmund would become England's foremost martyr-king and he would become a prominent saint, which is ironic considering that many Christianised Vikings later set up their home in the country.

Wessex now stood alone, and the Great Heathen Army fell on it in 870. Ivarr was now absent from the army – he is known to have been active in Scotland and Ireland at about this time – and the force was led by Halfdan and a new leader by the name of Guthrum. In the succeeding year, the Great Heathen Army moved deeper into Wessex in a campaign that included nine battles and undoubtedly many other skirmishes. There was supposedly a great Anglo-Saxon victory at Ashdown, but in fact this made little difference to the course of events.

The Viking war machine moved inexorably on, winning victories at Basing, Meretun and Wilton. Sometime during the campaign the king of Wessex, Æthelred I, died – possibly of wounds suffered in one of the battles – and his place was taken by his young brother Alfred. Alfred had grown up quickly during the campaign and negotiated a truce with the Viking force – an arrangement that cost him a lot of money. The Vikings, satisfied with the takings from their extended foray but possibly also needing to regroup and reinforce, moved out of Wessex for the time being; but they would not be away for long. Their absence gave the soon-to-be great Alfred a chance to rally... and plan his revenge.

> "They slaughtered the incumbent king, Ælle. In one lurid account, he was subjected to a brutal ritual execution"

When Vikings Ruled the Waves

Portrayed as bloodthirsty pirates pillaging innocent villagers, Vikings also ruled the waves with a lucrative trade network

The great white sail cracked as the vicious Atlantic wind lashed against it, but still the ship sailed on. Long and sleek, the warship, crafted from mighty oak, crashed through the waves, sending a sharp spray of water across the deck. The men inside rowed as one, their mighty muscles straining as they plunged the oars deep into the water and drove the ship forward through the turbulent waves. Their strength alone brought the ship to land and they poured out onto the beach. Dressed in thick woollen tunics, the warriors were armed with an array of weapons, from long sharpened spears to hefty battle-axes. With a booming voice one man yelled to the others, thrusting his sword into the air, and the rest bellowed in response. Then onward he ran, as the united force thundered uphill against the billowing wind. Their destination? A coastal monastery bursting full of gold, gems and hefty food supplies ripe for the taking, and only a collection of quiet, unassuming monks to protect it.

This image of monstrous invaders laying siege to innocent monasteries and pillaging them of their precious items is the first one that leaps to mind when many are confronted with the word 'Viking'. The portrayal of the Norse tribesmen as rapists and pillagers is so prevailing that it's often forgotten that the word Viking itself means to go on an expedition. It is easy to fall into the assumption that these people were nothing more than pirates – taking from those too weak to defend themselves. And it is undeniable that this happened: the Viking invaders sailed from Scandinavia to coasts of the British Isles and beyond, invading villages and monasteries, killing the inhabitants and stealing their riches. It's spoken about in first-hand accounts and it's still being evidenced today in the Viking hoards left by anxious townsfolk who hurried to hide their riches from the invaders.

However, this only tells half the story. Two things powered the Viking civilisation: the vicious raids they're famous for, and something else – trade. Not only did Vikings set up new colonies in the lands they invaded, but they also created powerful trade routes that helped their nation to become one of the most prosperous in the world.

For the majority of the year, the same Vikings who had pillaged the towns worked the land, tirelessly toiling in the fields, or creating intricate and valuable ornaments and jewellery to fund their blossoming civilisation.

> Contrary to modern preconceptions, Vikings had excellent hygiene, with many bathing at least once a week

When Vikings ruled the waves

Vicious Vikings

Meet Scandinavia's most terrifying plunderers

Erik the Red 951-1003
Infamous for: Being exiled from Iceland for murder. He went on to colonise Greenland

Guthrum Unknown - 890
Infamous for: Waging war against the king of the West Saxons – Alfred the Great

Ingvar the Far-Travelled Unknown
Infamous for: Pillaging the shores of the Caspian Sea

Rodulf Haraldsson Unknown - 873
Infamous for: Leading raids in Britain, France and Germany

Ivar the Boneless Unknown
Infamous for: Invading Anglo-Saxon kingdoms of England using the Great Heathen Army

47

Viking voyages

As expert ship builders, the Vikings were able to voyage further and wider than any civilisation before...

Centuries before Christopher Columbus would stumble upon the land now known as America, the Vikings had claimed the Atlantic Ocean as their own backyard. They had mastered Russia's river system and reached the Middle East; their impressive voyages helped them to become leaders of a rapidly developing world and this new Viking civilisation thrived thanks to the power of a single creation: the ship.

The entire Viking society was built around their ships, which were bigger, lighter and faster than any before. These vessels had been perfected over many years, with the power to brave the vicious storms of the Atlantic Ocean, but also the sleek construction to skim through shallow rivers. These powerful and efficient ships enabled their mighty passengers to create colonies all over the world, and the building and maintaining of these vessels became the basis of Viking society.

Vikings were using their mighty sea power to trade around the coast of Europe while the British Empire was merely a collection of scattered kingdoms unable to defend their shores. The Viking sailors were aware that it was often easier to take the same journey by water rather than land, with some journeys taking five days by sea, compared to a month on land, and they used this to their advantage. Longer voyages were carried out by those settling in strange and exciting foreign lands, and the Viking civilisation spread to Iceland, Greenland, and even to Canada and North America.

The image of a Viking longboat crashing through the waves with its fierce dragon figurehead and its long, sleek curves is certainly an inspiring one, but for those onboard, life was not quite so glamorous. With no shelter, at night the sailors used the sail as a makeshift tent that they would sleep under, shivering beneath blankets or animal skin sleeping bags. The only sustenance would be dried or salted meat with water, beer or sour milk to drink. The sinking of vessels was no great tragedy, but rather expected on long journeys. There would be no rescue sent as usually nobody knew about sunken ships for weeks, months or even years. It was not unusual for any number of ships to go missing on voyages across the brutal Atlantic Ocean. When Erik the Red travelled to Greenland, only 14 of his original 25 ships managed to arrive safely.

However, it was the determination and hardiness of the voyagers willing to take these risks that led the Vikings to valuable and exotic treasures and trade lying along the coastlines of the world. Toward the end of the 8th century, Viking voyagers began an invasion of England that would forever determine the fate of the island nation. By 860 this pioneering spirit led them to the assault of Constantinople, then some 20 years later, in 885, Viking ships attacked the mighty city of Paris. Driven by the quest for trade, territory, plunder and a thirst for adventure, the impact of these historic voyages can still be felt around the world today.

Some dead Vikings were laid to rest in boats surrounded by their weapons, valuable property, and even living slaves

Woollen sail
Longships featured one large square sail approximately ten metres wide. These were most likely made from wool, though no sails have survived to confirm this. To keep the sail's shape when it got wet, the wool was covered with criss-crossing leather strips.

Wooden hull
All Viking ships were made in the same way, using planks of oak or pine overlapped and nailed together. The ships were then reinforced and made watertight by using tarred wool or other animal furs to fill in the gaps between the planks.

Oarports
These were holes for the oars that ran along the entire length of the ship on both sides. The holes would also be used to tie shields in place, but only when the ships were in port as the risk of losing their vital protection while the ship was in motion was too great.

Frightening figurehead
The front of the ship was often decorated with a carving of an animal head, usually a mix between a dragon and a snake. These figureheads were removable and would only be put up when the ship was approaching land, as they risked heavy damage while out at sea.

When Vikings ruled the waves

Steering oar
This rudder-like oar, also known as a 'steerboard', was attached to the back of the ship on the starboard side. It was used to steer the ship and would require a large amount of physical exertion compared to modern alternatives. The position of the 'steerboard' is where the term 'starboard' originated from.

Keel for strength
The keel of the ship would be made first and provided the ship with strength beneath the waterline, while also allowing navigation in shallow waters. Sometimes ships would feature a false outer keel, which would take the brunt of the wear when ships were dragged onto beaches.

Oars for speed
Oars differed in length depending on where they would be used. There were no seats on Viking ships, so the oarsmen sat on storage chests. Oars were usually used to gain speed quickly when near a coast or in a river, then stored out of place when out at sea.

Small hold
The longship was designed for war, so it was vital for it to be fast. Because of this, they had a small loading capacity, with room for only high-value goods and booty. The merchant ships would be able to carry far more cargo, with room for livestock to be transported onboard.

Navigation

Before some of the greatest explorers in history were born, Vikings had already navigated their way around the world. But with no compasses, satellites or radios, how did this tribe of Scandinavians manage to map the globe so impressively? The answer is simpler than you might expect – experience. Rather than relying on devices, Viking travellers trusted nature to guide them. They would study the position of the stars and Sun, and even the colour of the sea and movement of the waves would give them an indication of how close they were to land.

Once a journey was complete, sailors would recount their voyage to others who wished to make the same journey. This ancient wisdom would be passed through generations of sailors.

The only tools Viking sailors needed were related to the Sun. For example, a sun-shadow board would be used at noon to check whether the ship was on course. A sun-stone could also be used on foggy days when the Sun was not visible. This stone would change colour to indicate the position of the Sun behind the clouds.

Images Source: Wikipedia Commons / Public Domain

49

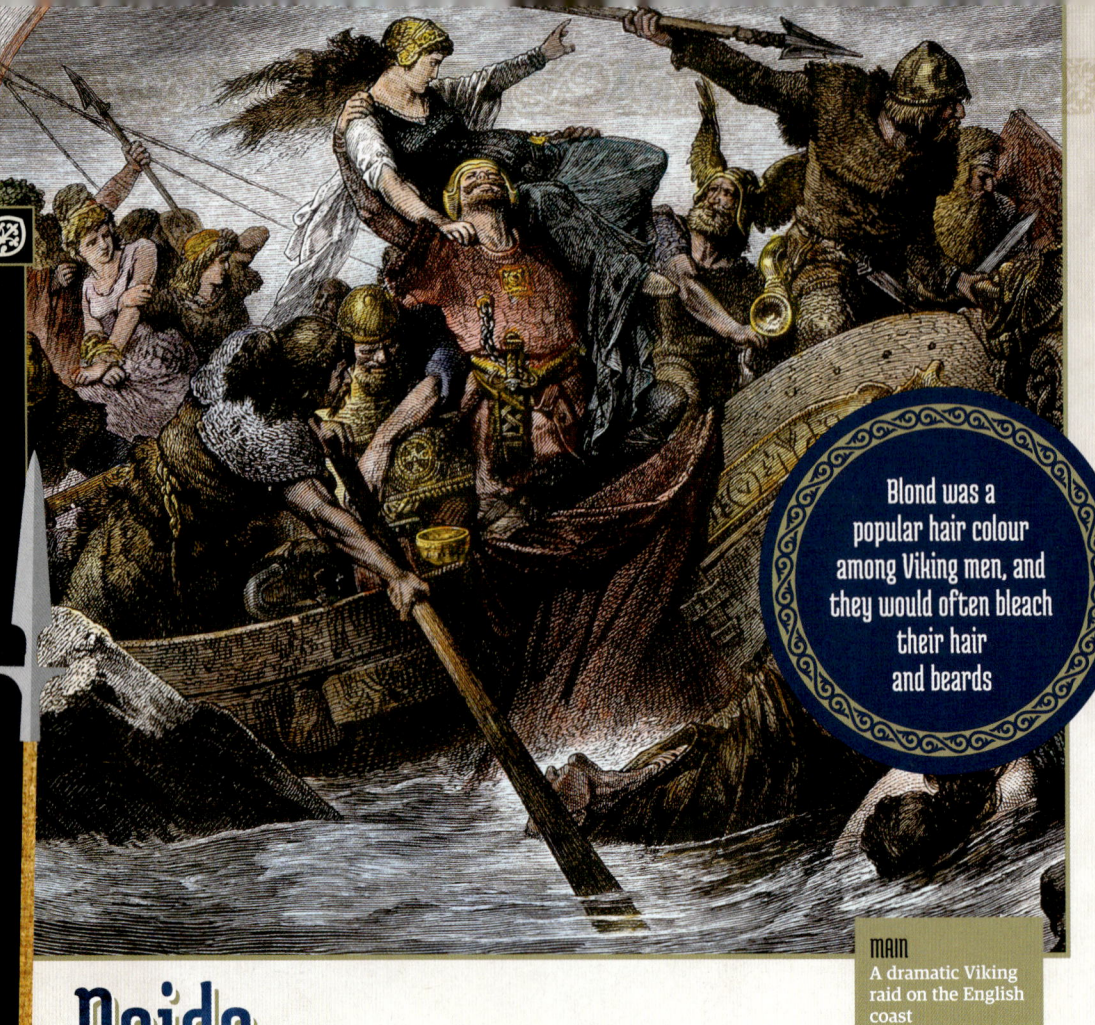

Deadliest weapons

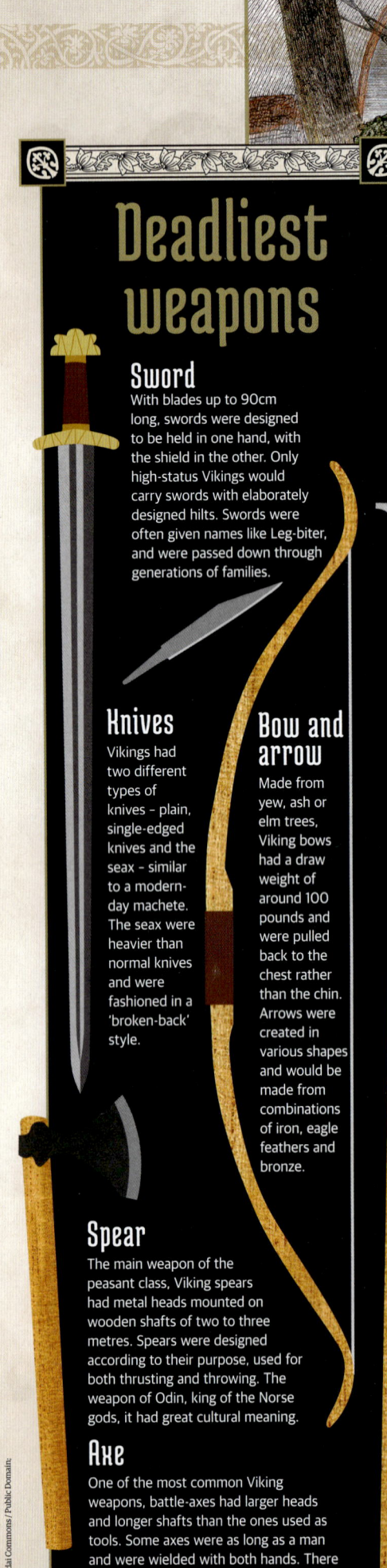

Sword
With blades up to 90cm long, swords were designed to be held in one hand, with the shield in the other. Only high-status Vikings would carry swords with elaborately designed hilts. Swords were often given names like Leg-biter, and were passed down through generations of families.

Knives
Vikings had two different types of knives – plain, single-edged knives and the seax – similar to a modern-day machete. The seax were heavier than normal knives and were fashioned in a 'broken-back' style.

Bow and arrow
Made from yew, ash or elm trees, Viking bows had a draw weight of around 100 pounds and were pulled back to the chest rather than the chin. Arrows were created in various shapes and would be made from combinations of iron, eagle feathers and bronze.

Spear
The main weapon of the peasant class, Viking spears had metal heads mounted on wooden shafts of two to three metres. Spears were designed according to their purpose, used for both thrusting and throwing. The weapon of Odin, king of the Norse gods, it had great cultural meaning.

Axe
One of the most common Viking weapons, battle-axes had larger heads and longer shafts than the ones used as tools. Some axes were as long as a man and were wielded with both hands. There were also smaller throwing axes.

Blond was a popular hair colour among Viking men, and they would often bleach their hair and beards

MAIN
A dramatic Viking raid on the English coast

Raids

No monastery was safe from the fiery scourge that swept over the land from beyond the sea

They had arrived in the dead of night; the darkness had been so thick that the monks had not seen their ship until it landed on the shore. It was too late, they all knew it, to call for help. A brother had run into the halls, waking the monks from their beds with shrill cries of "The demons are here! They're coming! They're coming!" Some of the brothers began to scream for help, while others leapt into action, grabbing precious items and concealing them in the folds of their cloaks. But already the doors were down and already the invaders were here. They were huge – bigger than any man the humble brethren had ever seen – with their wild blond hair and mighty weapons grasped in hand. They leapt upon the monks immediately, hacking at their bodies with a frenzied ferocity. Some pleaded for mercy, some did not have time to plead. There was no time for negotiations; how can one negotiate with pure, unbridled violence? There was only death, destruction and blood as they swung their axes and jabbed their swords. One brother alone had managed to escape the massacre. He speedily weaved through the figures and threw himself down into the tall grass outside. He watched as body after body was thrown from the doors of his home; he watched as men still alive were cast off the high cliff into the sea; and he watched as the heathens set the holy walls alight with flame. The hot wind lashed against his face and robes in the flickering darkness. He grasped a golden chalice in his hands numbly, the only thing he had been able to rescue before fleeing. The invaders had the rest of it, all the precious items loaded into sacks on their large ships. And almost as quickly as they had arrived, they slipped away from the shore and returned to the darkness.

In 793, a Viking crew sailing near northeast England raided a Christian monastery at Lindisfarne. For the Vikings the strange, exposed building packed full of valuable treasures was an opportunity too good to miss, but for many in England this shocking and unprovoked attack marked the beginning of the scourge of Viking raids. These sporadic but violent assaults continued across the coasts of England, and by 855 a force known as the Great Heathen Army had arrived in East Anglia. The army made their way across the country, capturing cities as they went, overrunning and overpowering the land. The Scandinavian warriors also launched invasions across the coasts of Ireland and all over mainland Europe. These raids even stretched to the Baltic Sea and Persia. The initial reasons for such rapid expansion are hotly contested between historians, with some believing the raids were a brutal response to the spread of Christianity, that the Scandinavian population had grown too large for their land, or perhaps they were the actions of men simply drawn by the thrill of adventure. Whatever the reasons, the invasions left a lasting scar on those who lived to see them.

When Vikings ruled the waves

How the Vikings raided

1 Preparation
Vikings did not strike haphazardly; their raids were planned down to the finest detail. They would first identify a weak target to attack along the coasts, which they knew perfectly. Because they had the fastest ships in the world they would launch their attack without any prior warning, ensuring that no help could reach their targets in time. Towards the mid-9th century these attacks had escalated to great fleets of 300-400 ships.

2 Gather horses
Viking ships were designed to row up river, but if the target was some distance away they would leave their ships and travel by horse. With no horses on the ships, they would raid nearby villages for mounts. These would be used to transport themselves and their booty over land.

3 Surprise attack
The pious and humble monks did not stand a chance faced with their fierce opponents armed with superior weapons. The well-trained Vikings would launch a sudden, vicious attack on the monastery, slaying the holy men. Some would be stripped naked, and cast outside, some taken prisoner, and others thrown into the sea.

4 Loot and burn
Once the monks were dealt with, Vikings pillaged at will. They plundered any valuables they could get their hands on, including food, but especially precious relics. However, they often ignored the valuable bibles. Once they had looted the buildings they set fire to the monasteries and the surrounding villages.

5 Escape
Laden down with their prisoners and booty, the Vikings would ride back to their ships, load them and sail away. They would later sell the gold, jewels and sacred emblems, and the monks would also fetch a high price in the European slave market.

Anatomy of a Viking warrior

Helmet
Vikings did not, in fact, have horned helmets. Instead, they were round with a guard around the eyes and nose. There is only one complete Viking helmet in existence – others may have been passed down through families then sold for scrap.

Hair
Long hair was favoured by both men and women. It would also be acceptable to shave one's hair or to wear it rolled in a tight bun near the nape of their neck. Men would also carefully groom their moustaches and beards.

Armour
Mail shirts or metal armour would have been expensive for the average raider, as would leather, so these were reserved only for those of high status. Ordinary Vikings likely fought wearing their everyday clothes, made from wool.

Shoes
Shoes were most often made from one long piece of leather sewn to the shape of the wearer's foot. Leather straps would be used to secure the boot to the foot, and thick woollen socks were worn to keep heat in.

Shield
Round shields were common and were made from light wood, such as fir or poplar and were reinforced with leather or iron around the edge. Round shields could get as large as 120cm in diameter, but most were around 75 to 90cm.

The attack on Lindisfarne

Lindisfarne is a holy island off the northeast coast of England, and during the Middle Ages was the base of Christian evangelising in the north of the country. However, in 793 a Viking raid on the monastery of Lindisfarne sent a wave of dismay washing over Christians worldwide. On 7 June, Viking raiders invaded the monastery and "destroyed God's church on Lindisfarne, with plunder and slaughter." Although the attack was not the first in the country, it was unusual in that it attacked the heart of the Christian nation in the north. A contemporary scholar wrote of the attack, "Never before has such terror appeared in Britain as we have now suffered from a pagan race [...] The heathens poured out the blood of saints around the altar, and trampled on the bodies of saints in the temple of God, like dung in the streets."

BELOW
Lindisfarne priory remains a place of pilgrimage to this day

51

What were the goods worth?

- 1 FEMALE SLAVE = 1 COW AND 1 OX
- 1 SUIT OF CHAIN MAIL = 2 HORSES OR 4 MALE SLAVES
- 1 HORSE = 3 COWS
- 1 STIRRUP = 1 SWORD OR 125G OF SILVER

WALRUS IVORY, WHALEBONE, ANIMAL FUR, ANIMAL SKIN

Finland

ANIMAL SKIN

Norway

SOAPSTONE

Sweden

Scotland

WHEAT, WOOL, HONEY, TIN

Denmark

Russia

England

Poland

Germany

Ukraine

SLAVES

France

SALT, WINE

SILVER, WINE

Turkey

WINE, SPICES

52

When Vikings ruled the waves

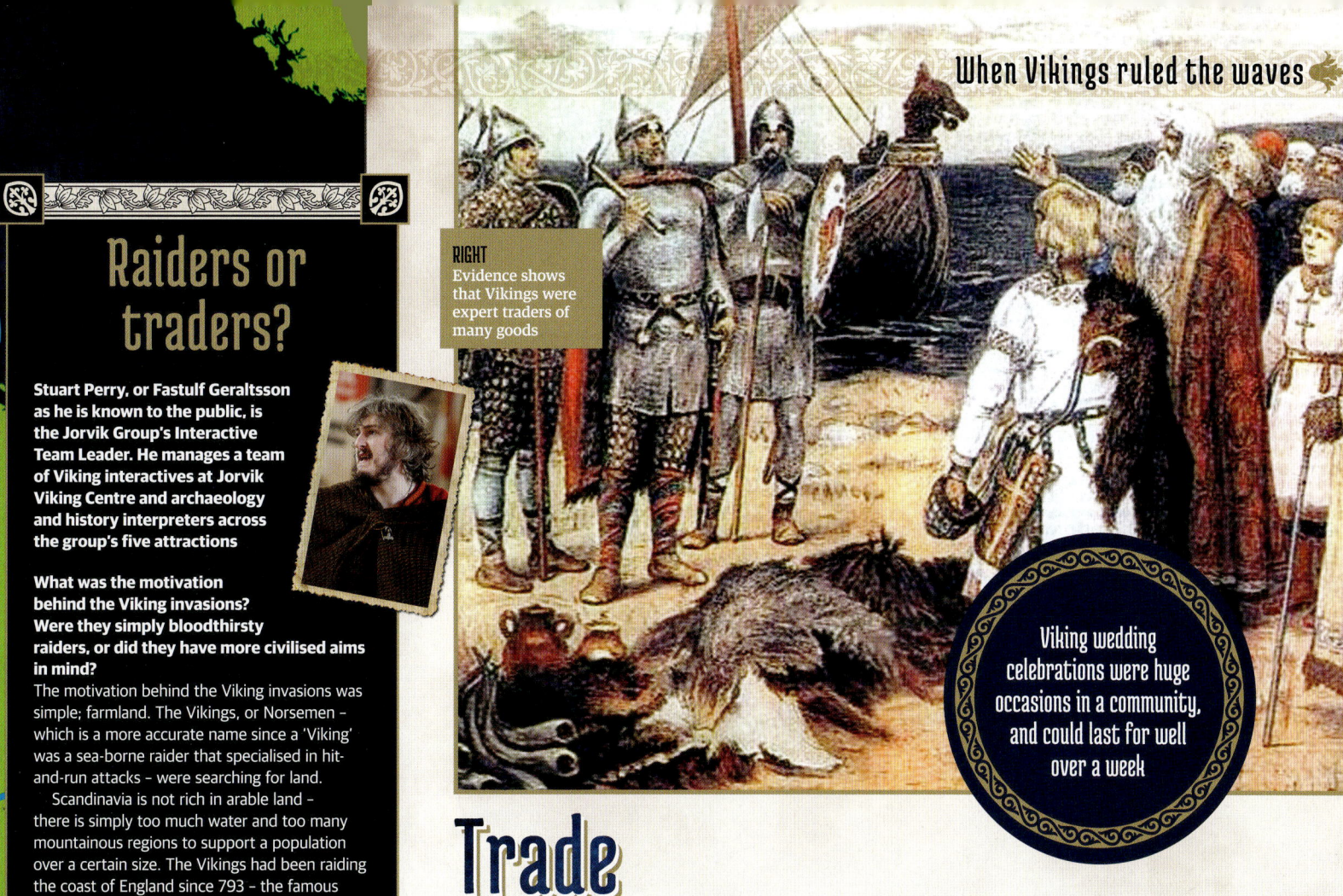

Raiders or traders?

Stuart Perry, or Fastulf Geraltsson as he is known to the public, is the Jorvik Group's Interactive Team Leader. He manages a team of Viking interactives at Jorvik Viking Centre and archaeology and history interpreters across the group's five attractions

What was the motivation behind the Viking invasions? Were they simply bloodthirsty raiders, or did they have more civilised aims in mind?

The motivation behind the Viking invasions was simple; farmland. The Vikings, or Norsemen – which is a more accurate name since a 'Viking' was a sea-borne raider that specialised in hit-and-run attacks – were searching for land.

Scandinavia is not rich in arable land – there is simply too much water and too many mountainous regions to support a population over a certain size. The Vikings had been raiding the coast of England since 793 – the famous attack on Lindisfarne – and would have had plenty of opportunity to see the abundance of good farmland, healthy crops and fat cattle all over the country. Combine this with the riches presented in the monasteries and towns they were so fond of raiding and England became a perfect area for expansion.

As for being 'bloodthirsty raiders', there is that element to the culture, yes, but it was not simply for violence that the Vikings went raiding. It was for profit. Rarely would the Vikings destroy an entire settlement, and the reason is simple; they wanted to come back and do it again! Raiding was a job for young impetuous men – but it was not the main focus of life in early medieval Scandinavia. It is this message that we convey at every opportunity here at Jorvik Viking Centre.

SILVER

SILK, SILVER, SPICES

RIGHT Evidence shows that Vikings were expert traders of many goods

Viking wedding celebrations were huge occasions in a community, and could last for well over a week

Trade

Vikings were not powered by brutality but instead a complex and prosperous trade network

Although raiding and pillaging provided a quick intake of wealth, it was not a stable way to live or to build a civilisation. Instead, the Vikings dedicated far more of their time to building up a prosperous and powerful trading network. Because of their superior ship-building skills they were able to travel to trade in faraway lands, obtaining a host of exotic and valuable goods. Their specially designed trading ships were able to carry up to 35 tonnes of cargo onboard them, including silver and even livestock.

Trading markets began to emerge along the west Baltic Sea in the mid-8th century where people came from far and wide to trade an array of goods. As these markets flourished, traders decided to settle permanently along the routes and they transformed into trading towns. Birka in Sweden, Kaupang in Norway and Hedeby in Denmark all grew to be prosperous and bustling trading settlements, with the inhabitants all working as craftsmen and merchants. Prosperous trading routes also emerged along the British Isles, with York and Dublin developing into major trading centres.

As the trade boom increased the Vikings travelled further afield, across the Baltic Sea and along the Russian rivers. They founded more trading towns in Kiev and Novgorod. The Viking traders even went as far as Istanbul, the capital of the mighty Byzantine Empire across the Black Sea. This perilous journey was one only the Vikings dared attempt, through vicious rapids and battling hostile natives. The Vikings continued their trading journey inland, bringing their goods to Jerusalem and Baghdad. The lure of the Silk Road and the exotic riches of the East were too good to resist, and Vikings met with traders from the Far East in their trading centres in Russia, trading fur and slaves for silk and spices.

Silver coins were the most common form of payment, but this was unlike today's currency where different coins are worth a particular value. The coins were weighed in scales to determine their value; this is because a lot of coins were melted down and crafted into intricate and beautiful jewellery to trade on. The great extent of the Viking trade network can be seen today in the hoards of silver coins, created in England, which have been found in Sweden, not to mention the 40,000 Arabic coins and the 38,000 German coins also uncovered there. Nordic bowls, Mediterranean silk and Baltic axe heads have even been discovered buried under English soil.

This vast trade network attracted a wealth of eager and talented artists and craftsmen. Viking bead-makers would import glass from Western Europe to create an array of simple and decorative beads for the wealthy to adorn themselves with, while the ample supply of amber from the Baltic lands was fashioned into pendants and playing pieces. Skilled Viking craftsmen transformed their imported bronze to fine ornaments and mass-produced brooches, and deer antlers could even be used to make delicate and beautiful combs.

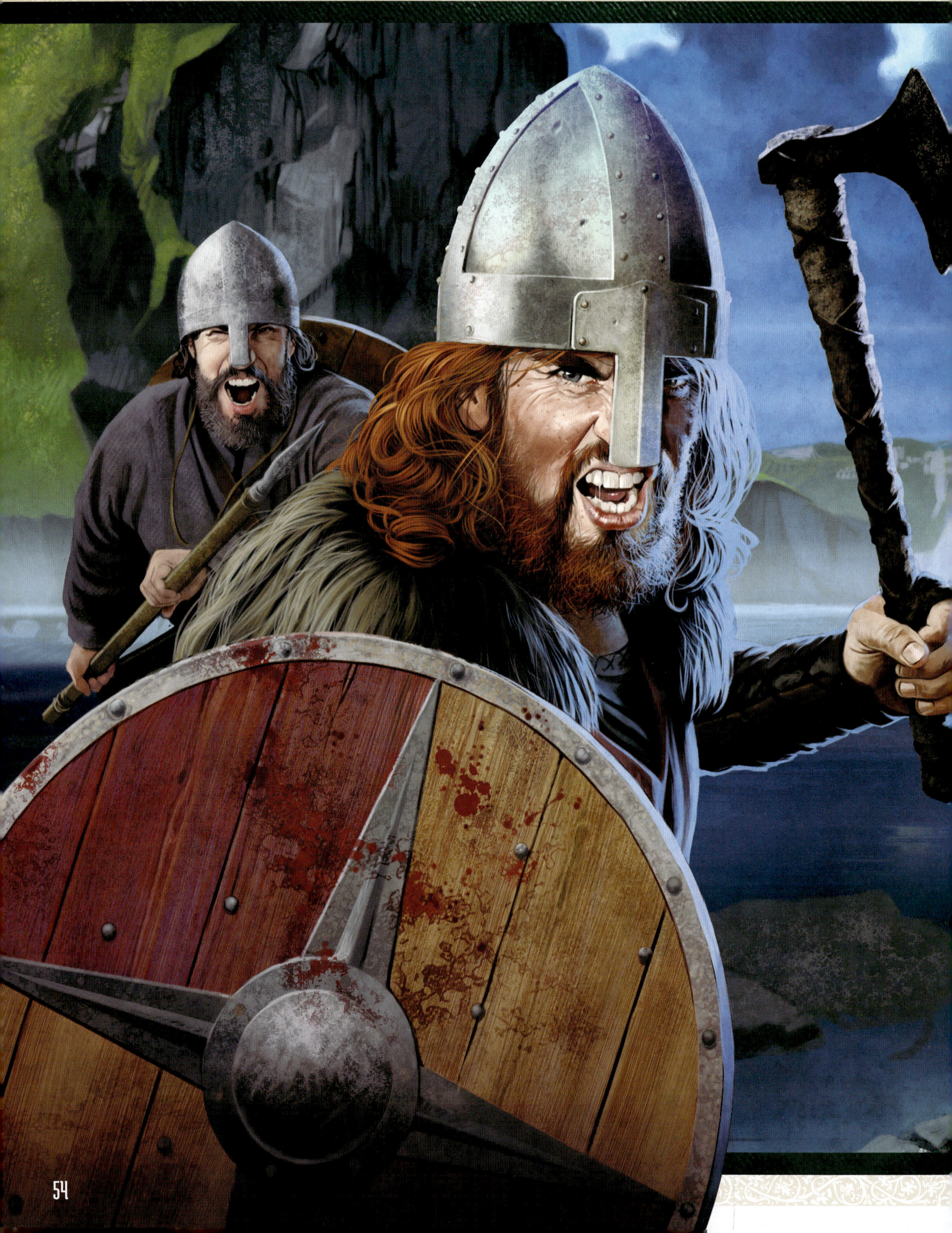

Lost Kingdoms of the Vikings

From Canada to Constantinople, the Norse raiders pillaged and plundered the known world in search of treasure and territory

Often portrayed as bloodthirsty raiders, the Vikings were a civilisation that travelled to more of the Early Medieval world than anyone else. Originating from Scandinavia, they branched out into mainland Europe to find food, land and riches, establishing kingdoms across the known world. For hundreds of years a fleet of longships on the horizon struck fear into the hearts of European peoples like the Franks, Saxons and Byzantines. The men from the north were traders as well as raiders, though, and commerce helped fund their lengthy expeditions. Bringing with them fur, wool and whalebone, they traded their goods for silver, silk and spices, which they then sold on. To trade or raid? It all hinged on the best way to make profit.

The Vikings are perhaps most famous for their attacks on the British Isles, the forced establishment of the Danelaw and battles against Alfred the Great. However, they sailed their longships all across Europe and ruled over many diverse lands. They even made forays into parts of Asia, America and Africa. From Newfoundland in the west to Kiev in the east, the Norsemen braved treacherous oceans and faced deadly adversaries. They may have seemed like savages, but it's the Norsemen we have to thank for the establishment and development of many of the European kingdoms that flourished after their decline.

Viking expansion

- 8th century
- 9th century
- 10th century
- 11th century
- Areas the Vikings raided frequently but never settled in

Ireland

For more than 200 years the Vikings exerted influence over vast swathes of the Emerald Isle

ABOVE At Clontarf, the Vikings amassed allies from both the Orkneys and the Isle of Man, but the reinforcements were not enough for victory

Norwegian Norsemen first appeared in Ireland at the end of the 8th century with a hit-and-run attack on a monastery on either Rathlin or Lambay Island. These sporadic coastal attacks continued for 30 years, and despite later spreading to the mainland, actually had no great effect on the Irish settlements that would rebuild during the lulls in fighting. At this stage, the marauders were content with staging assaults that lasted no longer than a few days before returning to Scandinavia to sell their spoils. At the start of the next century, however, the Vikings grew in confidence and the pillaging intensified. Ship enclosures (known as longphorts) were established in Dublin, and these fixed positions allowed the raiders to ravage the countryside at will. It wasn't long until Irish kings had had enough. The king of Tara, Máel Seachnaill, took the fight back to the Vikings, and near Skreen in County Meath, killed no less than 700 of the Nordic raiders.

The increase in assaults had a profound effect on the Celtic-Irish society for more than two centuries. Norse-Irish alliances became common, but by the start of the 10th century, Vikings from Denmark were added to the mix. To differentiate, Vikings from Norway were known as the 'Lochlainn' and the Danish Norsemen as the 'Danair'. The Viking success on the British Isles only increased the number of attacks, and in the years leading up to 1000, they tactically used their longships to travel up rivers and attack further inland. The Norwegians dominated initially, financed by all the monasteries they plundered, but the disorganised nature of their attacks meant the Danes' power base grew steadily.

On the Irish side, one man rose above the others, the king of Munster, Brian Boru. With his support base in the southern kingdom, Brian assembled a unified confederate army, which imposed itself as the major force in the region. The army destroyed Dublin's fortress, allied with many of the Viking leaders and was even powerful enough to expel several Norse clans from Ireland entirely. Brian claimed kingship in league with the Dublin Norse, and no one dared challenge him. His supremacy lasted until 1012, when a series of intense Viking attacks culminated in the critical Battle of Clontarf in 1014. Taking place on 23 April,

> Historic Viking settlements can be easily identified by '-by' and '-thorpe' suffixes, which in Old Norse meant homestead and farm. Therefore, cities and towns such as Derby, Grimsby, Whitby and Scunthorpe were once Nordic settlements

■ English territory ■ Danish or Norse territory
■ Celtic lands ■ Swamp

Vikings in the British Isles

The areas of Viking conquest that became known as the Danelaw

The first significant Viking attack on the British Isles was in 793, when the Vikings carried out a brutal raid on the island monastery of Lindisfarne. The almost constant assaults on Britain's coastline over the next few centuries were too much for the Anglo-Saxons and Celts, who surrendered a vast swathe of land to the Norse raiders.

Clontarf was a battle between the majority of the Irish kingdoms led by Brian against Vikings supported by Máel Mórda, the king of Leinster, who had switched allegiances after a dispute. Brian had approximately 7,000 troops at his disposal, and they marched to Dublin to engage 4,000 Leinster men and 3,000 Norsemen who had landed on the shoreline at sunrise. As the armies brawled, Mórda's men scored an early advantage as his vicious Viking centre proved devastatingly

The theories behind the Viking expansion

Exhausted farmland
Scandinavia has a variety of landscapes but none were ideal for farming. Norway was too mountainous, Sweden had extensive forests, while Denmark could be too sandy.

Desire for treasure
Searching far-off lands for plunder is something the Vikings became associated with. Raids were carried out and a settlement would be built to cement their claim to the loot.

Overcrowding
As the Viking population swelled, many sought to move elsewhere. The eldest son inherited family lands, so younger brothers would venture in search of territory.

Wanderlust
A sense of adventure was common trait. Even when the treasure dried up, the Norsemen were keen to seek out new lands in far-off places overseas.

New trade routes
The popularity of Christianity meant that many of the nearby Christian kingdoms refused to trade. As a result, the pagan Vikings would either invade the lands or look elsewhere.

Lost Kingdoms of the Vikings

Norse words that invaded the English language

Old Norse	Modern English
Sala	Sale
Klubba	Club
Beit	Snack
Rannsaka	Ransack
Fiall	Hill
Berserkr	Berserk
Hloppa	Flea
Burðr	Birth
Kalla	Call
Kasta	Cast
Krafla	Crawl
Hús bóndi	Husband
Leggr	Leg
Uggr	Ugly
Rotinn	Rotten
Renna	Run
Traust	Trust
Sloegr	Sly
Slatra	Slaughter
Lauss	Loose
Gervi	Gear
Kiþ	Kid
Knifr	Knife

effective. The pendulum swung in the other direction, however, when the Viking champions Brodir and Sigurd were defeated. As afternoon came, Brian's men managed to cut off the Viking access to their longships. This was a critical blow to Morda's forces, who began to flee towards the one bridge over the nearby River Liffey to safety. As they tried to escape, the returning Máel Seachnaill and his men emerged and cut off access to the bridge. The Vikings and the Leinster men were now trapped and subsequently routed.

The battle was the bloodiest single conflict in ancient Irish history. Brian lay dead in the mud with 4,000 of his own men and, crucially, 6,000 Leinster men and Vikings lay slaughtered alongside them. The battle resulted in the end of a period of great turmoil in Ireland and initiated a time of relative peace in which the Irish and the remaining Vikings lived together. The Norsemen who stayed in Ireland were absorbed into Irish culture and started to intermarry. The Danish kingdom of Dublin had stood for more than 200 years prior to Clontarf, but just 52 years later, Harald Hardrada would lose at Stamford Bridge and the great Viking age of the British Isles would be over.

> "The Battle of Clontarf in 1014 was the bloodiest single conflict in ancient Irish history"

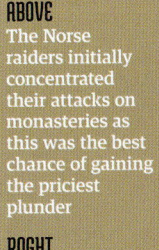

ABOVE The Norse raiders initially concentrated their attacks on monasteries as this was the best chance of gaining the priciest plunder

RIGHT This excavation site shows a Viking footpath in Dublin. 'Dubhlinn' was a prominent area of Viking activity during the Norse occupation

57

North America

With parts of Northern Europe ransacked, the Vikings turned their attention to the other side of the Atlantic

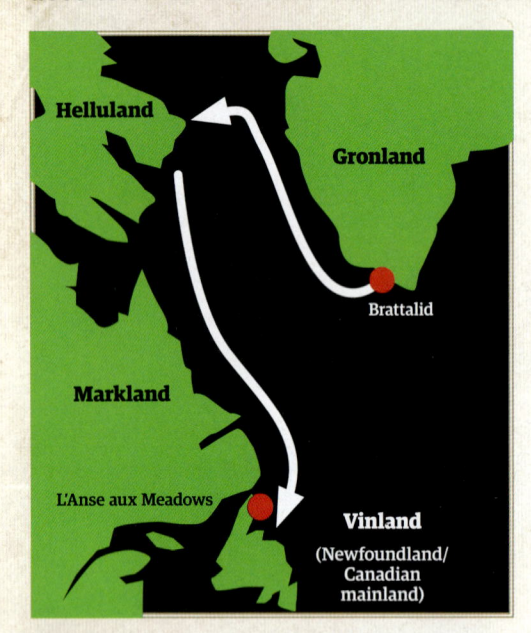

The true extent of the Viking presence in North America is hotly debated, but it will always be one of the greatest achievements of maritime exploration. After the Norse Vikings populated Iceland in about 870, Greenland was next to follow, with its conquest instigated in the 980s by the notorious Erik the Red. The rough seas of the Atlantic were much tougher than the Vikings had previously experienced on the North Sea. To combat the difficult conditions, the Norse mariners used a type of ship known as a knarr. Larger than the standard longship, it could carry much more cargo and would stand up to whatever the Atlantic had to throw at it. This allowed for longer and more fruitful journeys. By 1150, 72,000 Norsemen were living in Iceland while 5,000 resided in Greenland.

The adventuring continued, and the first Viking sightings of North America came in about 985, when Icelander Bjarni Herjólfsson spotted uncharted land after being blown off course on his way to Greenland. The stories of a new land encouraged others to seek it out. In about 1000, Leif Eriksson, the son of Erik the Red, was the first to set foot on this unexplored territory. Eriksson and his 35-man crew may have been sent by Norwegian king Olaf I to spread Christianity (Olaf was one of the first Vikings to do so) and discovered three places around the Gulf of Saint Lawrence., naming them Helluland (land of flat rocks), Markland (land of forest and timber) and Vinland (land of vines)., known today as Baffin Island, the Labrador coast and Newfoundland.

After this initial excursion, the westward journeys only continued. The most extensive voyage was undertaken by Thorfinn Karlsefni, who intended to settle in this new found land for good, taking more than 100 men and women as well as tools, weapons and farm animals on his expedition. His wife gave birth to the first child from the Old World to be born in the New. As more Vikings made the journey, it was inevitable they would make contact with the native population. Norse men and women called the native people Skrælingjar and became trading partners, benefiting from the fur given to them by the locals. The Skrælingjar were a pre-Iron Age civilisation and most likely the ancestors of the modern Inuit. They were given their first taste of iron weaponry and tools by these visitors from across the sea.

The settlements built by the Vikings in North America consisted of sod walls with peaked timber roofs. The most prominent settlement, and what is seen as proof of Viking occupation, is today called L'Anse aux Meadows. Located on the northern tip of Vinland, the area is believed to have been home to about 75 people and would have probably acted as a base camp for repairing ships that had made the perilous journey. After approximately two or three years of attempted colonisation, the Skrælingjar began to see the Vikings as a threat and unrest broke out. As a result of the violence, trade visits were no longer a worthwhile venture. Viking activity in North America was dramatically reduced, as the settlements in Greenland could no longer support further trade missions that lost both men and valuable resources. Greenland wasn't a fully functioning Norse colony, and these less than favourable economic conditions made journeys to North America more and more difficult.

The Viking failure to colonise the Americas on a long-term basis was due to both natural hazards and native resistance, but also confirmed the limitations of nautical conquest in the early Middle Ages. The distance from Greenland to Vinland is about 3,500 kilometres, which was a tough journey for any medieval vessel, and the small population didn't have the manpower to overpower the natives. They may have discovered North America 500 years before Columbus, but the Vikings were unable to sustain a stable colony in the New World.

Lost Kingdoms of the Vikings

ABOVE The Vikings made it to Greenland in 982 and established both eastern and western settlements with about 300 farmsteads

LEFT The journeys to America were long and hard and would sometimes result in casualties or longships straying off course

BELOW Norse technology was not significantly more advanced than that of the natives meaning the Vikings found it difficult to assert their authority

What became of Vinland?

Expert bio: Dr Alex Sanmark is reader in Medieval Archaeology at the Centre for Nordic Studies, University of the Highlands and Islands. She specialises in various aspects of the Viking Age, from religion to law and gender, in Scandinavia and overseas settlements.

How important is L'Anse aux Meadows to our understanding of Viking settlements in the New World?

It is hugely important because it is the only Viking settlement in the New World. There are other types of archaeological evidence, though. Two Icelandic sagas, for instance, tell us about the Vikings sailing to Vinland from Greenland and Iceland. This has, of course, spurred people's imagination, and many have been looking for evidence of Viking presence a lot further south, especially in the US. Others have faked the evidence by producing their own runic inscriptions. The Viking settlement of the New World is an important political issue for some who are keen to show that 'Europeans' were there from early on. The sagas are highly problematic as sources as they are very late, dating from the 13th century onwards, and they are also literature, meaning that they don't necessarily tell us exactly what happened. We can't rely on them for evidence, so this settlement is of great importance.

Are there any similar Viking settlements to L'Anse aux Meadows in the Americas?

No, but a possible Viking camp has been identified on Baffin Island in recent years. There is also an increasing amount of archaeological evidence from Canada that shows that the Vikings were there and traded with the natives. It is possible that established trading networks were in place and the Vikings may well have travelled a lot further inland than previously thought. Viking presence is above all traced through artefacts that the native people did not have, such as finds of metal, strike-a-lights and woollen cloth. These finds are important as they point to friendly interactions, which is not always the image provided by the written sources.

Why did the Vikings survive hundreds of years in Greenland but could not establish themselves in Vinland, with its richer resources and better climate?

The settlement at L'Anse aux Meadows was probably never intended to be permanent, but rather a base for resources, such as wood, which they could not get in Greenland. The Vikings seem to have stayed there for short periods of time as the number of Norse in Greenland was never very large, and setting up a new colony would have required a substantial group of people to be successful. Also, L'Anse aux Meadows was not a very useful area for resources that were unavailable in Greenland, for these the Vikings had to travel quite far inland. The journey between Greenland and Canada was long and could take up to a month, which of course made regular journeys between the two areas difficult. It may be, although there is no evidence to prove this, that the relationship with the natives was so difficult that the settlement was abandoned.

What were relations with the Native Americans like?

We don't know very much about this. The sagas tell us both about trading with the native population and about fights between them. On the other hand, there is increasing evidence of interaction between the two groups and it may be that the whole situation was a lot more positive than the image provided by the sagas. The sagas are literature after all, and it may have been more interesting to describe fighting than trading. In view of recent archaeological finds, I'm sure more evidence will be appearing in the future.

How could a longship or a knarr make it all the way across the Atlantic?

It may seem strange to us that people set out across the North Atlantic in open ships, but we need to see this in its context. It was of course a very long and dangerous journey, and the sagas contain stories about ships being lost on the way. People in the Viking age were, however, very used to travelling in this way and they didn't start by crossing the Atlantic. People in Scandinavia were using ships with sails from the early Iron Age and developed their ships and sailing skills over several hundred years. They were extremely talented seamen and knew when and how to sail, following currents, fish and seabirds.

France

Across the Channel, Vikings threatened the Franks in Normandy, Brittany and Aquitaine

ABOVE The longship could easily make the trip from Scandinavia to France and was nimble enough to traverse rivers as well

LEFT The journeys to America were long and hard and would sometimes result in casualties or longships straying off course

- Devastated by the Vikings
- Surrendered to the Vikings
- France after 843

By the end of the 9th century, Vikings from Denmark had increased the amount of coastal assaults on Western Europe and would proceed to populate significant amounts of territory in Normandy, Brittany and Aquitaine. Their leader, Reginherus or Ragnar, thought by some to be the legendary figure Ragnar Lodbrok described in Old Norse poetry, had the confidence and the audacity to siege Paris in 845.

Ragnar led an army of 120 longships and 5,000 warriors – fierce men who had already scorched the earth all over Europe. After plundering Rouen, the siege of Paris began on 28 March. Although the attackers were stopped in their tracks by a plague that spread through the camp, they still managed to take the city, and were only stopped from burning it to the ground by a last-ditch Frankish ransom of 7,000 pounds of silver.

Despite being primarily Danish territory, a Norwegian leader emerged by the name of Hrölfr, or, as he is more commonly known, Rollo. Already a veteran of conflicts on the British Isles, his military forces besieged the city of Chartres, forcing the king of the Franks, Charles III, to sign the Treaty of Saint-Clair-sur-Epte in 911, granting Rollo feudal rights in the area around Rouen.

Viking land now stretched from Normandy in the north to Aquitaine in the south, and remained under Viking control for about two centuries. Even though they had foreign invaders in their lands, this was actually of benefit to the Franks as it meant the Norsemen would effectively provide them with a buffer zone against coastal invasions from other enemies of the realm.

It was not long until Christianity and Frankish customs started to take over from Nordic culture. Rollo himself was baptised and the Normans that invaded England in 1066 were descendants of the Normandy Vikings. The medieval French word for a Scandinavian is 'Normand', a term that was then given to the area (Normandy) and the people that inhabited it (Normans). Harald Hardrada may have been defeated at Stamford Bridge, but William the Conqueror's forces that were victorious at Hastings were more Norse than many think.

Russia and Eastern Europe

Using the river systems of the Baltic to their advantage, the Vikings travelled east for further trade and conquest

One of the greatest Viking achievements is perhaps their foray deep into eastern Europe. In the 9th century, the Slavic tribes in Russia and eastern Europe were fast becoming exhausted by constant inter-tribal wars that were stretching their resources and affecting their commerce. Capitalising on the broken alliances, the Viking ships arrived from the Gulf of Finland in huge numbers. Using large rivers such as the Volga, Neva and Volkhov as waterways, the men from the north vastly expanded their territory.

The town of Novgorod on the banks of Lake Ilmen became one of the main strongholds for the Nordic invaders, who were known as the 'Rus'. The East European plain provided the Vikings with forest and grassland that was ideal for hunting, fishing and farming. The plentiful food supply helped trade routes expand further northwards towards Lake Ladoga and southwards down the River Dnieper. The Rus people traded with local Slavic tribes and travelled into modern-day Russia, helping give the nation its name in the process.

The three Swedish kings who came from overseas were Rurik, Sineus and Truvor, who settled in Novgorod, Beloozerg and Izborsk. Rurik's heir, Oleg of Novgorod, travelled 600 miles south to take control of Kiev in 882 and went on to pillage lands even further southwards, knocking on the door of the Byzantine Empire in the process.

Like many of the areas that the Vikings inhabited, their influence steadily declined and was replaced by local customs. This happened once again in Eastern Europe as the Russian identity began to become distinct from Norse. One of the rulers of Kiev, Vladimir, took the decision to make Greek Orthodox the area's religion in 988, decreasing the impact and relevance of Viking paganism even further. The culture change of the Norse people to more Slavic customs resulted in the growth of a Russian dynasty that rivalled the Carolingian Empire in Western Europe. The founders of the Russian tsardom were descendants of the Rurik Dynasty, a Viking dynasty that became one of Europe's oldest royal houses.

LEFT
Trade and negotiation were essential to Viking conquests. Here, a Norseman is bargaining with a Persian merchant over the price of a female slave

Seven other travelling civilisations

Normans
The Normans were descendants of the Vikings. A realm was established in Sicily and southern Italy in the 10th century and the Norman people also established states in North Africa and even as far east in what is now Lebanon.

Phoenicians
The Phoenicians were one of the finest trading civilisations of the ancient world. The most powerful city-states were Sidon and Tyre, which became almost too tough for even the notoriously powerful Alexander the Great to conquer.

Venetian Republic
Venice was the greatest seaport in Late Medieval Europe. The Venetians were excellent shipbuilders thanks to the marshy lagoon in which they lived. The Republic controlled states such as Istria and Dalmatia until its decline and fall in the Napoleonic era.

Genoese Republic
Genoa benefited from a natural harbour that led to the Ligurian Sea. Its booming maritime economy allowed it to be an independent republic for 800 years. Genoa's trade helped the West in the Crusades and had links as far away as Crimea.

Kalmar Union
The people of the Kalmar Union were great travellers. The post-Viking kingdoms of Denmark, Norway and Sweden were incorporated under one crown with Copenhagen as the capital. The Union also incorporated Iceland and Greenland.

Srivijaya
Another civilisation that based its power on sea trade, the Srivijaya Empire prospered between the 7th and 13th centuries. In its heyday, the civilisation had trade links with India, China and the Malay Archipelago. Their power waned after attacks by the Chola and Malayu people.

Abbasid Caliphate
The Abbasid Dynasty became the strongest empire in Asia Minor and northern Africa until the Mongols in 1258. The caliphate presided over the 'Golden Age of Islam' as Muslim merchants traded in the Mediterranean and Indian Ocean.

Constantinope

The Vikings venture to the gates of the Byzantine Empire

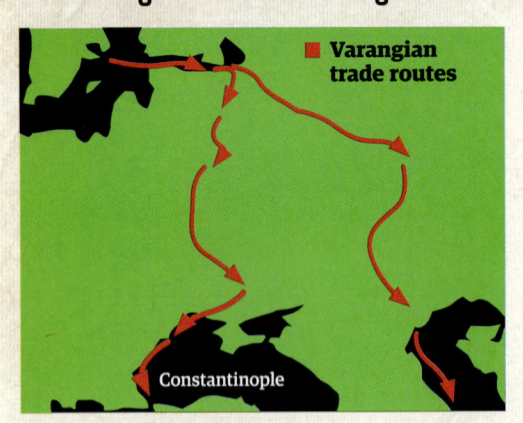

Viking lands were growing ever southwards, and by the early 10th century, an encounter with the Byzantine Empire was imminent. The movement came to a head in 860 during the siege of Constantinople, as a flotilla of 200 Viking warships emerged from the darkness and headed for the city they knew as 'Miklagard' (the Great City). After this, accounts become quite hazy, but the most likely outcome is the Vikings could only conquer the suburbs and not the fortified inner city without siege equipment. Determined to plunder the wealth of what was the biggest city the Vikings had ever seen, assaults continued, eventually resulting in the 2 September 911 commercial trading treaty. This brought friendly relations between the two states and frequent trade across the Black Sea as the Vikings took control of the Volga Trade Route from the Baltic Sea to the north and the Caspian Sea to the south. By 944, the relations soured, and Oleg's successor, Igor of Kiev, led an unsuccessful campaign against the Byzantines in 941. A new treaty introduced restrictions on Rus attacks on Byzantine lands in Crimea and a complete ban on fortress construction at the mouth of the Dnieper River. As time went on, the overstretched Vikings reasoned they could not conquer Constantinople, so many decided instead to go into the service of the emperor.

The Vikings that had ventured further south were called Varangians, which was the name given to them by the Greeks. After the final failed siege of Constantinople, the Byzantines were so impressed with the Varangian fighting mentality that the emperor, Basil II, hired them as warriors as part of his personal guard in 988. The Byzantine military was very multicultural in nature, so Viking men were warmly welcomed. This new breed of soldier travelled far and wide to the likes of Syria, Armenia and Sicily under the Byzantine banner as the attacks from non-Byzantine Varangians ended in 1043 after the Rus-Byzantine War. The loss signalled the end of the Varangian advance towards Asia as the area became either Slavic or Byzantine, not Norse. The Varangian Guard soldiered on until the 14th century, though, ensuring that there were still some Vikings standing in Constantinople.

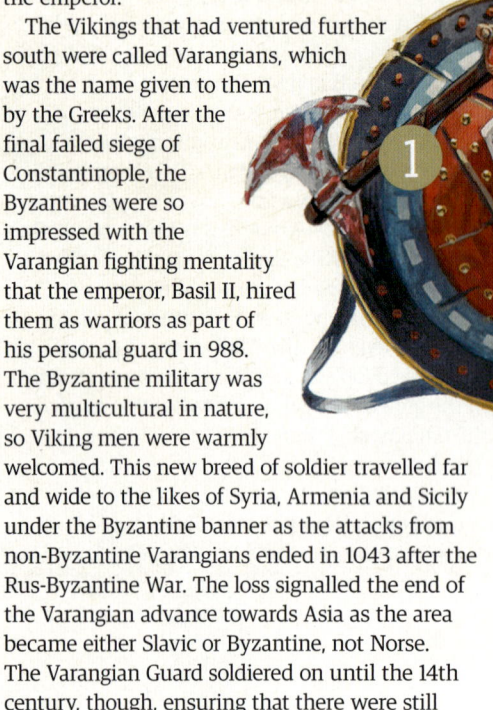

LEFT Constantinople had 12 miles of walls, so even the Vikings had almost no hope of besieging it

Anatomy of a Varangian guard

The fearsome warriors who became the most brutal bodyguards of the age

1 Axe
Wielding a foot-long bladed axe, when the Varangian guards arrived, the Byzantine emperor's presence on the battlefield was confirmed.

2 Weaponry
Double-edged swords and spears would also be used if an axe wasn't available, or it was favourable for the conditions of battle.

3 Shield
Shields would be in the classic Viking round style and would be worn on the back when warriors were wielding a two-handed weapon.

4 Helmet
Varangian guards wore an iron conical helmet but were also happy to don a headdress instead in the hot Mediterranean weather.

5 Boots
Tough leather boots were covered by greaves or leg guards to protect the lower legs from hacks and slashes.

6 Clothing
A standard tunic would be worn under the armour along with metal strips that protected the wrists and forearms from slashes.

7 Armour
This elite unit had a choice of lamellar armour made out of iron or bronze plates or a chain mail hauberk.

8 Mounted infantry berserkers
The Varangian guard rode to battle but did their fighting on foot. Their heavy armour had pros and cons depending on the battle.

Lost Kingdoms of the Vikings

Legacy
The fearsome warriors who became the most brutal bodyguards of the age

The influence left by the Vikings is greater than many are led to believe. From the Normans in the west to the Rus in the east, many civilisations that went on to dominate the late Middle Ages and beyond owe their roots to Viking expansion. The Vikings helped open the doors to pan-European trade and established urban centres at Dublin, Kiev and Reykjavík, cities at almost opposite ends of Europe. The effect of Norse culture is restricted more than it could have been as the Vikings never truly settled south of Denmark. They were an exploring people who lacked mass land armies and huge cities to stamp their authority and leadership on areas outside their own sphere of influence. They simply did not have the construction nous to establish a citadel as large or as powerful as Constantinople or Rome. Additionally, the Christianisation of Europe watered down the Nordic influence further and ended it completely when Scandinavia was fully converted in the 12th century.

Outside of Europe, Africa and Asia Minor were only briefly settled upon, so the influence seen today is from the Mongol Empire and Islamic caliphates. America suffers from the same problem, and that is why Columbus is and always will be seen as the first to discover the New World. The Viking Age lasted for hundreds of years, and whether it's a city name in northern England, a type of axe or French surnames, the legacy is there for all to see.

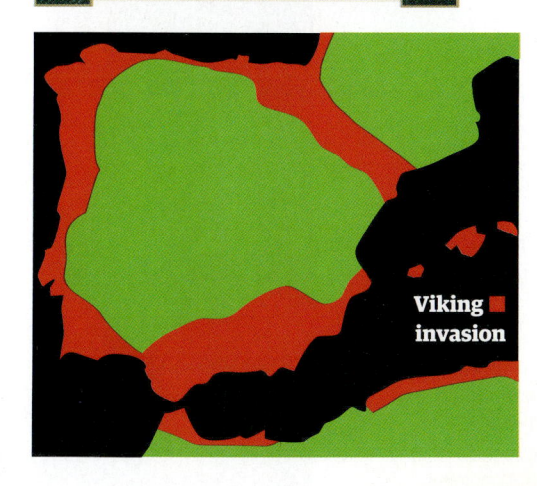

RIGHT The Christian Reconquista was well under way by the time the Vikings began their raids

Iberia
The Norse expansion into the Christian north and Islamic south of Spain

After controlling the Bay of Biscay and establishing themselves on France's western coast, the Vikings moved even further south to the Iberian Peninsula. The first known attack was made up of 100 ships launched from Aquitaine in 844 and raided both Gijon and Coruna. After meeting strong resistance, the seafarers changed tack and headed for what is now Portugal. The raids were initially small and infrequent and, as with most Nordic attacks of the age, the coast was the worst affected. Prisoners were taken and monasteries were destroyed.

The first few assaults were mostly concentrated in the north of the Christian kingdoms of Asturias and Galicia. The southern Islamic part of Spain, al-Andalus, was targeted as well. Seville became a Viking city for six weeks in 844 and Lisbon was plundered for all its worth. The attacks came at a bad time for the Muslim population, who were enduring the start of the Christian Reconquista. Despite the ability for longships to sail from Normandy in less than a week and evidence of longphorts, Iberia would soon become a bridge too far for the Norsemen.

As the attacks subsided, the lands were regained from the Vikings. The Muslim leader, Abd al-Rahman II, took back Seville and sent the heads of 200 Viking warriors to his Moroccan allies. The Vikings returned in 859 led by Bjorn Ironside and Hastein. They sailed around the peninsula in search of southern France and Italy. This turned out to be a shrewd move as both the Muslim and Christian settlements were too strong for long-term attacks to be worthwhile and repelled the Vikings before they could get close to Seville. The Norsemen returned north to France but their descendants, the Christianised Normans, would be back in the Mediterranean in later centuries.

Viking invasion

Images: Joe Cummings; Source: Wikipedia Commons / Public Domain

63

Charlemagne

The 'father of Europe' and ruler of much of France and Germany, Charlemagne made his name as a king but left a legacy as the first Roman emperor since the 5th century

Over 300 years, Europe had fallen into darkness. With the power of the Pope and the once mighty Roman Church beset by enemies, the legacy of the Western Roman Empire toppled as steadily and as surely as the Caesars had themselves, stability withdrawing like overstretched legionnaires and knowledge fading away like the crumbling Roman roads that cross-hatched the continent.

Europe needed a strong leader to pull it back from the precipice, and it got a brace of them in the form of the Carolingian dynasty, a family of self-made kings who stabilised their lands by force, expanded their frontiers with terrifying aggression and ensured the primacy of the Christian Church. Yet, through this crucible of violence emerged a western Europe reforged to survive another 1,000 years.

By the 6th century, most of what is now France, western Germany, Switzerland, the Netherlands and Belgium was inhabited by the Franks, a Germanic tribe split into several small kingdoms that had rushed into the power vacuum left by Rome. These petty principalities had been united not by their monarch - the rois fainéants, the 'do-nothing kings' of the Merovingian dynasty, had been increasingly sidelined by their own ministers - but by the Mayor of the Palace, the executive of the royal administration who was half-prime minister and half-Shogun-esque warlord.

Pepin of Herstal had warred his way to stability between 680 CE and his death in 714 CE, bringing the other Frankish lands to heel and taking Christianity to their furthest and most pagan reaches. His son, Charles Martel, was a stronger hand yet. Though Pepin had nominated his grandson as successor, Charles - born out of wedlock and excluded from the court - was having none of it, and took the not-quite-throne by force. Despite not being Pepin's choice of heir, he more than honoured his father's vision, expanding the centralised control of the Frank lands and extending his rule further into what are now modern Holland, Denmark and Germany with a formidable standing army and revolutionary use of heavy cavalry, the foundation of Europe's knights. He defeated the pagan Saxons in the east and halted the advance of the Moors - the North African and Spanish Muslims of the powerful Umayyad Caliphate - who attempted to follow up their conquest of Spain by pushing across the Pyrenees mountains into France. 'Charles the Hammer' was even offered high office by the Pope, which he declined, but it was an auspicious omen of his grandson's own journey to come.

Succeeding his father Pepin the Short in 768 - who had given up the pretence of being anything other than supreme ruler by forcing the last Merovingian king into a monastery and taking the title of 'King of the Franks' - Charlemagne,

> In later life, Charlemagne came into conflict with his doctors after they advised him to stop eating roasted meat

Charlemagne

LEFT
Charles Martel, grandfather of Charlemagne, defeats the Moors at the Battle of Tours in 732

BELOW
St Giles pardons the Emperor. Although a popular legend, there's no evidence that the two ever met

which means 'Charles the Great', shared the zeal of his predecessors. At war for most of his life, Charlemagne took Charles Martel's fight against the Moors into northern Spain, continued the conquest and conversion of the Saxons and launched new campaigns against the Lombards of northern Italy, the Slavs in Croatia and the Avars in Hungary.

Leading his personal guard, the scara cavalry, into battle with his sword Joyeuse, Charlemagne's exploits have one armoured foot in myth and the other in fact, with separating the two being a difficult task, but his journey from king to the first Roman emperor since the fall of the Roman Empire has little to do with his legend as a warrior king and everything to do with the insecurity of the Church.

Pope Leo III succeeded Adrian I on the day of the previous pontiff's burial, so fearful was he that the Frankish king to whom his predecessor owed his lands and safety would feel a right to interfere in the election of the new pope. Yet, despite his wariness he was quick to bring Rome's most powerful ally on side; along with the letter that announced his succession, Leo included the keys to St Peter's Basilica and the Pope's banner. The not-so subtle message was that he viewed Charlemagne as the defender of the Holy See, and trusted him with Rome's protection. The Frank was equally magnanimous in return, congratulating the pontiff and sending vast riches, the spoils of his war against the Avars, but not without condition, suggesting that as he happened to be the stalwart defender of Christianity, the pope had a duty to pray for the Frankish armies as they continued their conquest.

Charlemagne would honour his side of this implied bargain, and in return Leo elevated him to an office left vacant since the 5th century.

While Leo engaged in his letter-writing campaign with the monarch to the north-west and used the Avar loot to become a patron of the arts, the family of the late Adrian I launched a conspiracy to remove him from his post and replace him with his nephew Paschal the Primicerius. On 25 April 799 CE, during the procession of The Greater Litanies through the Eternal City, Leo was attacked by armed thugs who stabbed him in the eyes and attempted to tear out his tongue at the root. After dragging him to the church of San Silvestro in Capite and trying to gouge out his eyes again, the bloodied pope was left unconscious as a prisoner at the monastery of St Erasmus. Accused of perjury and fornication by his rivals, the wounded – but amazingly not blinded or voiceless – Leo fled Rome to Spoleto, 126 kilometres (78 miles) north of the city, where under the protection of the Duke of Spoleto he was able to make his way to Charlemagne at Paderborn in Saxony.

That such a loyal servant of the Frankish king could be found so close to Rome, deep within Italy's central Umbria region, neatly underlines the unbalanced relationship of power between the Franks and the Roman Catholic Church that had initially caused Leo such anxiety. Though the territory had been given to Rome in 776 after the defeat of the Lombards, the king retained the power to choose the Duke, making papal control as meaningless as that of the last Merovingian kings under Charlemagne's ancestors.

Clearly, the threat of political interference from Charlemagne had been trumped by that of actual bodily harm, and Leo begged for the monarch's aid. He had no authority to do so – neither he nor the conspirators in Rome were subjects of the Franks, and no law yet existed that would make bishops subordinate to secular authority. With conflict left in Saxony to pursue, Charlemagne let the matter stew for a year and kept the recovering pontiff as his guest. Finally heading to Rome in November 800 with a sizeable (and no doubt fairly threatening) entourage, Charlemagne summoned a council of the

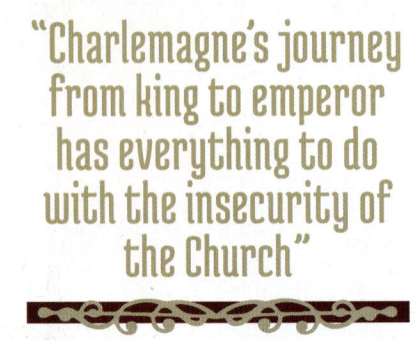

> "Charlemagne's journey from king to emperor has everything to do with the insecurity of the Church"

city's religious authorities and patiently listened to the accusations put to Leo, before allowing the deposed pontiff to make an impassioned plea of innocence.

Unsurprisingly, Charlemange took Leo's side, and ordered the conspirators' executions, but Leo requested that they instead be exiled, with the unpopular pope perhaps seeing an opportunity to impress with capacity for forgiveness.

Crowned 'Emperor of the Romans' on Christmas Day that same year by the grateful pope, the official report insists that Charlemagne was ambushed like some sort of early-medieval surprise party. The king's biographer, the monk Einhard, claimed that his liege had such "aversion [to being crowned Emperor] that he declared he would not have set foot in the church… if he could have foreseen the designs of the pope."

It's entirely possible that Charlemagne and Leo came to some agreement during their year together. After all, the idea of grinning priests hiding a bejewelled imperial crown as if it were a birthday cake is too ludicrous to contemplate. Documents from his reign reveal that Charlemagne preferred using the title 'Charles, the most serene Augustus crowned by God, the great, peaceful Emperor ruling the Roman Empire' rather than the simpler and more often used 'Emperor of the Romans'. These aren't entirely the actions of someone with an aversion to the role, and the king's apparent humility may have been as expertly stage-managed as Leo's mercy. Nonetheless, with his rule over the Frankish lands uncontested and his empire secured through sheer military prowess, Charlemagne no more needed to declare himself Roman emperor than the fearsome Charles Martel needed to be king. The vulnerable pope, however, required an emperor in order to protect himself and the vast empire with the Church at its heart. Only Rome had nostalgia for its lost empire; the Franks held

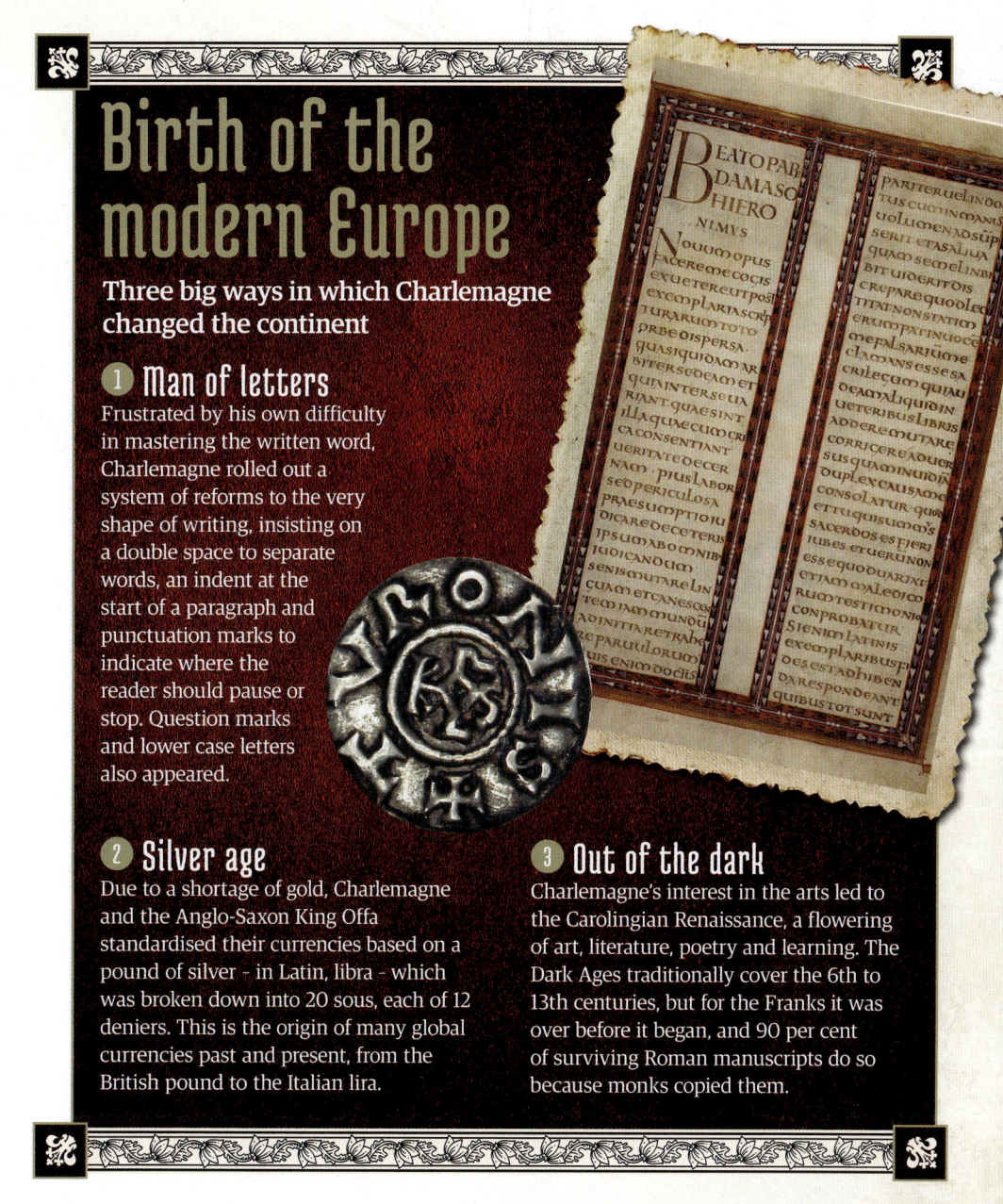

Birth of the modern Europe
Three big ways in which Charlemagne changed the continent

1 Man of letters
Frustrated by his own difficulty in mastering the written word, Charlemagne rolled out a system of reforms to the very shape of writing, insisting on a double space to separate words, an indent at the start of a paragraph and punctuation marks to indicate where the reader should pause or stop. Question marks and lower case letters also appeared.

2 Silver age
Due to a shortage of gold, Charlemagne and the Anglo-Saxon King Offa standardised their currencies based on a pound of silver - in Latin, libra - which was broken down into 20 sous, each of 12 deniers. This is the origin of many global currencies past and present, from the British pound to the Italian lira.

3 Out of the dark
Charlemagne's interest in the arts led to the Carolingian Renaissance, a flowering of art, literature, poetry and learning. The Dark Ages traditionally cover the 6th to 13th centuries, but for the Franks it was over before it began, and 90 per cent of surviving Roman manuscripts do so because monks copied them.

Charlemagne orders the construction of a city to ford the River Main - Frankfurt, or Frank Ford

their 4th century resistance to Roman rule, and their role in dismembering the Roman Empire, as a point of fierce pride. Ultimately though, the way Charlemagne signed his name changed nothing of the way he conducted his affairs, and the impact of his ascension - reluctant or willing - to Europe's highest office would take another 150 years to make itself fully known.

The first Holy Roman Emperor, Otto I, took the title in 962 CE and reinvented himself in the Frankish king's image, creating a powerful multi-ethnic state and a crown that would endure for over 1,000 years.

Through the Holy Roman Empire, Charlemagne's rule defined not just the primacy of France as one of Europe's imperial, religious and cultural superpowers, but of numerous Austrian, German and Italian states too.

A career that began for Charlemagne as king of the Franks ended not just as emperor, but also as the father of the Europe that we can still recognise today.

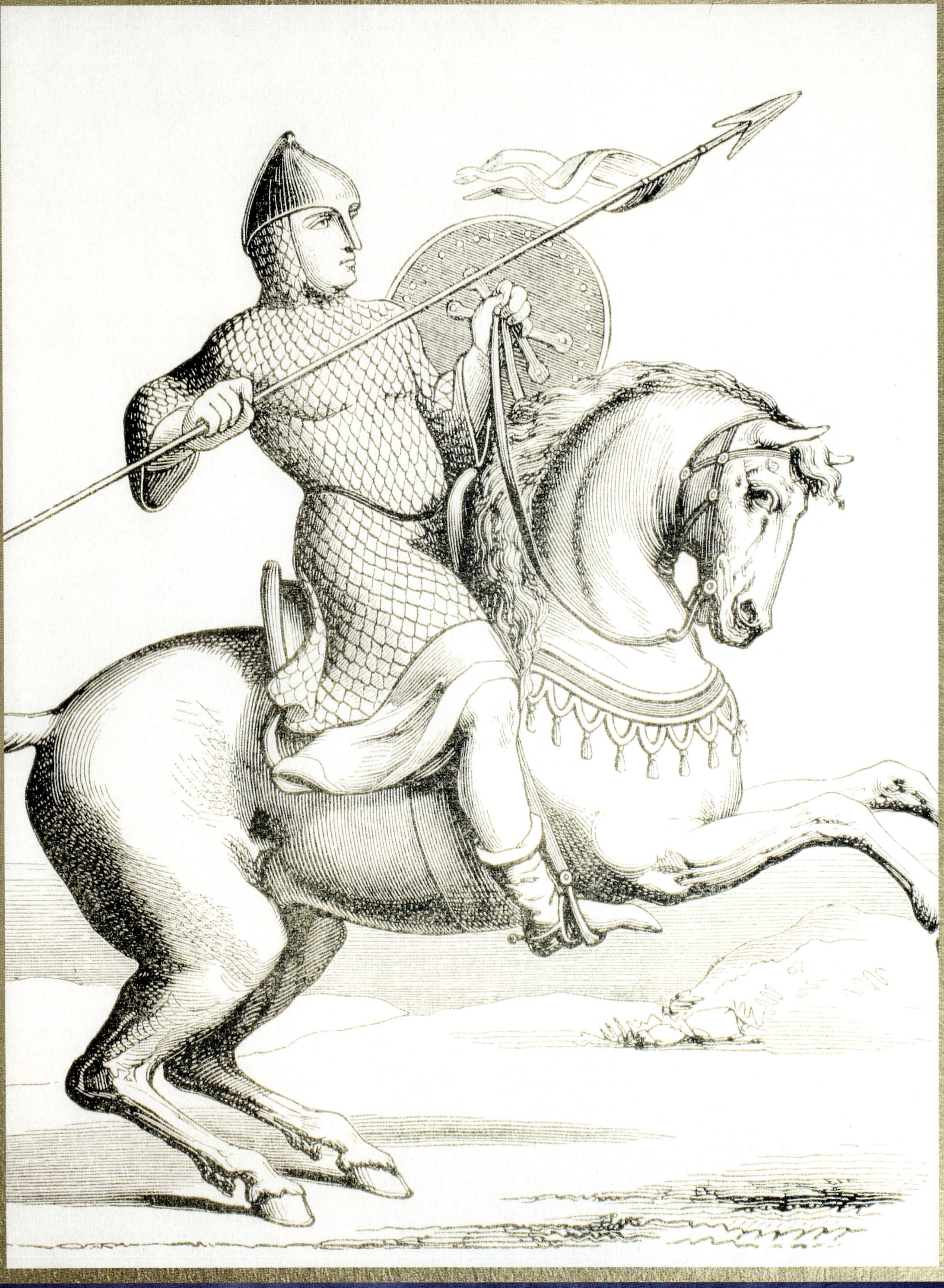

Kingdom of the Northmen

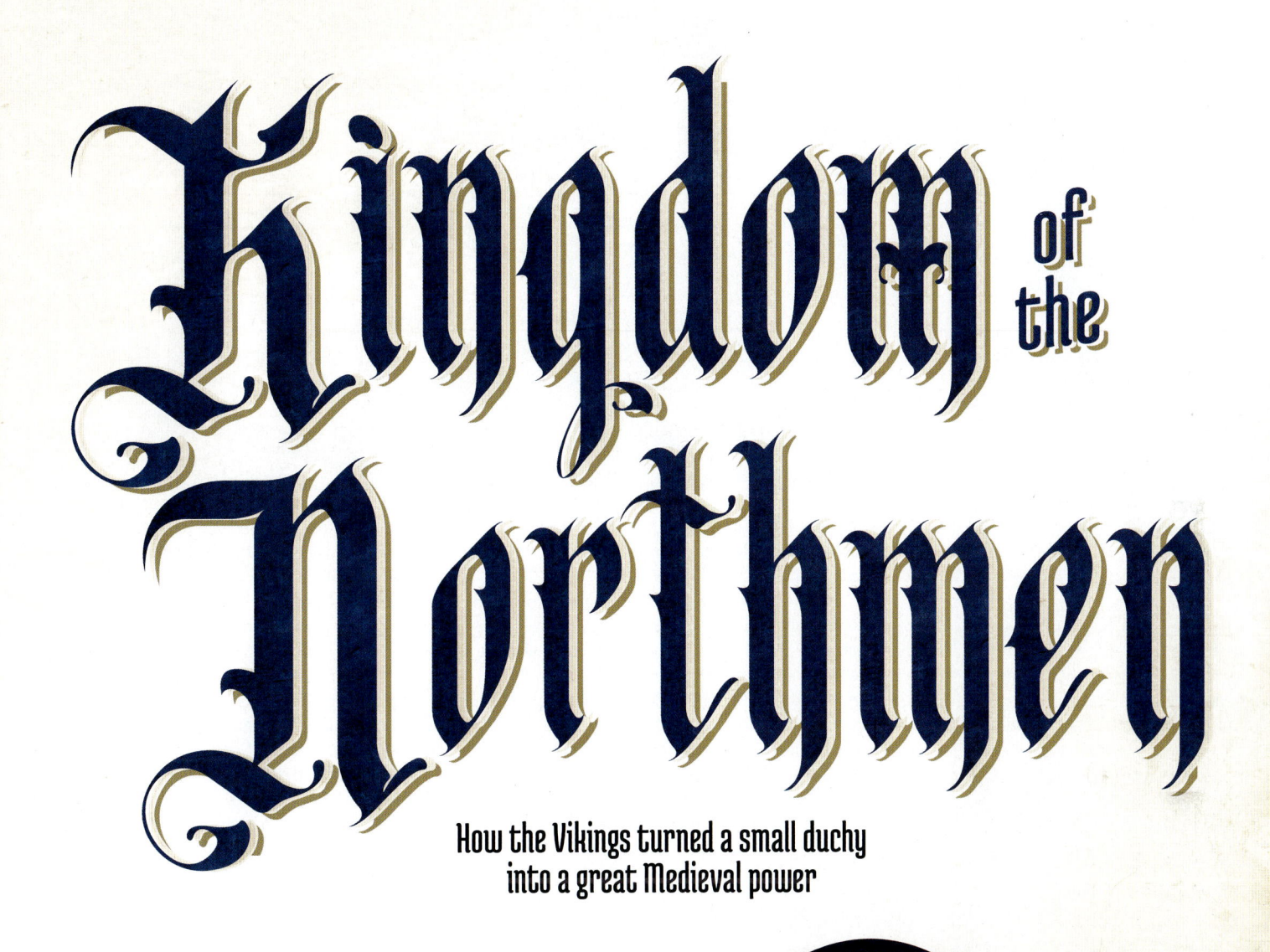

How the Vikings turned a small duchy into a great Medieval power

Visit Normandy today and you will find a settled agricultural land dominated by the bocage that caused Allied troops so much difficulty in the weeks after D-Day. But this quiet atmosphere belies the area's turbulent past.

Normandy was fought over for centuries. The area enters recorded history in 53 BCE, when Julius Caesar conquered its Celtic and Belgic inhabitants as part of his campaigns to bring Gaul under Roman control. After vigorous resistance, the local people settled comfortably into Roman rule until the crises of the 3rd century CE brought the first devastating raids by Saxon pirates. After the temporary stabilisation brought about by the emperor Diocletian, the region again fell prey to invading Germanic tribes from the beginning of the 5th century. But by the end of the 5th century, one of these tribes, the Franks, had become dominant under their king, Clovis. The Franks were devout Christians, and their patronage brought the foundation of many monasteries in the area, most famously the tidal island monastery of Mont-Saint-Michel, on which Saint Aubert built the first oratory in 709.

However, by the latter part of the 8th century and on into the 9th, what would one day become Normandy came under attack from a fresh wave of pagan raiders: the Vikings. The Carolingian Empire assembled by Charlemagne began to dissolve after his death and the Vikings exploited the political weakness attendant upon civil wars all they could.

Among them was a Northman called Rollo (Hrólfr in Old Norse) of uncertain origin - the extant sources identify him as either Danish or Norwegian, but the difference might have seemed moot to contemporary chroniclers. Rollo, having unsuccesfully laid siege to Paris, set up his base on the estuary of the River Seine near Rouen, from where he raided for a decade. Unable to expel him, Charles the Simple, King of the Franks, hit on the strategy of turning poacher into gamekeeper: officially cede the territory that Rollo had occupied to the Northman, in return for Rollo swearing allegiance to him as king. The two men signed the Treaty of Saint-Clair-sur-Epte in 911: Rollo was ceded the land from the River Epte to the sea, in exchange for defending the kingdom from Viking raiders.

As part of the treaty, Rollo and his men agreed to convert to Christianity, and Rollo was formally baptised, taking the name Robert and being

> Charles the Simple gave what would become Normandy to the Viking chieftain Rollo to stop him raiding Frankish lands

The Crusades

As the power of the dukes of Normandy grew, so did their reliance on the protection of their great patron, Saint Michael. In 1020, Richard the Good, son of Richard the Fearless, commissioned Abbot Hildebert to build a new abbey church upon Mont Saint-Michel. Romanesque architecture was in its infancy, but in their ambition to glorify the archangel, Richard and Hildebert asked extraordinary things of their new church.

The rock of Saint Michel was shaped like a sugar loaf, rising 78.6 metres (258 feet) above sea level. The obvious architectural choice would have been to cut the top off the mountain to create a solid and level foundation for the new church. But that would have been to step down from heaven. Instead, Abbot Hildebert took the apex of the rock for the ground level of his new church, and built out in all directions to provide the foundations of his building.

ABOVE
Norman military success rested upon their ability to keep conquered land, an ability that arose from their mastery of military architecture

promised the king's daughter in marriage - although whether the marriage was ever finalised is still unclear.

As a sign of his allegiance to Charles, Rollo had to formally place his hands into the hands of the king. To drive home the point that Rollo was the subject of the monarch, the bishops attending proposed that Rollo kiss Charles' foot as well. The proud Northmen were not at all keen on the idea and came up with a compromise: one of Rollo's men would perform this obeisance on his chief's behalf. But when the nominated warrior stood before the king, he grabbed Charles' foot and hauled it up to his lips, causing the king to fall over. The Normans were to remain a disrespectful thorn in the side of the French monarchy for another three centuries.

The treaty did not preclude Rollo from continuing to act as a Viking chieftain, so long as he did not attack the lands belonging to Charles. As such, in the following decades he expanded the territory under his control until, by his death around 932, it included almost all the land that would become the Duchy of Normandy.

The Viking settlers also acquired a name during this time: Normanz, the plural form of an Old French word (singular Normand, Normant) that meant 'North man' that was itself derived from the Old Norse word Norðmaðr, which in Latin became Normannus or Nortmannus. By derivation, the land they had settled came to be called Normandy.

Along with a new name, the Northmen had become enthusiastic converts to their new religion. Rollo's son, William Longsword, conquered the

Defining moment
Vikings on the make 951
What to do about these Northmen? The question tormented all the monarchs of northwestern Europe. With their supremely manoeuvrable longships, the raiders could achieve tactical local superiority in a time when communications and land-based travel were slow. So Charles the Simple, proving himself not so stupid, decided to grant the Viking leader, Rollo, the region north of the River Epte up to the coast, on the understanding that Rollo would prevent other Viking raiding parties sailing up the River Seine to attack Paris. It proved a masterstroke.

Timeline

57-56 BCE
Roaming Romans
- Julius Caesar, campaigning to clear his debts and gain glory, attacked north and northwest Gaul over two campaigning seasons, bringing the provinces under the control of the might of Rome.

Late 3rd century
Barbarians at the coast
- Raids by ship-borne Saxon and other Germanic tribes caused the building of the Saxon Shore system of forts in an ultimately futile effort to turn back the barbarian tide.

851
Vikings on the river
- Having been summer raiders, Viking war bands took to setting up camp over winter in the lower reaches of the Seine estuary, ready for a new season of plunder and slave taking the next year.

1002
Marrying up
Richard the Good, Duke of Normandy, married his sister, Emma, to King Æthelred of England. It was a good match, and it was the start of the fateful linking of the crown of England to the Duchy of Normandy.

966-996
Consolidation
- Richard I, known as the Fearless, expanded feudalism in Normandy, ensuring that his barons were personally loyal to him, and then for the last 30 years of his long reign stabilised the duchy.

Kingdom of the Northmen

Cotentin Peninsula in 933, bringing the tidal island of Mont-Saint-Michel under Norman control. The dukes favoured the Benedictine monastery there, and Richard the Good, son to Richard the Fearless, sponsored the building of the Romanesque church on the isle. The complex of buildings on the island became one of the wonders of the medieval world.

Richard the Good (Richard II) was the first duke of Normandy, his father, grandfather and great-grandfather having taken the lesser title of count of Rouen. Richard also numbered among the many leaders to inflict defeat on King Æthelred of England for, in 1000, the English attacked the Cotentin Peninsula intending to capture Richard to prevent Viking raiders using Normandy as a safe haven. The attack proved a failure, leading Æthelred to put his body on the line in a different way: he contracted a marriage with Richard's sister, Emma, thus fatefully linking the House of Normandy to the English crown.

The Norman dukes had become major players in French politics, their power so great that the dukedom, while nominally subject to the king of France, was virtually an independent state. However, it was plunged into civil strife when Duke Robert the Magnificent died while returning from a pilgrimage to the Holy Land, leaving his eight-year-old illegitimate son as heir. The boy, known as William the Bastard by his many domestic enemies, survived the turmoil of his childhood to become William the Conqueror.

William's conquest of England would, in the end, be the death of the Duchy of Normandy. William's sons disputed the succession, their quarrels being resolved on the battlefield at Tinchebrai in 1106 when Henry I of England defeated his brother, Robert Curthose, Duke of Normandy, holding him prisoner for the rest of his life. Thus was also sown the seed of future conflict between England and France: as dukes of Normandy, the successors to Henry I owed fealty to France, but as kings of England they were equals to the monarchs on the other side of the English Channel.

The duchy became part of the Angevin Empire when it was conquered by Geoffrey Plantagenet, count of Anjou and husband to Empress Matilda, the only surviving child of Henry I of England, in 1144, who then gave it over to his son, the future Henry II of England and the country's first Plantagenet king. The Plantagenet kings of England and the Capetian kings of France became locked into a decades-long struggle for power. At one point, the Angevins controlled half of France as well as England, but as dukes of Normandy, they remained vassals of the French king. Angevin power waxed under Henry II and Richard I, but fell apart when John took the throne and proceeded to acquire the nickname Lackland, as King Philip II gradually whittled away at the Plantagenet territory, finally winning a victory at the Battle of Bouvines on 27 July 1214. Normandy was now a duchy in the gift of the king of France, and the kings had no interest in returning it.

In 1259, Henry III of England, signed the Treaty of Paris, formally acknowledging that he no longer had a claim. The loss rankled deeply with the English monarchs, becoming one of the justifications for the Hundred Years' War, during which the duchy was reconquered early in the 15th century, only to be lost in 1450 following the Battle of Formigny.

> The Normans were to remain a disrespectful thorn in the side of the French monarchy for another three centuries

Independent Normandy

Although the French crown reconquered Normandy early in the 13th century, the duchy had been largely independent of France for 300 years. During that time, a body of local laws, privileges and rights had grown up that the Normans were reluctant to cede to the French kings, with their predilection for centralising everything under their increasingly authoritarian rule. Tensions grew, and riots flared up against the rule of Philip the Fair, the French king who suppressed the Knights Templar. In an effort to protect their ancient rights, the Norman barons presented to Philip's heir, Louis X, a charter that sought to preserve them. Louis had little choice but to sign, thus guaranteeing, in principle at least, that the monarch could not impose a new tax upon the Normans without their consent, that the rulings of the chief Norman court at Rouen were final and could not be overturned by royal courts, and that the king would forswear arbitrary acts and punishments against them.

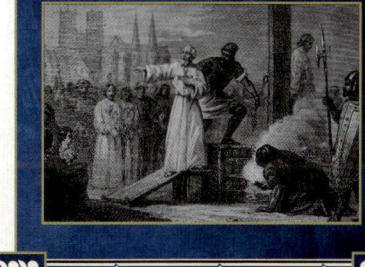

Defining moment
The Conquest 1066
England had been conquered before, by the Romans, and then the Danes in 1015, but the conquest by William in 1066 was pivotal. It replaced almost all the upper echelons of Anglo-Saxon society with Norman, Breton and French lords, leading to us having names like Robert and Richard rather than Ælfweard and Eadwig, and turned the sociopolitical orientation of England southwards. Before, the most significant links were eastward across the North Sea to Scandinavia, now they were south to the other side of the Channel.

Defining moment
Battle of Bouvines 1214
Alarmed by the conquests of Philip II, a coalition assembled, including King John of England, Holy Roman Emperor Otto IV and the count of Flanders. Although John was not present at the battle, his hopes of restoring the Angevin Empire rested upon the defeat of Philip II. The French charged repeatedly, winning a decisive victory. With no hope of regaining his lands in France, King John had little option but to sign the charter his barons brought him a year later, the Magna Carta.

---

28 September 1106
Battle of Tinchebrai
● Robert Curthose, William's eldest son, was bequeathed the Duchy of Normandy on his father's death. Rivalry between the sons of William led, finally, to Henry, by 1100 king of England, invading Normandy and defeating his brother in battle.

1144
Normandy conquered
● In 1128, Geoffrey, count of Anjou and a traditional Norman enemy, married Matilda, daughter of Henry I. Anarchy and conflict followed when Stephen of Blois was declared king of England and duke of Normandy.

18 May 1152
Angevin Empire
● Henry II, king of England and duke of Normandy, married Eleanor of Aquitaine, bringing England, Normandy, most of Wales, much of Ireland and the western half of France under his control in what would be called the Angevin Empire.

1202-1204
France conquers Normandy
● During a two-year campaign, Philip II, king of France, defeated King John of England – a defeat brought about in large part through John's ill treatment of his local allies – and by August 1204 Philip had conquered Normandy.

71

Alfred Vs the Vikings

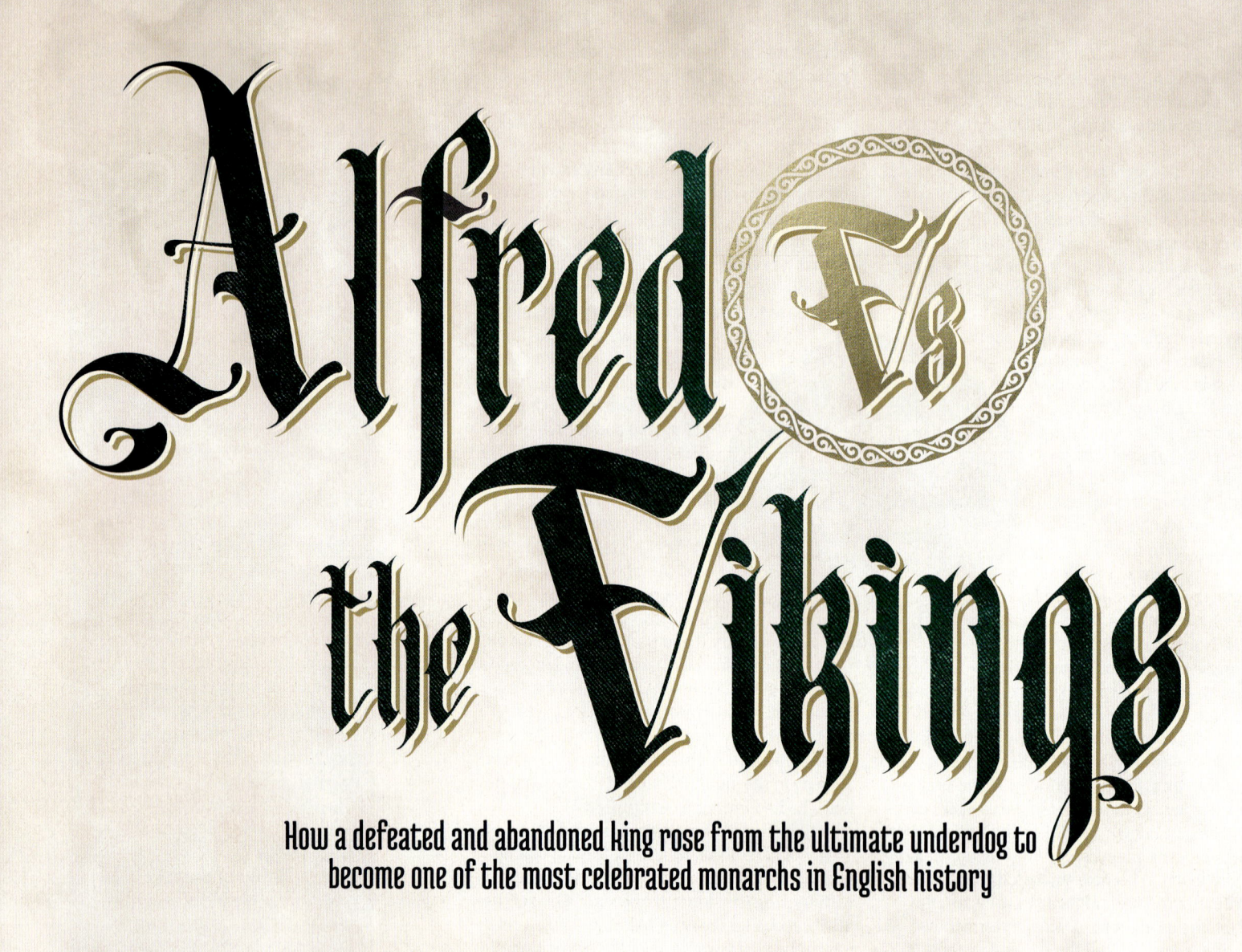

How a defeated and abandoned king rose from the ultimate underdog to become one of the most celebrated monarchs in English history

The rain thundered down on the wet, swampy moors of Wessex. A crack of lightning set the sky alight before the wasteland was plunged into darkness once more. Alfred staggered as he ran breathlessly through the plains, accompanied by a handful of men. They were all pale, shivering and soaked to the bone.

"We must find shelter." The words had barely left Alfred's mouth before his foot caught on a root and he crashed into the mud. "My lord," his companion offered his hand, but Alfred shook his head and pushed himself to his feet. Standing breathlessly in the wide, open plain, he glanced back to the land that was once his. The cities of Wessex were a mere glimmer in the distance, little lights where he had grown into a man, shot his first boar and fathered his children. Now they belonged to his enemies and he was an exile, betrayed by those he thought loyal, no longer a king and anything but great.

Alfred was not born to be king. He wasn't strong, he suffered with illness throughout his life and most of all, he was the fifth-born son. He seemed destined to a life of study in the priesthood, something he was perfectly happy about. Although far from a coward, he was milder and more thoughtful than his rowdy brothers. But he had been born in a time of unrest and war.

Since the attack on Lindisfarne monastery in 793, Viking raids all around Britain had increased in number and ferocity. In 865, a huge army dismounted from a fleet of ships, and while the previous attacks had been men eager for quick plunder, this was an army that didn't intend to return home. It wanted one thing: conquest.

This attack was very bad timing for the kingdom of Wessex. Alfred's father, king of Wessex for nearly 20 years, was dead. The throne passed between his two eldest sons, but death followed them both quickly, and in 865, the leadership fell to Alfred's older brother Æthelred.

In 866, the Viking army was on the move. At least 1,000 strong, it slaughtered its way across the country, felling any nation that stood in its way. East Anglia, Northumbria and even Mercia, Wessex's northern neighbour, became Viking property. Those kings who tried to pay the invaders off, such as the East Anglian monarch, Edmund, found themselves later repaid by swift and brutal conquest. Soon, the only Anglo-Saxon nation that remained unclaimed by the pagan raiders was the exposed kingdom of Wessex.

The Vikings were not hesitant about making their move; they captured Reading in the winter of 870 but suffered a surprising defeat at Englefield by a small Anglo-Saxon force. Spurred by news of this triumph, the young king and his brother were determined to stop the raiders in their tracks. Fuelled by the taste of victory, Alfred and Æthelred gathered their forces for a raid on the Viking stronghold in Reading.

Although they were filled with dogged determination, this was the first time both of the brothers had faced a real battle situation, and it didn't end well. Although they achieved initial success, when the gates of the fortress opened a wave of bloodthirsty Vikings poured out and laid waste to the Wessex forces. The English turned and fled for their lives, pursued for miles. It was a humiliating defeat for the man who would one day be known as 'great'.

For the Vikings, the victory was all the encouragement they needed. With Wessex exposed and the rest of England in submission,

Alfred vs The Vikings

The Legends of King Alfred
A powerful friend

Aged just four, Alfred is said to have travelled to Rome to meet the pope, who apparently "anointed him as king". This is surprising as Alfred was the fifth son, and could mean the young prince was confirmed or made a consul, as it was believed he would go into the Church.

73

Anglo-Saxon kingdoms

- CELTS
- ANGLO-SAXONS

NORTHUMBRIA
WALES
MERCIA
EAST ANGLIA
WESSEX
ESSEX
KENT
JUTES
SUSSEX

they stormed towards the centre of the region. The raiders outnumbered the fractured and broken Wessex forces considerably and this skeleton army could only watch as the Vikings moved closer to their capital. Although the Saxons put up a brave resistance, the battlegrounds transformed into scenes of slaughter, and as the brothers faced the Vikings for the ninth exhausting time, the Wessex army fled in panic.

The bodies of Anglo-Saxon dead were strewn about the field, and the king received a mortal wound. Within a month he was dead, and his passing was followed by the arrival of a fresh fleet of Viking ships.

Æthelred had sons, but they were young, and with the fate of Wessex dangling on a knife edge, it was agreed that Alfred would rule, in the hope that a strong ruler could unite the forces and claim victory from the jaws of defeat.

It is difficult to think of an English crown more burdensome than the one Alfred inherited in 871, aged just 22. With the Viking army ploughing its way through Wessex and drawing dangerously close to the capital, Alfred decided that he would try to settle things on his own terms. He set out to halt the army's advance at Wilton, less than 30 miles from his capital city of Winchester.

One thing was immediately obvious: Alfred was vastly outnumbered. He had struggled to quickly assemble a force and the Viking ranks were swelling with eager new conquerors and gold seekers. Aware that this was his first battle as king, Alfred knew he had no option but to lead from the front. He ordered his men to form the shield-wall and faced his mighty enemies.

Perhaps benefiting from the strength that only men defending their homeland are gifted, the Wessex forces somehow managed to hold their ground. What they lacked in numbers they made up for in will and they destroyed the enemy shield-wall. In mild disbelief at the unexpected victory, Alfred watched as the Vikings fled and his men celebrated around him.

But the young Alfred had made a crucial mistake: he had failed to take advantage of his victory by pressing the retreat. The Vikings regrouped and swarmed the field. They rumbled towards the unsuspecting foe and in a moment victory turned to slaughter. It was the Wessex men, not the Vikings, who fled for their lives.

For Alfred, this defeat was the worst one yet. His army, or what remained of it, was in tatters. He had watched all the other kingdoms fall and it seemed inevitable that his own would follow. However, little did he know that the Vikings' patience too was wearing thin. No other kingdom had put up as much of a fight as Wessex and even though they had won many battles, it had come at a great loss to their numbers.

With both forces spent, Alfred made

The Legends of King Alfred
Quick learner

Alfred's mother, showing her children a beautiful book of Saxon poetry, told them that whoever was first able to memorise it would get to keep it. Alfred was fascinated, but unable to read. So he took it to tutors and managed to learn it, receiving the book in reward.

ABOVE Accounts liken Alfred's ferocity during battle to that of a "wild boar"

Alfred vs The Vikings

'peace' with the Vikings. He most likely paid them a huge amount to withdraw, and for a good few years it worked. However, in 876, Alfred faced a new foe, the Viking king Guthrum. Guthrum had already managed, through great cunning, to travel through the heart of Wessex and seize the town of Wareham from under Alfred's nose. Although they made a treaty of peace, the arrival of hundreds more Viking ships indicated relations were anything but friendly. With his army reinforced, Guthrum headed straight towards Alfred's stronghold in Chippenham with one aim in sight. He didn't want a quick raid or a battle; he wanted Wessex, and to get it he would destroy the one thing holding it together: Alfred.

Guthrum planned his attack perfectly. The Twelfth Night was a festival that took over the entire city, a season of revelry with eating, drinking and merriment. Every person from king to peasant was part of the celebration and the defences of Chippenham were exposed and unguarded. Guthrum took advantage of this lapse and the city was overrun by Vikings within moments. Alfred had no time to summon an army and was forced to flee with his family to Wiltshire. However, it turned out that the powerful Viking king with his huge force presented a very convincing argument, and one by one the nobles of Wessex bowed to their new ruler. The leadership of Wessex was destroyed and Alfred, with nobody to call on, fled into the darkness of the moors.

This was more than humiliation for the king – it was the lowest point in his life. The loss of riches meant little, as Anglo-Saxon kings did not sit on golden thrones, but side by side on the mead bench with their faithful companions. And that was just it – he had no companions, he was alone. In a world where loyalty and faithfulness were prized above all, he had been cast out, a virtual exile because of a chain of swift and brutal betrayals by his liegemen.

Alfred could have easily succumbed to the hopelessness of his situation, but instead he decided to fight. He and a small band of followers built a hidden camp in a swamp in Athelney, Somerset, and used it as a base to unleash hell upon the invaders. For months Alfred and his men fought a guerilla war against the Danes, sneaking out of Somerset, killing small parties of Vikings they passed, looting camps and seeking out the enemies' vulnerabilities. Their number one target was the English who had betrayed Alfred, hoping their deaths would send a clear message to his people that the king had not abandoned them.

Tales of Alfred's deeds soon spread throughout the population, comforting those loyal that the king would

Anatomy of an Anglo-Saxon warrior

Shield
The crucial piece of equipment for any Anglo-Saxon warrior, one of the primary battle tactics was the shield-wall. Not only did this protect against the enemies' missiles, but it could also be used to push forward and break the enemy line. The first shield line to break would be the losers, so hardy, strong shields were essential

Spear
Possibly the most common Anglo-Saxon weapon, spears went hand in hand with the shield-wall tactic, being thrown as javelins and thrusting weapons. The size and material of spearheads differed hugely, as did the length – ranging from about five foot to over nine foot.

Helmet
Known as 'helms', the lack of evidence of Anglo-Saxon helmets have led many to believe that they were not commonly used, or were made from perishable materials like leather. The earliest Anglo-Saxon helmet discovered was found at Sutton Hoo and dates as far back as the 6th century.

Sword
Swords were very treasured items, with connotations of status, and not just any soldier could wield one. Rather than melting iron ore, the blades of swords were constructed from several small pieces of iron or welded together. Swords would also often be decorated with inscriptions, and one 6th-century example bears the mark "Sigimer made this sword".

The search for a king's remains

Although we don't know the exact circumstances of Alfred's death, it is known that he suffered from a lifelong condition that may have been Crohn's disease. After his death, Alfred was first buried in the Old Minster in Winchester in 899, but four years later his body was moved to the New Minster. According to legend, this was because his body wandered around the church, but it is more likely that New Minster was the original intended resting place. He didn't get to rest for long though, as in 1110 Alfred's body was transferred to Hyde Abbey. In 1539, during the reign of Henry VIII, the church was demolished, but the graves remained intact.

The site lay pretty much untouched until it was purchased to construct a prison in 1788. Convicts likely discovered the coffins while ridding the site of rubble, and promptly pocketed anything of value. Any bones found were simply tossed around the area. The prison was torn down between 1846 and 1850, and in 1999 an excavation discovered not only the foundations of the abbey, but also some bones. However, to much disappointment, these remains were found to belong to an elderly woman, and the rest of the excavation objects were placed in a store room in a Winchester museum. However, in 2014 it was announced that a fragment of pelvic bone from this find had belonged to a man aged between 26 and 45, who died between 895 and 1017. Although it has not yet been proven, this age and date range makes it very likely that the bone belongs either to Alfred or his son, Edward.

RIGHT Alfred later ordered the construction of a small fleet of longships

BELOW Viking invaders were intent on Wessex, which had held out longer than other lands

The Legends of King Alfred
Burning of the cakes

This legend is one of the most well known. While Alfred was on the run from the Vikings after the attack at Chippenham, he apparently sought refuge in the home of an old peasant woman. Seeing how run down, tired and hungry he was, she took pity on Alfred, unaware he was the king, and promised him food and shelter if he watched her cakes (small loaves of bread) while she went out. The king, consumed by his own problems concerning how he was going to beat the invaders, was distracted and let the cakes burn. When the woman returned, she scolded, and in some accounts even struck the king for his absentmindedness.

Alfred vs The Vikings

return and free them from their Danish suppressors. Slowly but surely a secret network of communication between the exiled king and his loyal earls formed. For Guthrum, the attacks by Alfred and his band of warriors were the last stumbling block to full control of Wessex, and he wanted rid of the persistent pest once and for all.

By the middle of April, Alfred was ready for war; he sent out a secret summons and assembled those faithful to him – an army of several thousand men – and headed for Guthrum's stronghold in Chippenham. Guthrum soon learned of this large gathering, assembled his own army, and headed to intercept Alfred. The time for pay-offs and promises was over. Guthrum didn't care how many riches Alfred could offer – he wanted to rule unrivalled, which is exactly what Alfred wanted too.

Before he was able to reach Chippenham, Alfred caught sight of his enemy; a menacing shield-wall of towering Vikings jeered the exiled king. Alfred hastily formed his own shield-wall, and fortified it not only with physical strength but with a rousing speech. He implored his men to summon their courage, damned those who would dare to run, and promised glory to those who remained. Then he joined the wall and advanced.

As the two walls drew close, the sky blackened with spears. Men were struck and fell, but both lines steadily advanced. As the Vikings mocked their opponents, Alfred made his cries of encouragement heard over the taunts. By now the walls were mere feet from each other, but the Vikings had one last trick up their sleeves. They unleashed their berserkers, savage warriors who used hallucinogens to drive them into a bloodthirsty rage. The naked men crashed into the Wessex shield-wall, but the effect was not as Guthrum had hoped. The Anglo-Saxons stood strong and unfazed, slaughtering the berserkers within moments.

When the two shield-walls crashed into each other, the Saxons were stronger than ever. Spears jabbed, desperate to find a weak point to expose and force the shield-wall open.

The battle waged on into the afternoon, the ground was littered with corpses and those who remained were crippled with exhaustion. It transformed from a battle of might to one of endurance. With their forces equally matched, only the men with more resolve would emerge as the victors, and the Vikings were flagging. The fact was simple – the men of Wessex cared more for their home than the invaders ever could.

Finally, the Viking shield-wall was broken. The Saxons unleashed hell upon their invaders. Chaos reigned in the Norse ranks and the desperate men turned and fled. Alfred was not going to make the same mistake that had cost him so dearly again and he led the charge after the retreating men, staining the plains red with Viking blood. Guthrum managed to make it to Chippenham and attempted to begin a siege, but Alfred's resolve could not be broken. He set up his forces outside, waiting for the inevitable surrender.

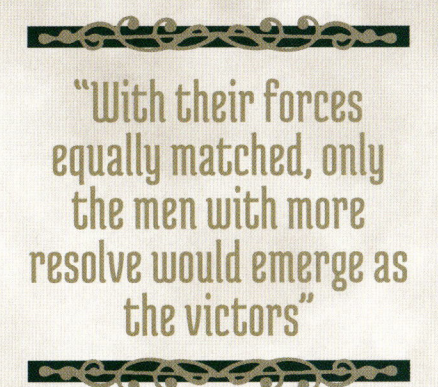

After 14 days, Guthrum's will was spent. He begged Alfred for a chance to escape with his life, he would give the king anything – as many hostages as he wanted – he just wanted to leave. No Viking leader in history had offered such one-sided terms to an Anglo-Saxon king. Some would have taken advantage of this sign of desperation, but Alfred, although a warrior, was not a brute. He granted Guthrum mercy with one condition – Guthrum would be baptised a Christian, and Alfred would serve as his godfather. Guthrum agreed – he would do anything to escape the kingdom of Wessex and its accursed king. The deed was done and the Viking king, for once, held up his side of the bargain. The two parted ways and Alfred returned to his capital in Winchester, finally free to begin rebuilding his shattered kingdom.

> "With their forces equally matched, only the men with more resolve would emerge as the victors"

ABOVE
Alfred was not actually taught to read until he was 12 years old, or even later

RIGHT
Guthrum and Alfred's territories were outlined in the Treaty of Alfred and Guthrum

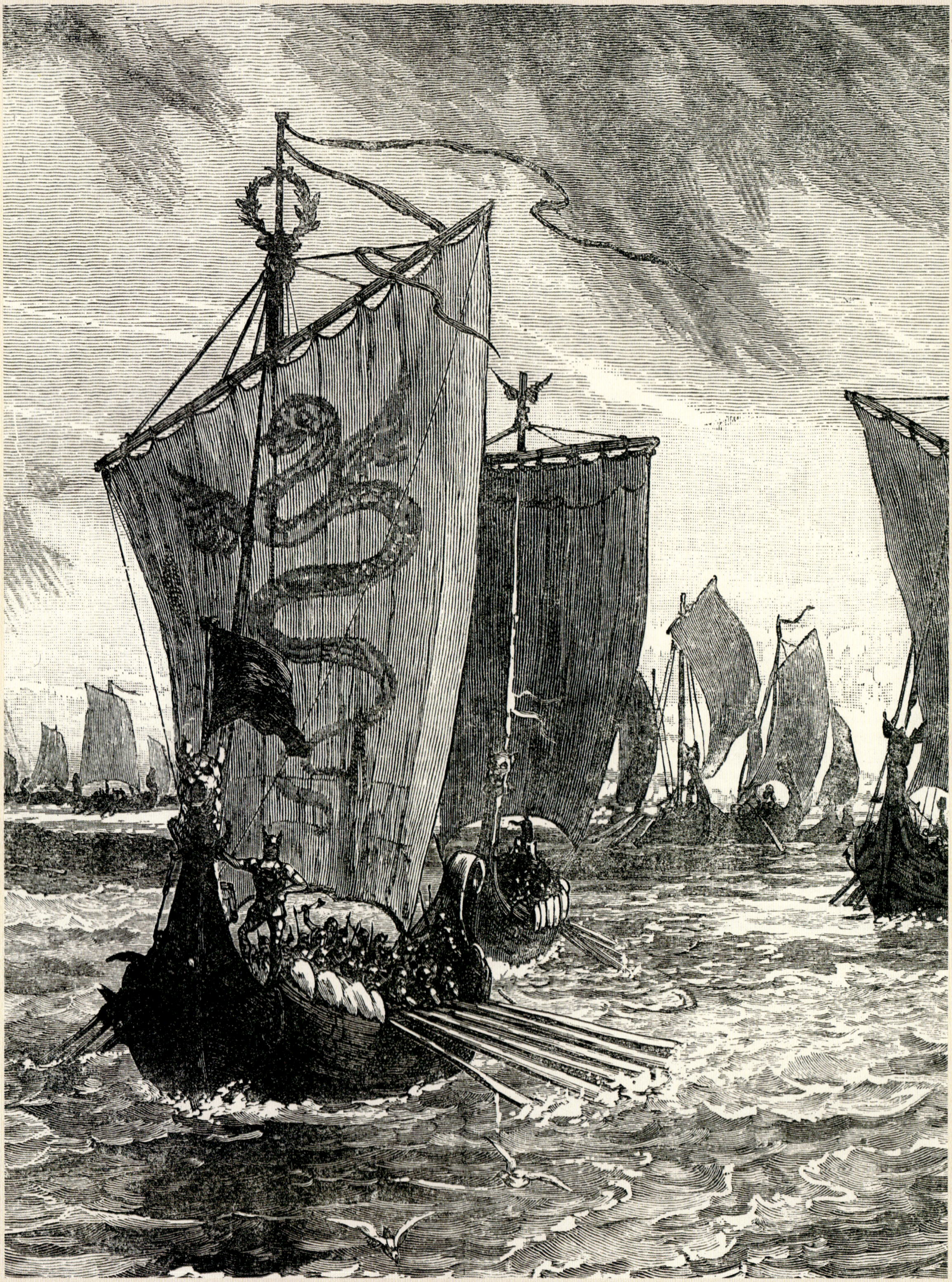

The Danelaw

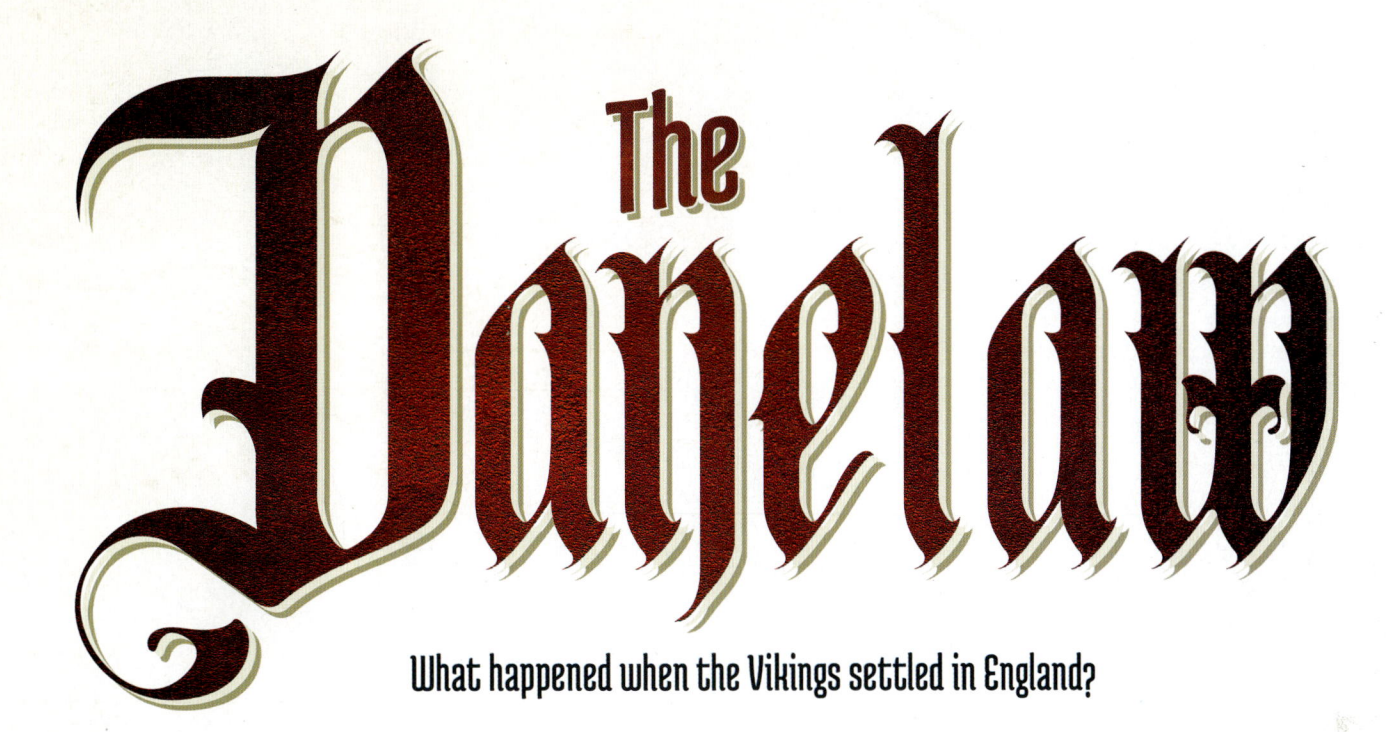

What happened when the Vikings settled in England?

With the defeat of Guthrum's army by Alfred, a frontier was established, running approximately from Wessex and the western half of Mercia (the English Midlands) with the Anglo-Saxons to the southwest of it and the Vikings to the northeast. To a large extent, this reflected the status quo, with Viking-conquered territories such as East Anglia, much of Mercia and Northumbria remaining in Norse hands. An uneasy period of truce followed, which was threatened and indeed broken from time to time, but despite this it managed to remain substantially intact for a while. Many settlers emigrated from Scandinavia, and they were more interested in building a sustainable existence in England than living the life of a raider.

This is not to say that the frontier between the two zones was frozen, and one important change occurred in 886 when Alfred conquered Lundenwic (London), which had previously been in Viking-held Mercian territory. It was rapidly increasing in importance, though it was several centuries away from taking over from Winchester in terms of political precedence in southern England. This followed Viking raids in the previous year, which had given Alfred the opportunity to conquer it with legitimate reason. The treaty that was subsequently agreed between the Vikings and Alfred set the frontier along the line of Watling Street, the old Roman road, and that of the rivers Thames, Lea and Ouse.

For a while, Anglo-Saxon England, in the southwestern part of the region, and the lands held by Vikings to the northeast co-existed peacefully enough. There were occasional Viking raids on England but they mainly came from new Viking incursions from the Continent or Ireland rather than from Viking-held territory in England. There were certainly rules in place governing relations between the two domains of England that now existed, but they were largely those of two equivalents rather than of one party dominating the other.

Guthrum, who had been baptised as part of the peace treaty with Alfred, adopted a completely different approach than the swagger of the stereotypical Viking warlord he had previously adopted. He used the 'Christian name' of Æthelstan, and for the rest of his reign as ruler of Viking Mercia and East Anglia (Northumbria was in different hands at the time) continued to use this name on the coinage that he issued. Baptism into the Christian faith was an increasingly common move across the Viking world as former pagan warlords began to see the political advantages that Christianity offered. The Viking-held territories were later given the generic name of Danelaw (although this name did not start to be used until the early 11th century, over a century after the first permanent Viking settlements in England were established). As the name suggests, in this part of England, Danish law and customs were used, in contrast to the convention in Anglo-Saxon territory. However, over time the two systems came to influence each other.

Although the initial settlement of England by the Vikings was undoubtedly bloody and violent, the situation stabilised significantly as Viking settlers began to assimilate with the indigenous population. While Viking leaders may have assumed the role of local rulers, they still needed the pre-existing population to work alongside them, to tend the land and generate taxes (often paid in kind rather than currency). So although we cannot be sure, in the absence of detailed records, that there was not the occasional brutal warlord ruthlessly exploiting the local population,

LEFT
A 20th-century image of the Viking fleet invading England in the build-up to the Battle of Brunanburh in 937

RIGHT
A Viking coin-maker at work at the Jorvik Centre in York

Erik Bloodaxe

The last Viking king of York?

The last Viking king of York was called Erik. Later sagas suggest that this was a man famed as a ferocious Viking warrior known evocatively as Erik Bloodaxe. Erik Bloodaxe had been involved in a bitter fight for supremacy in Norway with his half-brother, Hákon – a battle that he ultimately lost. Erik Bloodaxe therefore went into exile and lived his life as an adventurer overseas.

The last Viking king of York was almost certainly called Erik, but modern historians are not convinced this is necessarily the same man as Erik Bloodaxe – Erik is, after all, a common enough Norse name. Other accounts have Erik Bloodaxe living out his life raiding in Spain and suggest that he died there. The Erik who became king of York, whether or not he was of the Bloodaxe variety, seems to have come to power with the active connivance of the then archbishop of York, the Anglo-Saxon Wulfstan. But his grip on power was tenuous and he was ejected from the city in 954. Soon after, he was killed in what appears to have been an ambush at Stainmore, a pass in the Pennines, the 'stony moor' on the frontiers of Yorkshire, Durham and Cumbria.

ABOVE
An atmospheric view of a Viking funeral

LEFT
The division of England into Anglo-Saxon Wessex and the Danish-controlled Danelaw

RIGHT
A reconstruction of a Viking settlement in a Scandinavian landscape

it is far more likely that the two populations in the Danelaw routinely (and for the most part, peacefully) co-existed.

The Viking invasions had an unexpected role in the development of a unified country that would be called England. Following Alfred's death, the baton was picked up by two extraordinary people, his son Edward (known sometimes as 'The Elder') and his daughter Æthelflaed, who had married the ealdorman of Mercia. Between them, they pushed forward the boundaries of Anglo-Saxon territory by progressively taking over settlements in the Danelaw. Following a crushing victory in 910 at Tettenhall (near Wednesfield – 'Woden's Field') close to Wolverhampton, where Edward and Æthelflaed between them led a combined army from Wessex and Mercia that decimated their Viking opponents, the frontier crept forward as previously Viking-held settlements like Leicester and Derby fell into the hands of their Anglo-Saxon opponents.

However, even when the Danelaw gradually returned to Anglo-Saxon hands, the rulers of Wessex (who became the dominant force in England) wisely allowed the settlers in the Viking-populated territories to maintain their own customs and laws, so a distinct identity developed, even if politically it came to be part of Anglo-Saxon England. A number of major towns emerged as urban life started to develop. The major ones – Leicester, Derby, Nottingham, Lincoln and Stamford – became known as the 'Five Boroughs'; it is notable that all but the last of these remain as county towns in modern England. Each of these was built around a fortress with its own jarl (Scandinavian for 'lord', which is linked with the English word 'earl'). These became significant commercial centres as the Viking settlers shifted their focus from raiding to trading. These settlers left their mark, not least in the English language and on the English countryside. A number of everyday modern English words have their roots in Scandinavian origins: 'anger', 'husband', 'sister' and 'egg' are just some examples of how deeply Norse is woven into English. The inclusion in a

> "They pushed forward the boundaries of Anglo-Saxon territory by progressively taking over settlements in the Danelaw"

The Danelaw

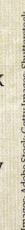

ABOVE Alfred's children built on his great legacy of resistance

place name of '-thorpe' (Scunthorpe, Cleethorpes) or '-by' (Derby, Whitby, Grimsby) is a clear sign of a settlement that was in Viking-held territory during this period. So Viking influence lives on into contemporary life, albeit in ways that are now often forgotten.

Rather than resenting the Anglo-Saxon takeover in the reign of Edward the Elder and his successors, the Viking inhabitants of the Danelaw seem to have come to terms with it well enough, at least in the region south of York. A decisive moment came in the year 937, when a massive army descended on Anglo-Saxon territory from the north. The army was formed of the combined forces of men from Scotland, Strathclyde (then a British territory in what is now northwest England and southwest Scotland) and a Viking force which had sailed over from Ireland. The English king Æthelstan (not to be confused with King Guthrum, who had adopted the same name a few decades earlier) won a decisive victory over this coalition at Brunanburh, somewhere in the north of England. At his side were men from not only Wessex and Mercia, but also those of Viking descent from the Danelaw. They had looked at the stability they had achieved under Anglo-Saxon rule and, perhaps in some cases to their surprise, found that they preferred it to the old unstable ways of the Viking world that was on offer from the alliance they fought against. However, one part of Viking-held territory in England remained stubbornly resistant to Anglo-Saxon rule long after other parts of the Danelaw accepted it. This was the region of Northumbria, centred on York (Viking Jórvík). This maintained strong links with Viking Dublin and on a number of occasions would-be kings came over the Irish Sea in a sometimes successful (sometimes not) bid to be ruler of both. Northumbria had always, to an extent, been distinct from the rest of Anglo-Saxon England, probably a situation that was encouraged by its geographical remoteness. It is quite likely that the Northumbrians of the time were no more comfortable at the thought of being ruled by kings from Wessex far to the south than they were with Viking government.

Northumbria was composed of two sub-divisions; Deira in the south, centred around York and, further north around Bamburgh, Bernicia. Deira was the main centre of Viking territory in the north while Bernicia often remained as an independent Angle-held territory with a ruling dynasty whose head was almost invariably called Uhtred (made famous in modern times by Bernard Cornwell's historical novels on the subject). Jórvík became the bustling centre of the Viking North.

Modern excavations have revealed extensive reminders of the Viking era here, especially in the Coppergate area of the city. These reveal that this was an overcrowded and unsanitary area to live in, but local merchants clearly found compensation in the living they were able to make from it. There is widespread evidence of the manufacture of combs, for example, which at the time was an important industry. Despite the humble houses that archaeology has revealed, Jórvík became something of a powerhouse.

The wealth of Jórvík made it an attractive target for Anglo-Saxon kings in the south of England, and it changed hands on several occasions during the first half of the 10th century. Several times they succeeded in conquering it (for example during the reign of Æthelstan) but then lost it again in the uncertain period that often followed the death of an Anglo-Saxon king and the almost inevitable succession crisis that followed. Eventually, the demise of a Viking ruler called Erik in 954 marked the end of the Viking kingdom in Northumbria. This appeared to be the end of an independent Viking territory in the north, but they would return to England several decades later in a new and even more terrifying guise.

Emperor of the North

1,000 years ago, a young Viking warrior became king of England. No one at the time can have expected how remarkable his reign would be

Most famous now for his futile efforts to turn back the encroaching tide on the seashore, the life of Cnut was extraordinary. As well as being a strong, reliable supporter of the Church, he was also an archetypal Viking raider. Forming part of a dynamic marital alliance with his wife, Emma, he was also accused of the murder of his brother-in-law, Ulf. As well as ruling England and Denmark, he was also for a short time king of Norway. His government of what has been called an 'Empire of the North' was a unique achievement, setting Cnut apart as a remarkable man.

Cnut's roots were in Denmark. His great-grandfather, Gorm the Old, was the founder-figure of the Jelling dynasty in Jutland. Gorm was a formidable pagan warrior, but his son, Harald Bluetooth, became an enthusiastic Christian ruler. Harald was involved in a bitter civil war with his own son, the renowned Sweyn Forkbeard, a conflict that ended with him fleeing the country and dying shortly afterwards in exile. Sweyn took over and won a reputation as a ruthless and ferocious Viking raider, frequently launching attacks on Britain, Ireland and elsewhere.

Cnut, the son of Sweyn Forkbeard, was probably born in around 995, though no one knows that for sure. The chronicles of the time are equally silent about the first 18 years of Cnut's life and it is not until 1013 that we find him

Emperor of the North

first mentioned in the *Anglo-Saxon Chronicle*. But in that year he accompanied Sweyn on what was supposed to be the climactic campaign in the battle to conquer England. After several decades of raiding, increasing in scale all the time and often only ended by the payment of what later became known as 'Danegeld', Sweyn sensed that England was fatally wounded and, like a hungry predator, moved in for the kill.

He found support for his ambitions from the region of the Danelaw (around the East Midlands of modern England), and Northumbria also soon submitted to him. Moving into southern England, the defence against his forces quickly collapsed. The English king, Æthelred II ('the Unready'), soon after fled the country with his wife Emma and their children, Edward and Alfred. England, it seemed, had fallen. King Æthelred would later be painted as something of a pantomime villain, incompetent and cowardly in equal measure. It was a very harsh assessment given the enormous challenges that he had faced, but it could not be doubted that his reign had apparently ended in spectacular failure.

But just then, as if by a miracle, Sweyn died before he had been made king. Cnut was not with him at the time, having stayed in the Danelaw while Sweyn had moved into southern England. Shortly after, Cnut was badly caught out by a surprise attack on his camp launched by English forces. Æthelred returned from exile and Cnut, barely escaping with his life, fled to Denmark. Before departing, he left behind him a group of hostages minus their ears and noses. This was Cnut the Viking in action.

England's respite, though, was short-lived. In 1015, Cnut was back with 200 ships sailing through the "mouth of the Frome" into Dorset. This saw the beginning of a brutal war for the control of England between Cnut and Edmund Ironside, the son of the now-dying King Æthelred and his first wife. Both were very young warriors, in their early 20s, and the fighting that followed through several battles at Penselwood, Sherston and Otford was bloody and violent. Cnut also laid siege to London and it was a brutal contest that was fought out over a period of a year and more.

The last decisive battle took place at Ashingdon (or Assandun), Essex, in October 1016. It ended in a crushing victory for Cnut. Edmund survived the battle and a deal was struck that left him with Wessex but Cnut with the rest of England. The deal did not survive for long because on 30 November 1016, Edmund very conveniently died, leaving Cnut as the undisputed king of all England.

At the time, it was likely that the people of England were filled with trepidation at these developments. Given the ruthless nature of Viking raids on the country,

ABOVE
An illustration of Cnut taken from *History of England* by Hume, Smollett and Jones

RIGHT
The Anglo-Danish warriors of Cnut's reign, shown wearing the traditional dress of the time

there was a real chance that the new king would milk England for all it was worth, and early signs did little to dispel that impression. Within a year, Cnut was ruthlessly removing those who he felt were plotting against him, including Eadric Streona, Earl of Mercia, whose treachery to the old regime had soon become a byword for duplicity and untrustworthiness.

Then in 1018 he raised the highest Danegeld payment yet; £10,500 from London and £72,000 from the rest of England, massive amounts in the context of the times. But there was a sub-text to this move: Cnut's intention was to use the money to pay off Viking raiders that he no longer had a use for now that the war had been won. This would allow him to govern as he wanted to.

The first sign that there was something to this young man other than the attributes of a rip-roaring Viking raider occurred at around the same time. At a Parliament at Oxford, Cnut wisely adopted the laws of the late King Edgar, seen as one of the greatest of all English monarchs. Edgar's reign was perceived as a Golden Age, a time of peace and prosperity.

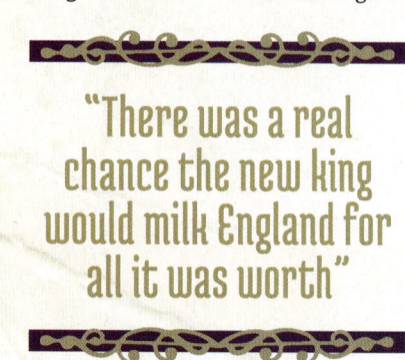

> "There was a real chance the new king would milk England for all it was worth"

BELOW
The new Roskilde cathedral that stands on the site of Ulf's death

ABOVE
An illustration from *British Costume During XIX Centuries* by Mrs Charles H Ashdown of Cnut and his second wife, Emma

It followed another notable step when he married Emma, widow of the late king Æthelred. Emma had two children from her first marriage; Edward (later King Edward the Confessor) and Alfred. Cnut also had two children from a previous relationship with Ælfgifu of Northampton, named Sweyn and Harold (later Harold Harefoot, king of England). Emma soon after her marriage to Cnut gave birth to another son, Harthacnut.

The death, soon after, of Cnut's childless elder brother, Harald, left Denmark open and Cnut soon installed himself as king there, seemingly with little opposition. Cnut, at around the same time, strengthened his hold on England by the judicious appointment of strong supporters in positions of authority in the country. Most prominent among these was Earl Godwin, who Cnut appointed as his representative in the crucial sub-kingdom of Wessex. Godwin would marry the sister of Cnut's brother-in-law. They would have a number of children, including Harold, who would himself become king of England and end his life, allegedly, with an arrow in his eye, at the Battle of Hastings in 1066.

Norway too had once been part of the empire of Sweyn Forkbeard, Cnut's father. However, it had not remained so for long before a rebellion there threw off Danish rule. The beneficiary of that uprising and the current king of Norway was

Emperor of the North

Murder in the cathedral

Cnut's involvement in the elimination of his brother-in-law Ulf

Although Cnut proved himself to be a strong and successful king, on several occasions during his reign he found himself at odds with his supporters and even members of his extended family. Ulf was Cnut's brother-in-law, married to his sister Estrid. In the lead-up to the Battle of Holy River, there were suggestions that Ulf's loyalty was suspect. Cnut's young son, Harthacnut, was in Denmark as its nominal ruler and it seems that Ulf tried to dominate political affairs there in the absence of a powerful king resident in the country.

Nevertheless, Ulf appears to have been with Cnut when he took part in the hard-fought battle at Helgeå. After, they returned to Denmark together to the royal capital, Roskilde. There was soon a family squabble, according to some accounts over something as trivial as a chess game. It may though have been something less insignificant such as a breakdown in trust between the two that led to Cnut's next action.

Clearly angered by something that had taken place, Cnut sent men to eliminate Ulf once and for all. They found him inside Roskilde Cathedral, though some accounts say Ulf was on the royal farm. However, the cathedral was not the imposing building that one sees now with the tombs of many of Denmark's later monarchs, but a much humbler wooden 'stave' church of simple design and intimate size. While some men hesitated to carry out orders given the sacred nature of the place, one of them, Ivar White, had no such scruples and struck Ulf dead.

This unchristian act must have created alarm and as Cnut was able to survive this incident with his reputation relatively intact speaks highly of his political skills. However, it would seem that his own sister was not prepared to give him the benefit of the doubt and her son Sweyn was sent into protective exile for the remainder of Cnut's life. Cnut paid large sums of money to Estrid to allow her to build a grander structure at Roskilde perhaps as a way of salving a guilty conscience.

85

ABOVE
A copperplate engraving of Cnut fighting Edmund Ironside, published in 1773

RIGHT
A coloured etching of Cnut convincing his courtiers that he cannot stem the tide

north that were virtually ungovernable. Cnut took advantage of the significant wealth of England to make gifts to disaffected nobles in Norway. When he arrived with a massive army, the position of Olaf quickly collapsed totally.

Olaf was forced to flee for his life, but he returned soon after in a vain attempt to reclaim the country. At his side was his half-brother Harald, who later – as Harald Hardrada ('the Ruthless') – was to become one of the most famous of all Vikings and would meet his end in a cataclysmic encounter at Stamford Bridge in Yorkshire in 1066. Olaf lost his life in the battle at Stiklestad. Olaf was a staunch Christian ruler and soon after his death was canonised. Saint Olaf would prove much more successful in death than King Olaf ever was in life.

But Cnut did not prove a success as king of Norway. He appointed his first wife, Ælfgifu, as his regent in the country along with their son, Sweyn. However, a disastrous famine undermined their position; this was a time of great suffering across much of the continent and not just in Scandinavia. Their rule was allegedly very harsh and there were a number of revolts that led to the collapse of Cnut's regime there. Olaf's son, Magnus, soon became king in his stead.

Norway was only ever a temporary part of Cnut's 'empire'. Perhaps the dispersed nature of the territories that Cnut ruled made them inherently hard to govern. Certainly the diversity of his subjects, and the relative 'newness' of all three core countries in it – England, Denmark and Norway – presented him with great challenges. It was a tough act for anyone to pull off and certainly there were indications that some of those around him, especially the sons who would have to run his territories after his death – and to a significant extent would be expected to do so when he was alive – were not up to the task, though there were as yet but young.

Cnut certainly had imperial pretensions. His visit to Rome made a great impact on him. He was so impressed at the grandeur and magnificence of the great Imperial Crown worn by Conrad II at his coronation that he had a replica made for himself. Letters back to England soon afterwards included several implicit imperial references – for example, when Cnut ostentatiously described himself as "King of England, Denmark, Norway [not at the time conquered] and part of Sweden". There was little doubt that Cnut had seen something of the magnificence and associated power that came from being an emperor that he took to modelling himself on one to a certain extent.

Yet, paradoxically, Cnut also became renowned for his humility. His great generosity to the Christian Church has already been mentioned, but his actions also won respect. On a visit

a man named Olaf Haraldsson. Olaf allied himself with the king of Sweden and together they raised an army with a view to attacking Denmark. Cnut got together an army of his own to face up to the threat. The two forces clashed in southern Sweden at the Battle of Helgeå. It was an indecisive confrontation, but Cnut succeeded in hanging on to Denmark.

Shortly after the ruthless elimination of his brother-in-law, Ulf, in Roskilde Cathedral, which followed on soon after, Cnut undertook perhaps the greatest mission of his life when he journeyed to Rome to be present at the coronation of the Holy Roman emperor, Conrad II. To be in attendance at this ceremony was a great mark of recognition for a man who was effectively a Viking king. It made a great impression on many at home and in Europe.

Perhaps the most significant part of Cnut's reign was the way in which he built close relationships with the Church. He was a generous patron of a number of religious establishments in both England and Denmark. He also appointed allies into key positions of influence in the Church, such as when Æthelnoth was made archbishop of Canterbury in 1020. This helped to build his influence and reputation, and further strengthen his position.

However, the question of Norway was unfinished business as far as Cnut was concerned. Following his return from the indecisive battle at Helgeå, King Olaf's position had become increasingly fragile back in Norway. It was then a very fragmented country with a number of regions, especially those positioned in the wild

> "Cnut certainly had imperial pretensions. His visit to Rome made a great impact on him"

Emperor of the North

Turning back the tide
Cnut's involvement in the elimination of his brother-in-law Ulf

Cnut is often remembered for the famous incident in which he sat on the seashore and commanded the tide to retreat with a predictable lack of success, but there is no contemporary reference to this event ever taking place. It was not until a century later that the tale appeared in the writings of the chronicler Henry of Huntingdon. However, there was something about his account that gripped the imagination of his readers and seemingly continued to do so into more recent times.

The story then is apocryphal, though several places have laid claim to the events associated with it. Southampton was one claimant – there is still a Canute Road there – and Thorney Island is another. Bosham in West Sussex is also linked with the legend; it was also said that here a daughter of Cnut was buried.

In the story, Cnut sat on his throne on the seashore and spoke to the sea in imperious tones, demanding that the tide retreat before his supreme earthly power. Of course it did no such thing, after which Cnut told his courtiers: "The power of kings is empty and worthless, and there is no king worthy of the name save Him by whose will heaven, earth and sea obey eternal laws."

Rather than being a mark of an arrogant king, the story came to be interpreted as an example of a ruler who realised that his power was finite compared to the omnipotence of God. Cnut, in this interpretation, knew exactly what would happen when he sat down in front of the advancing tide and undertook these actions to demonstrate the limits of his power to a group of sycophantic courtiers. So greatly impressed was he by this experience that it was said that he afterwards stopped wearing a crown. It is a good story, though we will never know whether or not these events actually took place.

to the north of England late in his reign, he walked five miles barefoot to visit the tomb of the revered Saint Cuthbert in Durham. Chroniclers of the time wrote of a man who was more monk than king. Although these attributes may have been exaggerated, as was common with the chroniclers of the time, this suggests a man who wanted to make a strong impression for his Christian acts.

This was an approach that was perhaps based as much on the political advantages that came from it as from any deeply held personal convictions. It made Cnut a 'modern' ruler, one who could sit at the high table of European politics as an equal rather than be regarded with suspicion by his fellow rulers as a potential raider.

This brought him great political benefits, and perhaps the most significant was his alliance with Conrad II. Denmark and the Holy Roman Empire shared a border – one that had been porous and problematic – but the alliance brought stability, enabling Cnut to concentrate his efforts on his unfinished business in Norway. Conrad's son married Cnut's daughter, Gunhilda – a sign of the great importance of Cnut in European affairs.

Alongside this, Cnut appeared to retain other more 'Viking' characteristics. From what we know, he was a lover of the sagas every bit as much as more traditional Scandinavian rulers had been before him. He himself appears in Viking sagas, though reflecting these extraordinary changing times the heroes here were now typically Christian rather than followers of Odin or Thor. This was a sure sign that the world was changing rapidly, though some parts of Scandinavia would stay stubbornly pagan well beyond the period covered by Cnut's reign. For example, Uppsala in Sweden was long a centre of worship for the old gods and half a century after Cnut's death the Christian writer Adam of Bremen was writing of the horrific rites of animal and human sacrifice that were still practised there.

However, Cnut lived a very active life and it seems to have taken its toll. There are a few hints that he was suffering from some illness that was wearing him down and on 12 November 1035 he breathed his last at Shaftesbury in Dorset. The place of his death is symbolically interesting as the tomb of the martyred English king and saint, Edward resided there. Throughout his life, Cnut had acted with great respect towards the English royal family that he had replaced. He, as we have seen, emphasised his appreciation of the late, great Edgar by adopting his laws. He even visited the tomb of Edmund Ironside at Glastonbury Abbey where he left behind a splendid gift of a lavish cloak adorned with peacock feathers, a potent symbol of both Imperial Byzantine grandeur and Christian resurrection.

His magnanimity marked him out as a wise man, able to build bridges with the people that he had conquered. Although he taxed his people heavily, they, for their part, seem to have accepted his right to rule them; he did at least give them peace and security, a welcome contrast to the four decades that preceded his reign. He was generally regarded by them with respect rather than love. But it was a welcome breathing space after the trauma of the reign of Æthelred 'the Unready'.

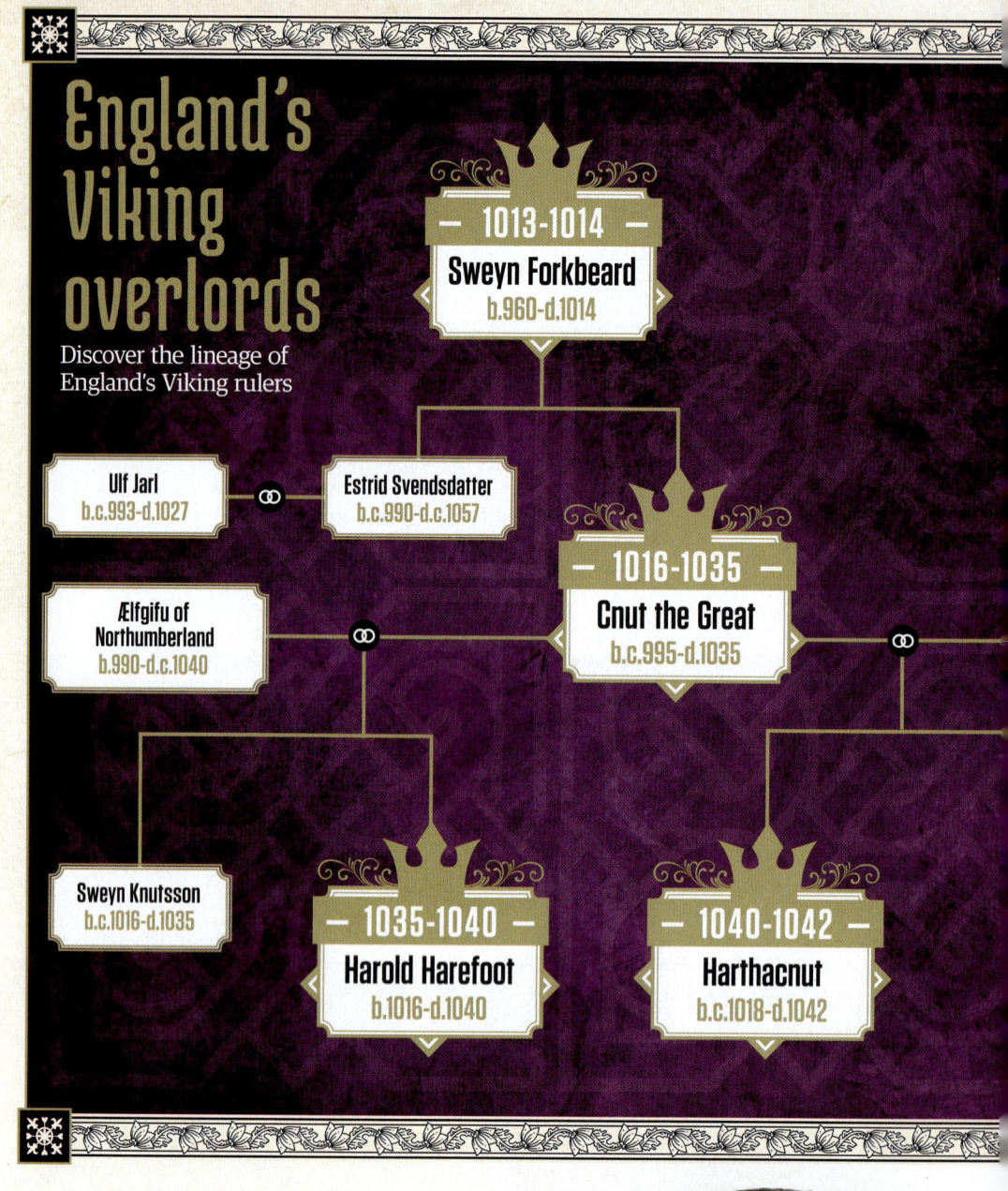

Cnut was buried in the great Anglo-Saxon royal mausoleum in Winchester. Here he metaphorically rubbed shoulders with other English kings and saints. In its own way it was another sign of a king who wished to assimilate with rather than dictate to his English subjects. Ironically however Cnut's bones were not to find peace in death. In the 16th century, his remains, and those of his wife, Emma, were packed together into a mortuary chest and placed high in the presbytery of Winchester Cathedral.

When Winchester Cathedral was entered by Parliamentarian forces in the great English Civil War of the 17th century, anti-monarchist soldiers broke open the chests and used the leg

England's Viking overlords

Discover the lineage of England's Viking rulers

1013-1014
Sweyn Forkbeard
b.960-d.1014

Ulf Jarl
b.c.993-d.1027

Estrid Svendsdatter
b.c.990-d.c.1057

1016-1035
Cnut the Great
b.c.995-d.1035

Ælfgifu of Northumberland
b.990-d.c.1040

Sweyn Knutsson
b.c.1016-d.1035

1035-1040
Harold Harefoot
b.1016-d.1040

1040-1042
Harthacnut
b.c.1018-d.1042

RIGHT The obverse (front) of a silver penny of King Cnut, dated c.1017-23

Emperor of the North

> "Cnut was the only king to ever rule both England and Denmark. He managed England's great wealth to full advantage"

RIGHT A stained glass image of Cnut from Canterbury Cathedral

Emma of Normandy b.c.985-d.1052

Æthelred the Unready 978-1013 1014-1016 b.c.966-d.1016

Gunhilda of Denmark b.c.1020-d.1038

Alfred b.c.1005-d.1036

Edward the Confessor 1042-1066 b.1003-d.1066

Edmund Ironside 1016 Unknown-d.1016

---

bones to shatter the splendid stained glass of the West Window. Following the restoration of the English monarchy in 1660 after the fall of the Commonwealth, the bones were gathered together and placed in the mortuary chests once more, but by this time they were hopelessly jumbled up; no one knew who went where. At the time of writing, a temporary laboratory has been set up in Winchester Cathedral to try and match the right bones with the right mortuary chests so that Cnut and Emma can once more rest side by side in peace.

The greatness of Cnut's achievements in building an extended kingdom that encompassed both England and Scandinavia can perhaps best be demonstrated by how quickly his 'empire' began to fall apart after his death. Without his great energy, vision and drive, his successors were incapable of keeping it together. Harold Harefoot, his son from his union with Ælfgifu of Northampton, and Harthacnut, from his marriage with Emma, both became king in due course, but neither lasted for very long, nor gave any indication that, had they lived, they would have actually been very successful monarchs.

Harold became the sole ruler of England after Cnut's death, but he died himself soon after. As a result, Harthacnut then became king, but he too did not survive very long, dying after overindulging at a wedding feast. With none of Cnut's sons now living, in 1042 the throne reverted back to the Anglo-Saxon bloodline when Edward 'the Confessor' became sovereign. He was able to trace his ancestry back to the line of Cerdic of Wessex, a 6th-century ruler who claimed descent from both Adam of biblical fame and the Germanic/Norse god Woden/Odin. In a somewhat diluted form, after several diversions across the centuries that have followed, traces of that bloodline still remain in today's British royal family. Edward the Confessor died without producing a child of his own, leading to one of th most notorious power struggles in British history.

Cnut was the only king to ever rule both England and Denmark (if we were to exclude the short reign of Harthacnut). He capably governed both, dextrously managing England's great wealth to full advantage and emulating some of the most significant elements of government to build a strong nation-state in Denmark. He used English churchmen to help build the young Church in Denmark as well as using more practical tools such as the employment of English moneyers to develop Danish coinage.

It would be true to say that the practical results of King Cnut's leadership were more deeply felt in the long run in Denmark than England, but his reign was nonetheless a fascinating period in English and European history and a remarkable achievement in its own right.

89

The Queen who ruled Kings

For 50 years, one woman stood at the centre of the affairs of three kingdoms

For 50 years, one woman stood at the centre of power and politics in northern Europe, her influence stretching from Normandy across the Channel to England and over the North Sea to Denmark and Scandinavia. Wife to two kings, mother to two more, Emma, daughter of Richard the Fearless, Duke of Normandy, was a pivotal figure in English, Norman and Scandinavian history. What is also clear is that Emma was no helpless female pawn in these dynastic and family struggles, but one of the most active players in the game. Emma made kings and brought them down; she legitimised rulers and sidelined others, and through it all she displayed the keenest sense for public relations of any medieval queen. Not bad for the initially illegitimate daughter of what was still essentially a Viking duchy.

In 1002, in a further attempt to deny raiding Vikings a sanctuary port with their cousins across the Channel in Normandy, King Æthelred of England contracted marriage with the sister of Richard II, Duke of Normandy. Æthelred was 36, Emma probably in her late teens. But for the daughter of a duke to marry a king was huge step up. The young Emma was, however, stepping into a pit of conflicting interests: Æthelred had been married before, his first wife, Ælfgifu, having provided the king with six sons and at least three daughters. As part of the marriage negotiations, Emma's brother had apparently insisted that any children produced by Emma and Æthelred would rank higher in precedence than the sons of Ælfgifu and Æthelred – an arrangement hardly likely to find favour with those six growing boys and their relations. Nor could they have been too happy with Emma being given the Anglo-Saxon name of Ælfgifu on her arrival in England in a strange attempt to write their mother out of history.

While incompetent in all other regal matters, Æthelred was extremely potent in the production of royal heirs: with Emma, he had a further three children; two sons, Edward and Alfred, and a daughter, Goda, despite the chroniclers intimating that the marriage was not the happiest of royal unions. It can't have been easy for the supremely competent Emma to be married to such a bungler. They had only been married a few months when she saw this at first hand: on 13 November 1002, Æthelred ordered the massacre of all Danes living in England. Fatefully, one of those caught up in the St Brice's Day massacre was Gunhilde, sister of King Sweyn Forkbeard of Denmark. What had before been purely business – raiding and plundering England – became deeply personal for the enraged king. During the following decade, Sweyn Forkbeard launched a series of devastating attacks on England, finally landing himself in 1013 and conquering the demoralised country.

Æthelred fled. To Normandy. Emma and their sons had already left for sanctuary across the Channel, although the *Anglo-Saxon Chronicle* notes laconically that Emma travelled separately from husband and children. But having conquered England – a feat for which he gets little notice – King Sweyn Forkbeard died only five weeks into his reign, on 3 February 1014. The English nobility, who had abandoned Æthelred, invited him back on condition that he would amend his ways and, a most telling condition, rule them justly. Cnut, Sweyn's young son, attempted to hold on to the crown but had to flee. So, for the first and only time in his life, Æthelred made a triumphant return to England. But the king was soon back to his old, capricious ways, forcing his eldest son, Edmund, to open revolt. With England riven by civil strife, Cnut returned at the head of a fresh invading army in September 1015. It was Edmund, now named Ironside, who led the resistance against Cnut over the next year and a half, Æthelred finally doing his country a service by dying on 23 April 1016.

With Edmund, the son of her rival, leading the fight and her own sons having taken refuge back

The Queen who Ruled Kings

91

ABOVE
After the death of her first husband, the ineffectual Æthelred, Emma was married to the famous King Cnut; her place on the English throne restored to her

in Normandy, Emma was for the moment only a bystander to the events shaping history. But when Cnut and Edmund fought each other to a stalemate, only for Edmund to conveniently die after signing a peace treaty with the Dane, Emma was soon right back at the centre of things. For what better way for Cnut to signal his legitimacy as king of England than for him to make queen the woman who had, until so recently, been queen?

According to the account Emma later commissioned, Cnut sent emissaries to her in Normandy to woo her acceptance of his proposal. According to a Norman chronicler, Emma was captured when Cnut took London and had little choice in the matter. But whether a forced or willing bride, Emma soon turned the situation to her advantage: she was queen again. And, what's more, with Cnut as her husband, she would become queen of a veritable North Sea empire, encompassing England, Denmark and Norway.

Leaving her sons, Edward and Alfred, in the care of her brother back in Normandy – as the sons of Æthelred and therefore direct claimants to the throne, the two boys would hardly be welcome at Cnut's court – Emma gave birth to a son, Harthacnut, from her union with Cnut. But the same problem as had attended her marriage to Æthelred applied to her union with Cnut: the king already had a wife, confusingly also called Ælfgifu, an Englishwoman from a prominent northern family, who had given birth to two sons. Although Cnut did not repudiate Ælfgifu, he accorded Emma high status at his court, her name frequently paired with that of the king.

But on 12 November 1035, Cnut died, throwing wide the question of succession. Emma threw her considerable political weight behind her son, Harthacnut, with the backing of Earl Godwin (father of the later King Harold), while Ælfgifu,

Emma's early life

Emma was born in Normandy c.985. An indication of her initial lack of prospects is shown by the uncertainty over her date of birth and the scanty information about her early life. Her father, Richard, was Duke of Normandy and the grandson of the Duchy's founder, Rollo, the Viking who settled in France with the permission of Charles the Simple, king of France, around 918, on the proviso that the settled Northmen would guard the kingdom against their wandering kinsmen. Rollo's son and grandson, and their people, assimilated rapidly into France, adopting French names (William and Richard), speaking French rather than Norse, and becoming enthusiastic and devout Christians. But up to Emma's father, Richard, it was common practice for the dukes to marry in the 'Danish fashion' ("more danico" in Latin), a practice that allowed marriage to a woman of lower rank but the possibility to put her aside should a more high-ranking bride become available. The Church disapproved of the practice, however, and Richard eventually formalised his marriage. In practice, children of these unions were not yet disadvantaged in terms of inheritance, the most notable example of course being William himself.

RIGHT
The children of Richard I, the Fearless, Duke of Normandy. Emma is in the last circle to the right

The Queen who Ruled Kings

LEFT A legend that tells that Emma was accused of adultery and forced to walk blindfolded over red-hot ploughshares to prove her innocence. She is said to have successfully done so

together with the powerful northern English families that she came from, backed her son, Harold. But Emma was hampered by the non-appearance of Harthacnut, who was tied up in Denmark trying to secure his rule there, whereas Harold earned the nickname 'Harefoot' by rushing to London in the immediate aftermath of Cnut's death to claim the throne. The negotiations split the country between Harold and Harthacnut, with Emma holding Wessex until her son was able to arrive and claim his crown. But Harthacnut did not come – his rule in Denmark being threatened by Magnus Olafson, who had taken Norway – and Earl Godwin switched sides. With her power leaking away – Harold had already commandeered the most valuable of Cnut's treasures from her base in Winchester – and no sign of Harthacnut's arrival, Emma had to look elsewhere for new levers on power. And just across the Channel, she had two sons, Edward and Alfred, both with claims on the throne of England. Edward attempted a half-hearted invasion, but Alfred was captured by Earl Godwin, then taken to Harold Harefoot's men, who blinded him – thus disqualifying him from kingship. The blinding was botched: Alfred died. The relationship between Emma and Edward, never easy and usually distant, suffered further as a result of these twin debacles.

With Harold Harefoot now firmly in charge, Emma was forced to flee England, but she did not seek refuge in Normandy, to which Edward had returned, but in Flanders. With her prospects looking bleaker than they had for a long time, Emma was buoyed by the arrival in Bruges of Harthacnut. He had come to claim the English crown. This proved much easier than might have been expected, for Harold Harefoot died on 17 March 1040. He was only 24. Harthacnut sailed to England with Emma and, on 17 June 1040, they landed at Sandwich. Emma was queen once more.

However, Harthacnut's rule was unpopular: used to ruling as an autocrat in Denmark, Harthacnut did not take kindly to the English expectation that a king rule in consultation with his chief nobles. By 1041, Harthacnut was probably also suffering the debilitating effects of the illness that would eventually kill him.

Realising that she needed to bolster her position, Emma arranged for the return of her son, Edward, who became king alongside his half-brother Harthacnut. Harthacnut had not married and had no recognised children, so he may have acquiesced to his mother's wish that he be succeeded by his half-brother. In any event, Harthacnut died on 8 June 1042. Earl Godwin, the most powerful earl in the land, supported Edward's accession and on 8 April 1043, Emma's eldest son by Æthelred was consecrated king.

But, not unreasonably, Edward harboured a deep resentment against his mother. Having been crowned king, he moved against her in November of the same year, appearing in Winchester, Emma's power base, with his three most powerful earls, Godwin among them, where he expropriated Emma's most valuable treasures. Edward shifted the centre of political power in England from Winchester to Westminster. Emma stayed in Winchester, and did eventually recover favour with her son, but she was decisively sidelined in the power struggles in England. From here on in, it was a contest between Edward and the Earl Godwin and his family, a contest that came to its bloody resolution at Hastings. Emma died on 7 March 1052. She was buried beside Cnut and Harthacnut in Winchester: wife to two kings and mother to two more. Few people have played such a central role, for so long, in English affairs.

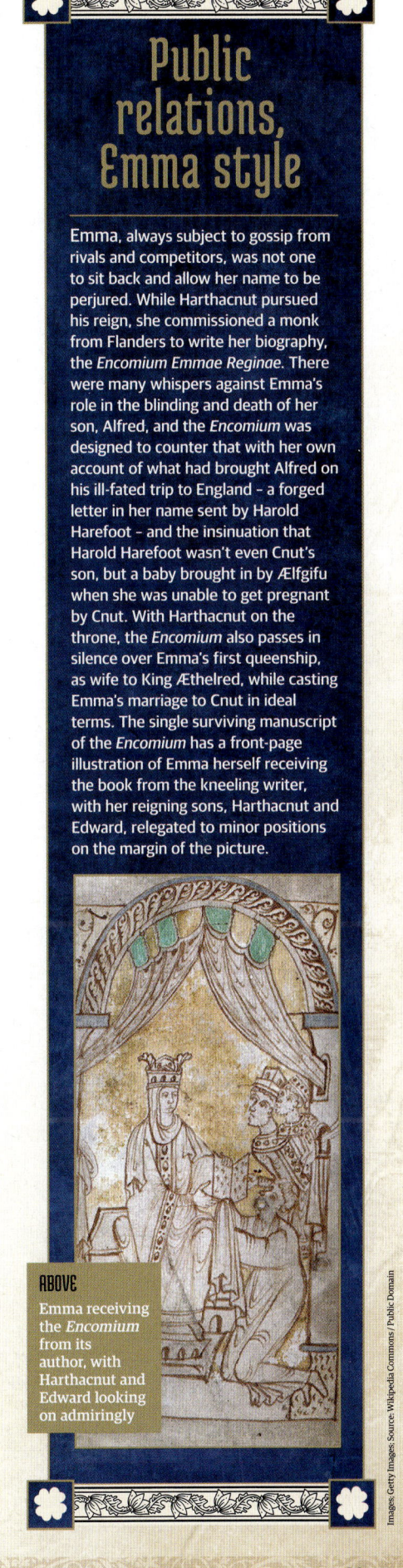

> Emma was the great-aunt of William the Conqueror. This connection gave William a claim to the English throne

Public relations, Emma style

Emma, always subject to gossip from rivals and competitors, was not one to sit back and allow her name to be perjured. While Harthacnut pursued his reign, she commissioned a monk from Flanders to write her biography, the *Encomium Emmae Reginae*. There were many whispers against Emma's role in the blinding and death of her son, Alfred, and the *Encomium* was designed to counter that with her own account of what had brought Alfred on his ill-fated trip to England – a forged letter in her name sent by Harold Harefoot – and the insinuation that Harold Harefoot wasn't even Cnut's son, but a baby brought in by Ælfgifu when she was unable to get pregnant by Cnut. With Harthacnut on the throne, the *Encomium* also passes in silence over Emma's first queenship, as wife to King Æthelred, while casting Emma's marriage to Cnut in ideal terms. The single surviving manuscript of the *Encomium* has a front-page illustration of Emma herself receiving the book from the kneeling writer, with her reigning sons, Harthacnut and Edward, relegated to minor positions on the margin of the picture.

ABOVE Emma receiving the *Encomium* from its author, with Harthacnut and Edward looking on admiringly

The Pious King with No Heir

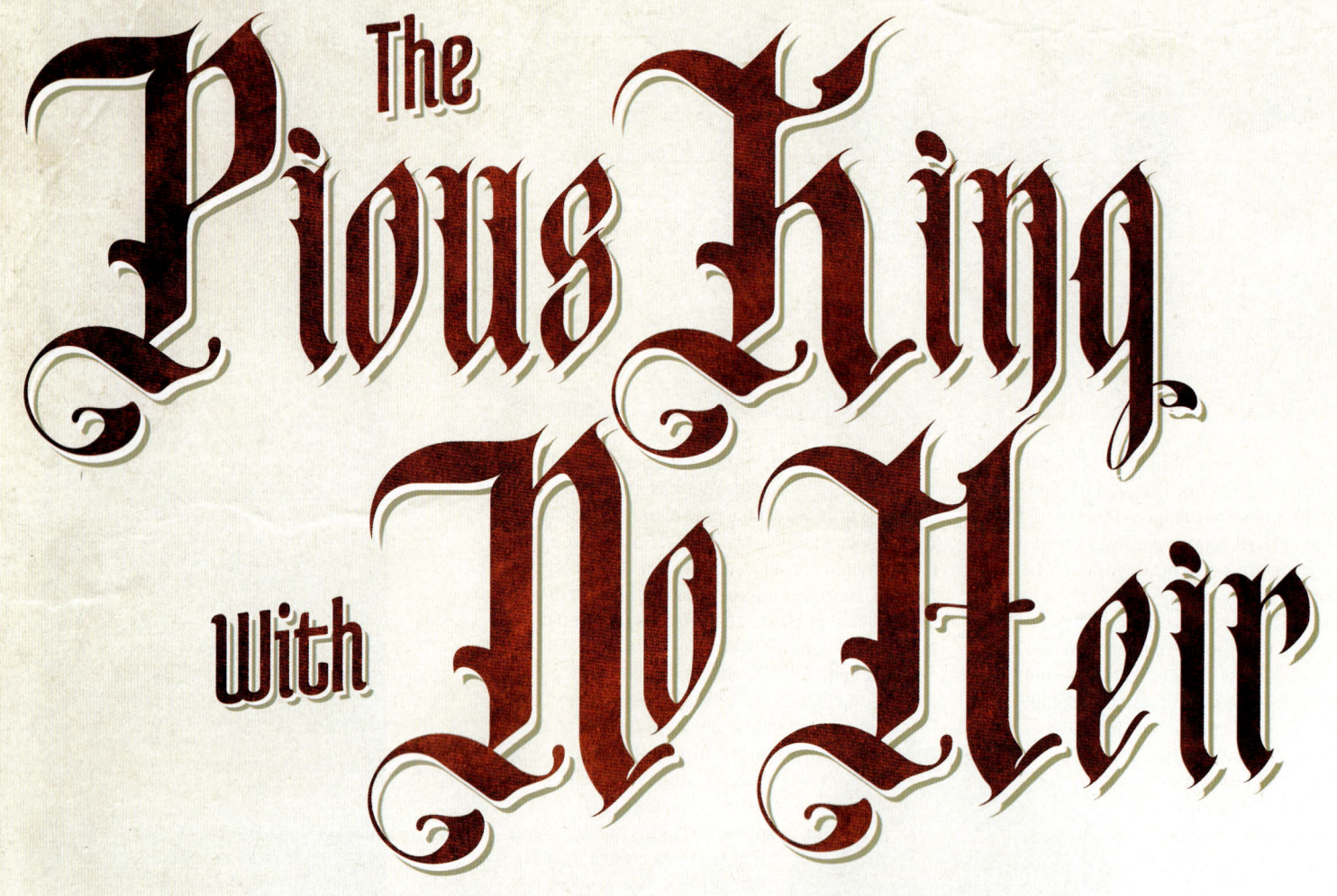

Edward brought the country stability and prosperity, but his failure to secure the succession to the throne left England open to war

Edward was born in to a country being torn apart by raiders and invaders. He was the eldest son of King Æthelred and his second wife, Emma of Normandy. Æthelred had already produced at least six sons by his first wife, so he was hardly in need of further heirs. But what he did need was to secure the ports across the Channel from Viking raiders.

The Normans were descendants of Vikings who had settled in the valley of the lower Seine in the early-10th century and been granted the land by Charles the Simple of France in return for securing his northern borders against Viking raiders.

A century later, with the Norman duchy well established, Æthelred attempted to do the same for his own realm. The Vikings who were harrying England were using the ports of Normandy as safe havens and they found a ready welcome among their Norman cousins. But the widowed Æthelred arranged a marriage with Emma, the sister of Richard the Good, duke of Normandy, in 1002.

Much good did it do him or England. Though the Normans largely kept their side of the bargain, Æthelred had made such a hash of defending England that, when Sweyn Forkbeard landed with his invading army in 1013, the demoralised defenders offered barely any resistance. In a telling comment on what she thought of her husband, Emma fled to Normandy with her two sons by Æthelred – Edward had a younger brother called Alfred – leaving the king behind. Æthelred himself followed later, only to return to England in 1014 when Sweyn Forkbeard died. His Viking army declared for Forkbeard's son, Cnut, but Æthelred's eldest son, Edmund Ironside, led the fightback and Æthelred was invited back – whereupon the resistance promptly crumbled again. On 23 April 1016, Æthelred finally did something for his country: he died. Edmund renewed the resistance to the Danish takeover, fighting Cnut through the summer and autumn and only losing the decisive battle through the treachery of Æthelred's chief adviser, Eadric Streona. Edmund died soon afterwards and Edward, who had been part of his half brother's army, fled into exile once more. With Cnut now secure on the throne, Edward can't have expected to return.

His prospects declined even further when Cnut invited Edward's mother, Emma, to come back over the Channel and take a second bite at being queen. Emma promptly accepted and, leaving her sons behind in Normandy, married Cnut – despite him already having sons through his handfast wife, Ælfgifu. As part of the marriage settlement, Emma probably extracted the promise that the children of her marriage

> Edward also had a sister, Godgifu, who married Drogo, count of the Vexin, and then, when Drogo died, Eustace, count of Boulogne

The Pious King with No Heir

would have priority in succession and so she set about producing another heir: Harthacnut was born in 1018.

All but abandoned by their mother, Edward and his brother Alfred grew to manhood in Normandy. With Cnut so dominant a king - and having three sons by two wives - there was little prospect of the young men ever returning to the country of their birth. In most such cases, they would have slipped into obscurity, forgotten by history. But Cnut died on 12 November 1035 when he was about 40.

Emma immediately swung into action, supporting her son, Harthacnut, for the succession. But the problem was that Harthacnut was detained in Denmark as he sought to establish his rule there - Cnut had ruled a North Sea empire comprising Denmark, Norway, England and parts of Sweden - while Cnut's son with Ælfgifu, Harold Harefoot, was on the ground in England and staking his claim to the throne. In some desperation, Emma remembered her other boys, living across the Channel, who also had claim to the throne. In 1036, Edward sailed back to England for the first time since he was a boy on a crown-fishing expedition. When he was met by an army rather than acclaim, Edward decided that his mother's assurances of welcome were as trustworthy as her maternal feelings and sailed back to Normandy. But later in the year, his younger brother Alfred decided to try his luck.

Alfred and his men were met by Earl Godwin, the most powerful Englishman in the land. The Godwin family had risen to prominence from obscure origins under Cnut. Godwin welcomed Alfred and his men and took them to Guildford, feasting and entertaining them. Then, as they slept off the feast, they were attacked. Alfred's men were variously killed, enslaved, mutilated and scalped. Alfred himself was taken prisoner but, in captivity, his eyes were put out: a blind man could not claim the throne. The young prince soon succumbed to his wounds. Earl Godwin had been, with Emma, a supporter of Harthacnut, but with this wet work Godwin successfully ingratiated himself with Harold Harefoot. In Harthacnut's continuing absence, Harold Harefoot was crowned king - and Emma was sent into exile. Not to Normandy - where Edward might have given her a frosty reception - but to Flanders. However, Emma was not yet finished with being queen. She commissioned her defence, a work exonerating her of all blame, and renewed her contacts with Harthacnut. In England, Harold Harefoot fell ill and died on 17 March 1040. Emma sailed back to England with her son, Harthacnut, a queen once more.

But then, in 1041, something really extraordinary happened: Harthacnut invited his half brother, Edward, over from Normandy to rule alongside him. Kings not being known for voluntarily sharing power, it may be that Harthacnut needed Edward to help shore up his increasingly unpopular reign. But a simpler

BELOW
Cnut from a 14th-century manuscript. Sometimes known as Cnut the Great, he ruled a considerable North Sea empire

When Sweyn Forkbeard died in 1014, Æthelred sent his ten-year-old son Edward to England to help negotiate his return

Defining moment
Born into interesting times c.1004
Edward, the first child of King Æthelred the Unready's second wife, is born somewhere around 1004. It could have been 1003 or 1005. The uncertainty shows how little attention was paid to him when he was young: as a prince with a distant claim to the throne, it was not worth recording his birth in annals such as the Anglo-Saxon Chronicle. Edward is born in the midst of repeated Viking attacks that are grinding down the ability of the English to resist.

Timeline

1013 — Into exile
Sweyn Forkbeard invades England. Emma, the queen, flees to relatives in Normandy, taking both her sons, Edward and Alfred, with her.

1014 — The return of the king (unfortunately)
Æthelred returns to reclaim the throne and promptly cripples the fight against Sweyn's son, Cnut.

23 April 1016 — Death of another king
Æthelred finally dies. His son, Edmund Ironside, leads the struggle against the Danes.

30 November 1016 — Death of a third king
Edmund Ironside dies. Sweyn's son, Cnut, is now the unopposed king. Edward returns to exile.

July 1017 — A queen again
Edward's mother, Emma, leaving her children in Normandy, returns to England to marry Cnut and reign as his queen.

1016-35 — The forgotten exile
With Cnut secure on the throne, Edward lives in exile with his relatives in Normandy.

12 November 1035 — The tide sweeps Cnut away
Cnut dies. Emma backs her son, Harthacnut, for the throne of England but he is delayed in Denmark.

1036 — Edward tries his luck
Edward lands in England with a small army but is forced to withdraw.

The Pious King with No Heir

ABOVE Edward the Confessor as portrayed in the medieval masterpiece, the Wilton Diptych (he's the standing figure in the middle). The artist who painted this extraordinary work is unknown, but possibly from northern France

explanation may be that Harthacnut was ailing and feared he had little time left to live. No doubt Emma, keen to install another of her sons on the throne, suggested Edward as both stop gap and potential successor.

Whatever the solution to this riddle, on 8 June 1042, Harthacnut died at a wedding feast. Edward, by this time in his late 30s, was, most unexpectedly, the new king of England.

Though king, Edward's position was unusually weak: he had no power base in the country and, in a time when power depended as much on personal relationships and ties as armed force, he was a stranger in a strange land. As such, he had no choice but to depend on his earls, of whom the most powerful was Godwin – the man he held responsible for the death of his younger brother. Besides, he could use Godwin's help to deal with a long-standing problem of his own: his mother.

In November 1043, with Earl Godwin by his side, Edward rode to his mother's base in Winchester and stripped her of her treasures. Although Emma did earn partial rehabilitation, her scheming came to an end and this most remarkable of women died on 7 March 1052, being buried beside Cnut and Harthacnut in Winchester.

Such favours required payback and Godwin's terms were steep: on 23 January 1045, his daughter, Edith, married Edward. Thus, this earl of obscure background and humble origins might look towards his grandson becoming king of England. It was a heady prospect.

Godwin's sons prospered alongside their sister, with his eldest sons, Sweyn and Harold, raised to earldoms. The family now ruled most of southern England – an uncomfortable, perhaps unconscionable, situation for the king. For, in 1051, Edward moved against the Godwin family.

The cause of the dispute was a struggle over the appointment of the archbishop of Canterbury, but it became a struggle for mastery of the realm. Edward called in the support of the northern earls, while Godwin and his sons raised their own armies. But, as the rival armies converged on London, Godwin's men, reluctant to fight the king, slipped away, leaving the earl in an untenable position. When he sought to negotiate with Edward, the king sent back the reply that Godwin could have peace, "when he gave him back his brother alive."

The Godwins fled in exile. As for the queen, Edward put her into a convent. As 1051 drew to a close, Edward could think himself now truly master of the land he ruled. But, in exile, the Godwins were planning their return.

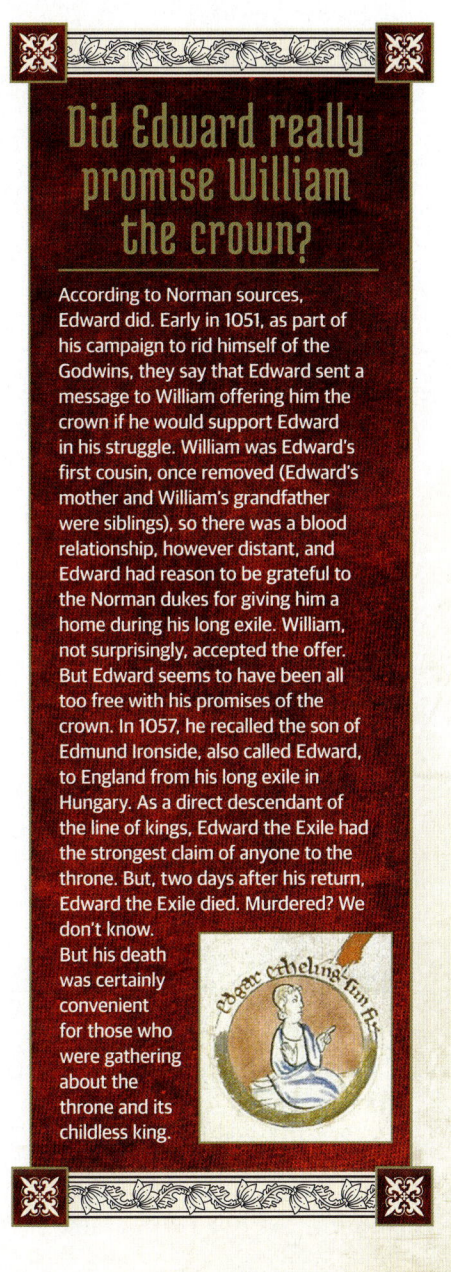

Did Edward really promise William the crown?

According to Norman sources, Edward did. Early in 1051, as part of his campaign to rid himself of the Godwins, they say that Edward sent a message to William offering him the crown if he would support Edward in his struggle. William was Edward's first cousin, once removed (Edward's mother and William's grandfather were siblings), so there was a blood relationship, however distant, and Edward had reason to be grateful to the Norman dukes for giving him a home during his long exile. William, not surprisingly, accepted the offer. But Edward seems to have been all too free with his promises of the crown. In 1057, he recalled the son of Edmund Ironside, also called Edward, to England from his long exile in Hungary. As a direct descendant of the line of kings, Edward the Exile had the strongest claim of anyone to the throne. But, two days after his return, Edward the Exile died. Murdered? We don't know. But his death was certainly convenient for those who were gathering about the throne and its childless king.

Defining moment
King after all c.1041
Harthacnut, against all precedent, invites Edward to return from exile and rule alongside him in England as co-regent. He does this either to shore up his own unpopular rule or because he knows he is ill and, being without any children, he is putting a successor in place should he succumb to his illness. Whichever it is, Edward, by now in his late 30s, finds himself, against all expectations, a king.

Defining moment
Taking down the Godwins c.1051
It started with a dispute over who would be Archbishop of Canterbury. Earl Godwin wanted his man, but Edward insisted on making his Norman cleric archbishop. It escalated into a full-on armed confrontation: the king and the northern earls against the Godwins – and the Godwins backed down. With support crumbling, Earl Godwin and his sons fled into exile, while Edward promptly put his queen, Godwin's daughter, into a nunnery. The kingdom was the king's, finally. Or was it…?

1036 – Alfred III's luck
Edward's brother tries for the crown, but is captured by Earl Godwin and has his eyes put out. Alfred dies from his wounds.

1037 – A new king
Harold Harefoot, another son of Cnut, is crowned king of England.

17 March 1040 – Another king bites the dust
Harold Harefoot dies. He is only 24.

17 June 1040 – And a new king arrives
Harthacnut lands in England and is crowned king.

8 June 1042 – The king is dead, long live the king
Harthacnut dies. Against all expectation, Edward finds himself king of England.

November 1043 – Mother troubles
Edward dispossesses his mother, Emma, of her treasures and banishes her from his court.

23 January 1045 – A married man
Edward marries Edith, the daughter of Earl Godwin.

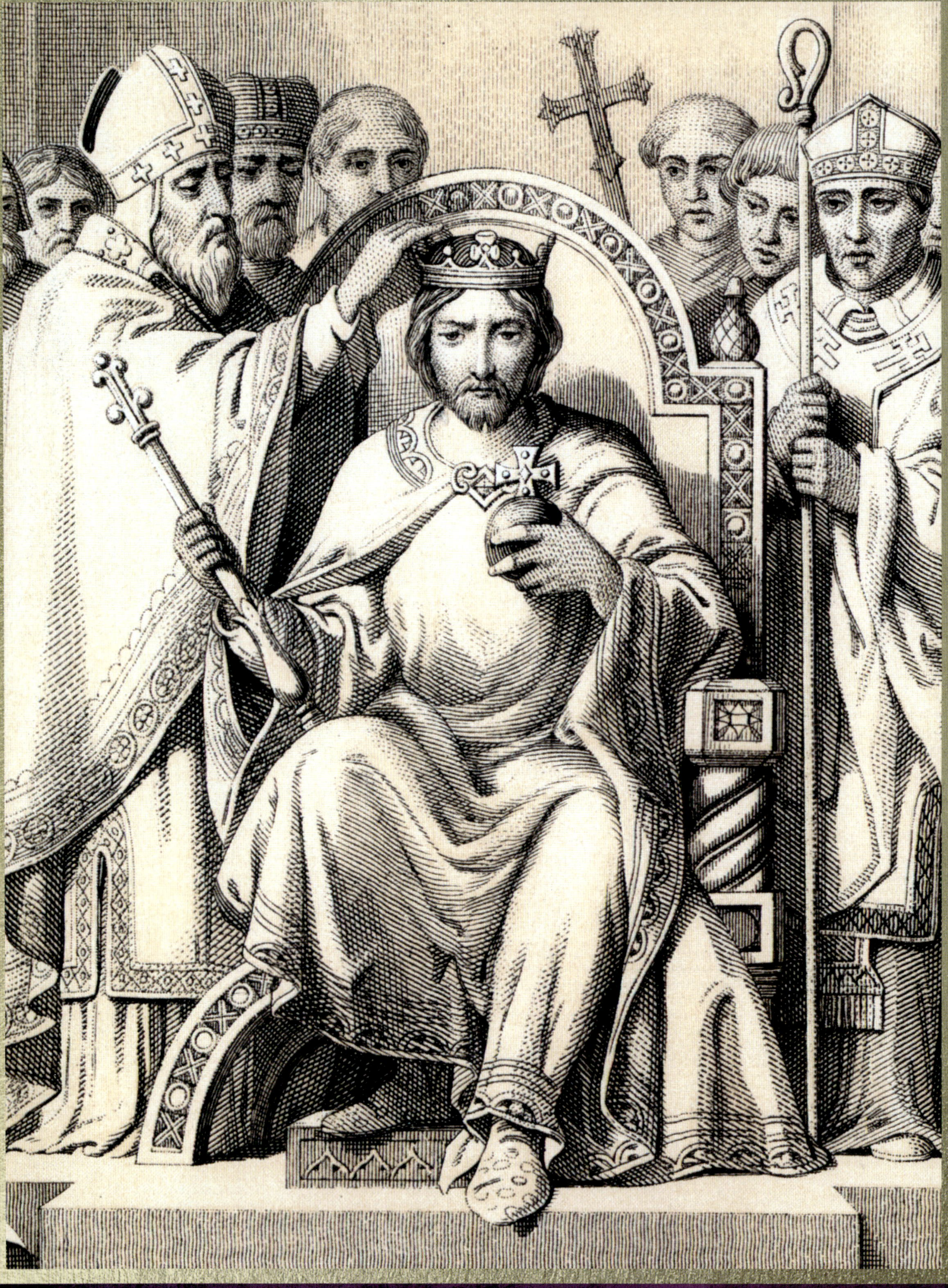

The Last Anglo-Saxon King

Harold, England's most powerful earl, claimed the throne on King Edward's death. But to hold on to the crown, Harold knew he would have to fight

The Godwin family had learned one thing through their years of service to the crown: while men might pay lip service to the rules of succession, in truth the crown went to who could claim and hold it. This knowledge was deep and bitter. Harold's grandfather, Wulfnoth, had been a victim of the plots and rumours that swirled around King Æthelred, but his father, Godwin, had risen to power through loyal service to King Cnut, becoming the most powerful man in the land after the king.

Then, when Cnut died, Godwin had been kingmaker, helping to raise first Harold Harefoot, then Harthacnut, to the throne. When Harthacnut had died, Godwin had eased the accession to the throne of Edward, the unlikely king, thus clearing - at least in the conscience of the earl - the bloodguilt he owed Edward for his part in the death of Edward's brother, Alfred. What's more, Earl Godwin had sealed his place as the power behind the throne by marrying his daughter to Edward. Now Earl Godwin could look towards the prospect of a future grandson of his taking the throne of England as Edward's heir.

But the king had not forgotten what had happened to his brother. And, in 1051, he moved against his over-mighty earl and his family. Edward installed one of his Norman clerics, Robert de Jumièges, as the new Archbishop of Canterbury, against the opposition of Earl Godwin. It is likely that Edward gave Robert the task of conveying to the duke of Normandy his offer of the throne when, in the spring of 1051, the priest left England for Rome to receive his pallium from the pope, the vestment signifying his status as an archbishop.

At the end of August, the simmering tension between king and earl broke when Godwin refused to carry out the harrying of the town of Dover that Edward demanded of him following an armed incident between the people of Dover and the retainers of Edward's brother-in-law. Dover was part of Godwin's earldom and he refused to injure the people. Earl confronted king. Godwin and his sons - Sweyn, Harold, Tostig, Gyrth, Leofwine and Wulfnoth - raised armies.

But the king had prepared for this confrontation. Calling the northern earls to his side, Edward raised his own forces and England trembled on the edge of civil strife. But, seeing such a spectre rise before them, both sides paused. Earl Godwin agreed to come to London to stand before the king and answer the charge of treason. With both armies on opposite banks of the Thames at London, the Godwins realised that the balance of power had shifted decisively against them, for much of their own forces had slipped away, unwilling to fight the king.

Edward, seeing this, delivered his terms to Earl Godwin: that he might have peace when he returned the king's brother to him, alive. There would be no terms.

Earl Godwin fled, with his wife and sons Sweyn and Tostig, to Flanders. Harold and Leofwine went

Harold's mistress, Edith Swan-neck, may have been Eadgifu the Fair, one of the largest landholders in England

99

The scandalous life and death of Harold's elder brother

Sweyn Godwinson, the eldest son of Earl Godwin and Harold's elder brother, led a tumultuous life. According to the man himself, he was the son, not of Earl Godwin but of King Cnut. However, his mother denied the claim vehemently. In 1046, Sweyn abducted Eadgifu, the abbess of Leominster, intending to marry her and claim the Leominster estates. When the king refused to agree to the marriage, Sweyn released Eadgifu, who returned to Leominster. But her abbey was disbanded, which suggests Eadgifu may not have been an entirely unwilling abductee. Sweyn fled to Flanders. In 1049, Sweyn returned, hoping to reclaim his territories, which had been split between Harold and a cousin, Beorn. Beorn eventually agreed to help Sweyn, but Sweyn ended up abducting Beorn too. The end for his cousin was worse than for the abbess: Sweyn murdered him. As a result, Sweyn was outlawed again. However, Earl Godwin engineered his forgiveness, but when the Godwins were exiled in 1051, Sweyn left the rest of the family to make the pilgrimage to Jerusalem and atone for his sins – these being so heinous that he went barefoot. But Sweyn, purged of his sin, died on the way back before he could sin again.

---

into exile in Ireland. The last remaining Godwin in England was the queen, and with her family fled, Edward put Edith into a nunnery.

The king had his country.

But Edward couldn't keep it. To guard against the Godwins' return, Edward had relied upon the levy of ships he could raise as king. Initially, it seemed to work. However, in 1052, when the Godwins raised their own fleet, the king's boats dispersed, having fulfilled their time of service, leaving the coast unguarded. Earl Godwin's fleet met with a separate armada raised by Harold and Leofwine in Ireland, and sailed unopposed up the Channel, round Kent and up the Thames. By 14 September, they had reached London, anchoring at Southwark. Edward had managed to scrabble together 50 boats to meet them, and again the two sides faced off against each other. The Godwins demanded the king return their land and earldoms. This time, however, support leached away from the king. The rising tide allowed the Godwin's ships to surround Edward's boats, anchored on the north side of the Thames.

The king had lost his country. Robert de Jumièges and Edward's other Norman advisers fled. In a display of political theatre, Earl Godwin met the king, begged his forgiveness and proclaimed his innocence of all charges against him. Edward, humiliated and outmanoeuvred, had no choice but to return to the Godwins all their lands and titles. Not long afterwards, Edward brought his wife and queen out of the convent he had confined her in.

To everyone in England it must have been clear that while Edward wore the crown, the Godwins had the power. But in 1052, the Godwins suffered a reverse with no return: Earl Godwin's eldest son, Sweyn, died.

A deeper blow hit the family on 15 April 1053: their patriarch, Earl Godwin, died. According to

> "The last remaining Godwin in England was the queen, and with her family fled, the king put her into a nunnery"

one chronicler, just before his collapse at the Easter Monday feast, the earl had asked that God not let him swallow if he had done anything to injure either the king or his late brother. From the descriptions of other sources, it seems the earl suffered a stroke. But with the father dead, his eldest surviving son, Harold, succeeded to the earldom of Wessex. As the senior Godwin, Harold moved to promote the interests of his brothers and, in 1055, he engineered the promotion of Tostig to the earldom of Northumbria, while by 1057 he had installed Gyrth as earl of East Anglia and Leofwine as earl of the counties surrounding London. Apart from Mercia, the Godwins were lords of England. And the king, apparently acquiescing, largely withdrew from affairs, contenting himself with attending mass each day, hunting and the building of a new minster, west of London, the Westminster Abbey.

Then, in 1064, the records tell us Harold crossed the Channel and became the guest of Duke William in Normandy.

Why should Harold, now indisputably the most powerful man in the land, let himself fall into the clutches of William? The Norman sources claim that Edward sent Harold to William with the promise that the crown would come to him after Edward's death. But even if the king still wanted this to happen, why should Harold carry such a wish? Edward was in his 60s and he had handed over the running of the kingdom to Harold – he couldn't have made Harold carry such a promise to William even if he'd wanted him to.

English chronicles claim it was all a mistake: a fishing trip blown off course by a storm. But there was reason for Harold to visit William: the Duke had one of his brothers. In the crisis of 1051, Godwin had handed over his youngest son, Wulfnoth, to Edward as a hostage. Some time between then and the Godwins' return in 1052, Wulfnoth had been taken across the Channel to Normandy, and left in the keeping of William. And there he had remained ever since. The most plausible explanation is that Harold set sail with

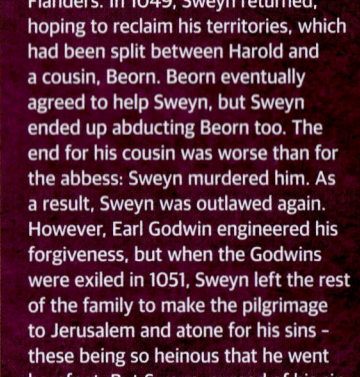

The estates of the Godwinsons produced an income of £8,500 a year in the 1050s; the king's estates returned £6,000

ABOVE
Harold setting out on his ill-fated journey to redeem his brother. Note the accompanying hawk and dog: hunting was such a major part of the life of the nobility that they took their hunting animals with them when they went abroad

The last Anglo-Saxon king

The deathbed of King Edward

Did King Edward give the crown to Harold Godwinson, his most powerful earl, as he lay dying on 6 January 1066? The sources disagree, although most do concur that Edward did give rule of the kingdom into Harold's hands. However, the *Life of Edward*, commissioned by his queen, tells us who was with him on that fateful day: Edith herself, her brother Harold, the archbishop of Canterbury and the steward of the palace. The Bayeux Tapestry reproduces this scene. But what exactly did Edward say? Again, according to the *Vita* (Life) of Edward, the king commended the queen and the kingdom to Harold's protection. Not exactly a ringing endorsement of Harold's kingship – although admittedly the king was dying at the time. But, in England, the king's wish did not determine his successor; in the end, that was a matter for the magnates of the country. And Harold had spent many years cultivating his contacts with them carefully. So it was no surprise that they chose Harold as king, and saw him crowned the same day as Edward died.

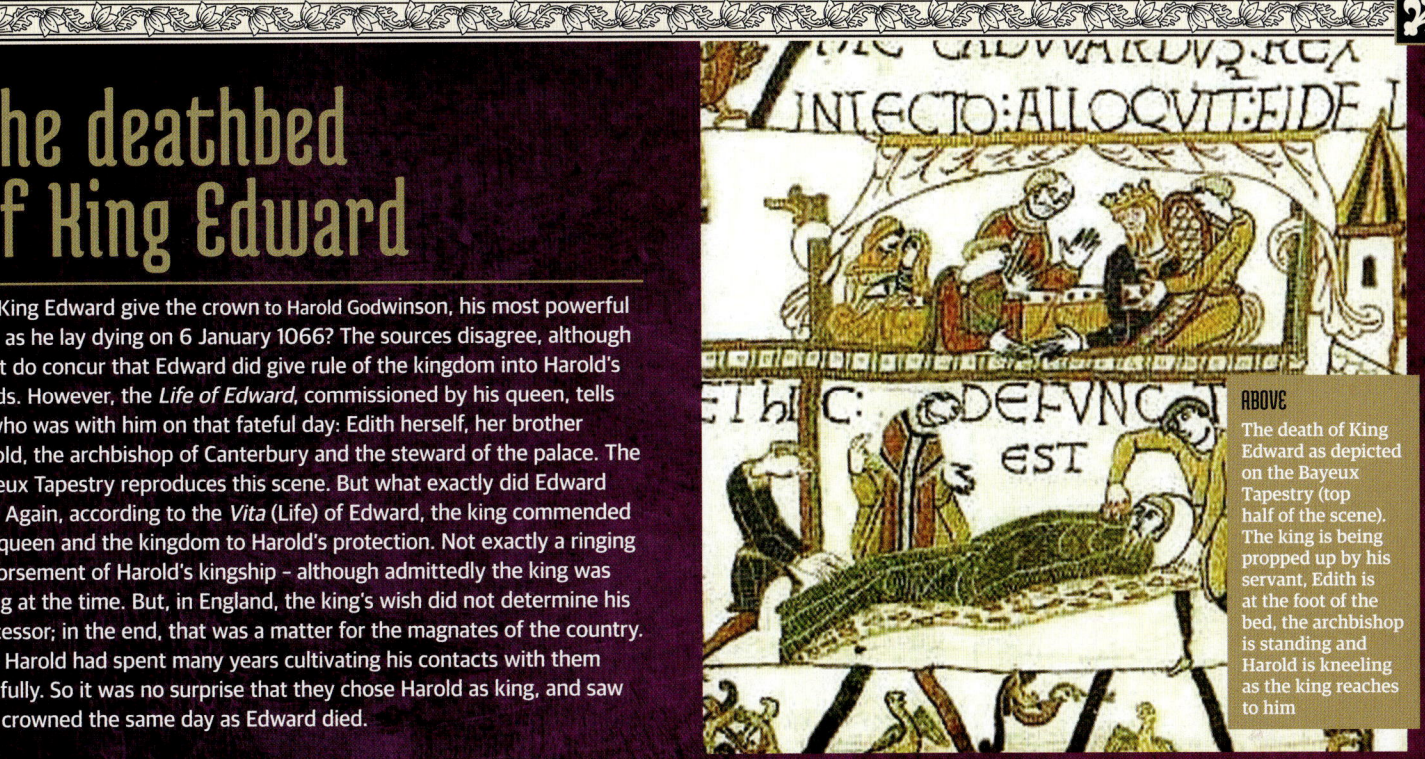

ABOVE
The death of King Edward as depicted on the Bayeux Tapestry (top half of the scene). The king is being propped up by his servant, Edith is at the foot of the bed, the archbishop is standing and Harold is kneeling as the king reaches to him

ABOVE
Harold giving his oath to William, his hand placed on holy relics, that he would uphold William's claim to the throne. As a 'guest' of the duke, Harold probably felt he had no choice

the aim of buying the freedom of his youngest brother. If that was his aim, it failed. Harold returned home without him. But William, for his part, had gained something from Harold: the promise to help William to the throne. For Harold, prisoner first to the Count of Ponthieu and then William's 'guest', there must have seemed little choice but to give his word to gain his freedom. But William seems to have been of a literal turn of mind: an oath, however extracted, was still an oath.

Harold returned home in 1065 to find his brother, Tostig's, earldom under threat. Rebels had united behind the son of the previous earl, intending to depose Tostig and install Morcar as earl of Northumbria. Unhappy with Tostig's governance, the rebels had assembled a great army. Harold went to negotiate with them himself. But the rebels would not accept Tostig back. Returning to the king and his brother, Harold reported their demands, only for Tostig to accuse him of treachery. That seems unlikely: the Godwins' greatest strength had always been their support for each other. But, in this case, Harold was not willing to fight for his brother's cause and on 27 October 1065, Harold told the rebels that they could have their demands: the installation of Morcar as earl of Northumbria and the restitution of their old laws. Four days later, the furious Tostig, with his family and retainers, went into exile. The unity of the Godwin family had been broken, with what would be fatal consequences for them all.

For, at the end of the year, the king fell ill. On 6 January 1066, Edward died.

Harold was crowned the same day.

101

The Last Viking King

With the Viking Age setting in the west, one man set out to reclaim the lands, power and culture of his forefathers. His name was Harald Hardrada, and this is his story

The Last Viking King

Conqueror, exile, mercenary and warlord; Harald Hardrada was many things during his bloody, brutal and eventful life. However, he was one thing above all others: a Viking. Descended, according to Scandinavian saga, from the legendary first-ever king of Norway, Harald Fairhair, Hardrada - named due to his style for 'hard rule' - came from a long line of war-loving Viking rulers who each, much to the terror of large swathes of Europe, had ravaged, pillaged and ransacked with a frequency that was previously unimaginable. The culture, landscape and language of Europe had irrevocably been altered by the Age of the Vikings, and Hardrada, born into one of its noble institutions, was brought up to be totally wrapped in its ideals and indoctrinated into a mindset the likes of which had seen the nations of Scandinavia dominate the known world for almost 300 years.

It was this in-built, centuries-old lust for war and conquest that saw Hardrada engage in his first ever battle in 1030 CE, a mere 15 years after his birth in Ringerike, Norway. Hardrada's brother Olaf Haraldsson had been forced into exile in 1028 CE after the Danish King Cnut the Great had taken the Norwegian throne for himself. However, upon Olaf's return in 1030 CE, Hardrada drummed up the support of 600 men from the Norwegian Uplands and joined with Olaf to take down Cnut. As such, on 29 July 1030 CE Hardrada took the fight to the Danish at the Battle of Stiklestad, fighting with his brother for control of his ancestors' country.

Unfortunately, despite showing considerable military might on the battlefield, Hardrada was defeated by the far larger Danish army, with Olaf being killed in the fighting. Hardrada barely escaped with his life, having been badly wounded in the melee. In fact, were it not for the covert help of his friend Rögnvald Brusason - the future Earl of Orkney - Hardrada would never have reached the remote farmstead in eastern Norway that he did a few weeks after the battle, nor been able to recover from his serious wounds. A month went by, and with each passing day the reality of what had occurred became all the more apparent to Hardrada. He had let down his brother, father, nation and revered forefathers. He had been defeated at the first hurdle, part-crippled by a foreign invader that remained in control of his country. Unable to bear the guilt any longer, one month after his defeat Hardrada exiled himself to Sweden, journeying north over the mountains by the cover of darkness.

Over the following year little is known of Hardrada's movements or activities, with not even the sagas of old recalling what transpired. All that is known today is that almost a year to the day after his defeat at Stiklestad, Hardrada arrived in the town of Staraya Ladoga in the Kievan Rus region of north-eastern Europe.

The native people were a wild bunch of Slavic tribes renowned for their hardiness, combat prowess and expertise in trade, with their geographical position placing them very much at the gates between the largely Byzantine-controlled east and the Scandinavian-

> *Harald's nickname was well given: it means 'hard rule' or 'stern ruler', which sums up his reign perfectly*

Images: Adobe Stock (All)

103

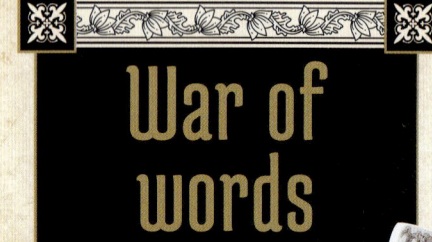

War of words

Battleaxe
The axe was the primary weapon for all the Scandinavian cultures of the Viking Age, with a multitude of designs used between nations with differing shafts and heads. One of the most popular designs was the Daneaxe, a large two-handed weapon with long shaft and crescent-shaped wrought iron head. Often the axe head would be granted a steel cutting edge, a factor that helped it generate skull-splitting force.

Sword
If a Viking carried a sword then it would be his primary weapon. The problem was that swords were more expensive to produce than axes, and so were only carried by the rich and powerful. Viking swords were 90 centimetres in length and took a Roman spatha-like design, with a tight grip, long fuller and no pronounced cross-guard. Hilts and handles were often inlaid with jewels or unique inscriptions.

Dagger
The standard secondary weapon for each Viking warrior, the dagger was an incredibly versatile weapon, granting an element of speed to the Viking's otherwise slow armament. In particular, the seax was a popular model that consisted of a symmetrical straight blade of various lengths with a smooth, wooden hilt. Seax daggers such as this could also be used for skinning animals and carving.

War of words
While it is true that Hardrada's reign was characterised by raiding, war and blood, he was also reportedly a sound diplomat and economist, and used his skills to bring a period of stability to Norway when much of Scandinavia was in turmoil. Two of the most notable examples of the king's ability to expand his empire by words rather than axe are, firstly, his arrangement of new international trade routes and deals - a decision that brought in much wealth to Norway - and, secondly, his dissemination of Christianity throughout the lands of Norway. Indeed, upon becoming king of Norway he implemented many policies geared towards promoting it, like the construction of churches.

---

occupied west. So when Hardrada emerged from the wilderness in 1031 CE, his ancestry and prowess in combat saw him warmly welcomed by the Rus' ruler Grand Prince Yaroslav the Wise, whose wife Ingegerd was a distant relative of his.

Badly in need of military commanders and recognising Harald's ability in combat, Yaroslav immediately made Hardrada leader of his forces and dispatched him to the western border to fight the Polish peoples at war with the Rus. The faith Yaroslav placed in Harald was well founded, with the warrior completing a crushing campaign, slaughtering hundreds and thousands of Poles and driving them back into their country's distant heartlands. Following this victory, Yaroslav left Hardrada to engage the Chude peoples of Estonia and the Pechenegs nomads that had been fighting on and off with the Rus for decades, with similar and horrific results. Hardrada was reportedly demonic on the battlefield, driven by some seemingly unnatural force in pursuit of his enemy's blood, transcending into a berserker state that no man could oppose.

> Harald was among one of the Viking Age's most well-travelled warriors, spending time in Europe and Asia

These victories for the Rus saw Hardrada gain a fearsome reputation, with a band of 500 men pledging their loyalty to him. Hardrada and his band of mercenary warriors were now the most feared fighting force in Europe and, after securing the Kievan territories in 1033 CE, they set off in a quest for fame and riches heading south to Constantinople, the capital city of the fabulously wealthy Byzantine Empire. Arriving there in 1034 CE and immediately introducing himself to the Byzantine Emperor Michael IV, Hardrada and his men were immediately employed in the Emperor's Varangian Guard, an elite fighting force controlled directly by the ruler. In theory, the Varangian Guard were supposed to simply protect the Emperor, but due to Hardrada's desire for battle he was soon fighting on almost every front of the empire.

From Arab pirates in the Mediterranean to rebel forces amassed in Sicily and onto Arab strongholds throughout Asia Minor, Hardrada became the scourge of any Byzantine enemy. He was deployed like a rampaging bull on the battlefield, one that could seemingly not be killed in combat no matter

RIGHT
Viking longships were light and manoeuvrable, and could reach a speed of up to 15 knots

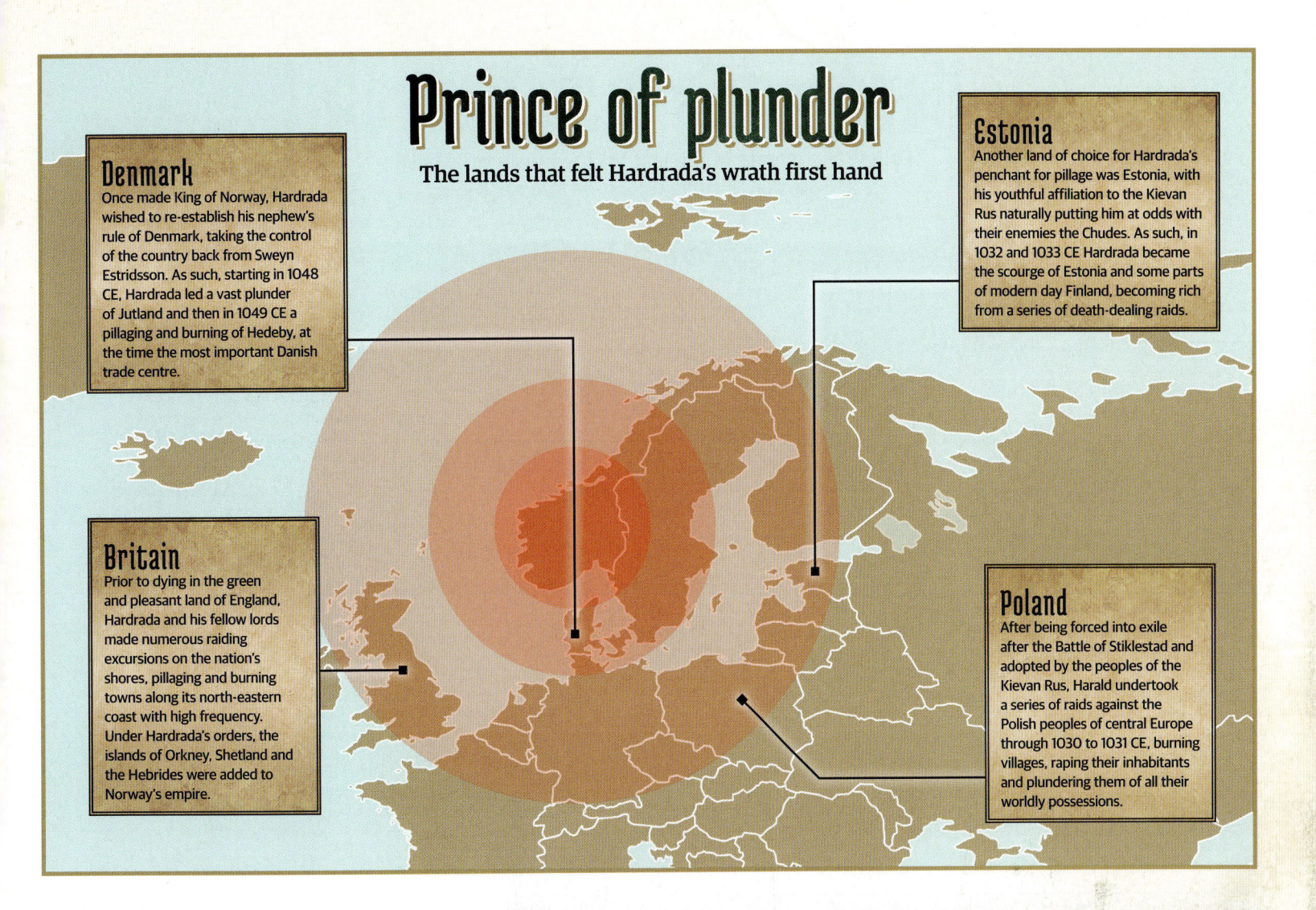

The Last Viking King

Prince of plunder
The lands that felt Hardrada's wrath first hand

Denmark
Once made King of Norway, Hardrada wished to re-establish his nephew's rule of Denmark, taking the control of the country back from Sweyn Estridsson. As such, starting in 1048 CE, Hardrada led a vast plunder of Jutland and then in 1049 CE a pillaging and burning of Hedeby, at the time the most important Danish trade centre.

Estonia
Another land of choice for Hardrada's penchant for pillage was Estonia, with his youthful affiliation to the Kievan Rus naturally putting him at odds with their enemies the Chudes. As such, in 1032 and 1033 CE Hardrada became the scourge of Estonia and some parts of modern day Finland, becoming rich from a series of death-dealing raids.

Britain
Prior to dying in the green and pleasant land of England, Hardrada and his fellow lords made numerous raiding excursions on the nation's shores, pillaging and burning towns along its north-eastern coast with high frequency. Under Hardrada's orders, the islands of Orkney, Shetland and the Hebrides were added to Norway's empire.

Poland
After being forced into exile after the Battle of Stiklestad and adopted by the peoples of the Kievan Rus, Harald undertook a series of raids against the Polish peoples of central Europe through 1030 to 1031 CE, burning villages, raping their inhabitants and plundering them of all their worldly possessions.

---

how far the odds were stacked in his opponents' favour. Returning back to Constantinople in 1041, Hardrada was now famed not just for his battle prowess, but also for his immense wealth, with almost seven years worth of plunder being amassed into a vast fortune that rivalled that of many kings. Indeed, Hardrada had raided so much that he had to send large portions of his loot back to Yaroslav for safekeeping - no boat was capable of carrying the sheer weight of the bountiful precious metals and jewels.

While Hardrada's position under the Byzantine Emperor Michael IV was unassailable, in December of 1041 CE he quickly fell out of favour, becoming caught up in the middle of a war of succession. Realising that his position was never going to be same again, Hardrada escaped a now turbulent Constantinople just months later, returning by boat through the Black Sea to the Kievan Rus. Upon returning to a rapturous welcome from Yaroslav, Hardrada promptly married the latter's daughter Ellisif and, for a short time, settled down in the Kievan capital, engaging in little combat and remaining in the Rus for a further three years.

However, as the days and years dragged by, Hardrada was still tormented by his defeat at Stiklestad. He hadn't set foot in his native Norway

Three ruthless victories

Asia Minor campaign
1035 CE

Following his joining of the Byzantine Varangian Guard, Hardrada was dispatched to Asia Minor to put down a widespread piratical Arab uprising. A series of running battles continued in which Harald pushed the Arab forces back into mainland Asia. Hardrada then led a search and destroy operation deep into the Asia Minor, slaughtering thousands and taking over 80 Arab strongholds.

Battle of Ostrovo
1041 CE

While the leader of the Varangian Guard, Hardrada led the Byzantine forces against a Bulgarian army in Greece. In 1040 Peter Delyan, a native Bulgarian, led an uprising against Byzantine rule and declared himself king. Hardrada killed his foe, crushed his forces in battle and re-suppressed Bulgaria to such an extent that it remained under Byzantine rule for another 145 years.

Battle of Fulford
1035 CE

Hardrada's last great victory, the Battle of Fulford saw him land in England and defeat northern Earls Edwin and Morcar of York in a battle involving over 15,000 soldiers. Harald's masterstroke was positioning his troops so he could absorb the heavy English infantry charge before countering down his right flank and breaking the enemy's lines. This won him the city of York.

Hardrada's last hurrah

Follow the events of the last Viking king's final battle at Stamford Bridge on 25 September 1066

7 Hardrada falls
Outnumbered and out-flanked, Hardrada entered a berserker state and with a trance-like fury began rending English soldiers limb from limb until he was hit in the neck by a stray arrow then impaled by English soldiers.

4 Shield wall formed
Hardrada mobilised his army, which descended towards the bridge on the eastern bank and erected a shield wall that halted their advance. Godwinson ordered his men to lock their shields and charge.

3 Retreat across the bridge
The western Viking force fled across the bridge, with a few elite warriors holding back the English at the choke point. However, the English beat the Vikings and crossed over.

5 Brutal melee
The two lines of men, thousands strong on each side, smashed together in an epic melee brawl. The vikings tried to hold the English assault, but they were ferocious and unstoppable.

6 Shield wall fragments
The Vikings were unable to repel the English, and holes began to form in the shield wall, with the defensive line splintering. Godwinson ordered extra troops through the gap to outflank the enemy.

1 Forces deployed
The Vikings were split into two groups, with the bulk of the army on the east side of the River Derwent and a smaller force on the west. The English force approached from the south-west, so at first the English were west of Derwent.

2 Norwegians surprised
Hardrada had not been made aware of the English advance, with the possibility that the English army had marched between London and Yorkshire in just four days unthinkable. That is exactly what happened though, and the battle began with a vast infantry charge on Hardrada's force early in the morning. Hardrada was unprepared and completely overrun.

Life after Harold

Despite a succession of other Norwegian and Scandinavian kings following Hardrada's death, none of them truly had Viking in the blood, and the Viking Age ended as abruptly as it began 300 years previously. Far from the war-loving, plundering and raiding mentality that won the Vikings almost all of northern Europe and 300 years of world history, these successors had neither the will nor the military might to maintain the Viking Age and their way of life, with Scandinavian influence subsiding, and gradually becoming subsumed into wider European culture over the following decades.

For example, Hardrada's successor was Magnus Haraldsson, who was left King regent upon Harold's departure for England. However, after only reigning for three peaceful and uneventful years, he died, possibly of ergotism, leaving his brother Olaf III to take the crown, who proceeded to rule Norway till his death in 1093. However, while his rule was long, it was not Viking, with the king renouncing any offensive foreign policies and diverting funds to the defence of Norwegian borders. This pattern of defensive and peaceful ruler continued, with the only combat experienced being that of the civil wars of the 12th and 13th centuries.

The domination of Viking culture had come crashing down with Hardrada's defeat at Stamford Bridge and Europe was now entering a new, more peaceful and civilised age. For Hardrada, in his last glorious stand, had being fighting on the razor's edge of a more savage time, one that saw the lands, language and laws of Europe changed forever. The last true Viking king was dead, and with him, so too the Viking Age.

BELOW
With Hardrada's fall in battle the Viking Age was over in Europe, and a new – but related – power would soon arise

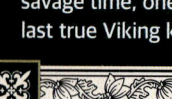

for almost 15 years and, despite his vast riches and subsequent victories, was haunted by the legacy left to him by his ancestors. Norway, he decided, must be returned once more to Norwegian hands. Setting forth from Novgorod in early 1045 CE, Hardrada journeyed back to the country of his birth, arriving in Sweden once more later on in the year. Here, Hardrada received excellent news: Norway was already back in Norwegian hands, with the illegitimate son of Olaf, Magnus the Good, sitting securely on the throne. Apparently, Cnut the Great's sons had abandoned Hardrada's much-loved Norway, and were currently fighting for control of England.

Hardrada set off immediately to Norway and, after arriving in 1046 CE and negotiating with Magnus directly, struck a deal that he would jointly rule the country in exchange for half of his immense wealth. For the next two years, both Magnus and Harald ruled Norway, holding separate courts and rarely meeting. Hardrada now had everything he could want, owning much land, ruling his country and being fabulously wealthy too. However, after two years of supposedly living an ideal life, the Viking blood within Hardrada's veins called once more, leading him into a campaign of revenge against Denmark for the death of his brother and the pillaging of his ancestral lands. As such, in 1048 CE Hardrada plundered Jutland, pillaged and burned Hedeby - the most important Danish trade centre in the entire country - and launched a colossal naval assault on the Danish royal pretender Sweyn Estridsson. This battle was the infamous Battle of Nisa, and saw Hardrada lead 300 ships against Sweyn in a conflict that left many ships on both sides 'empty'.

Despite defeating Sweyn at Nisa and successfully launching multiple Viking raids on Denmark over the next six years, Hardrada never did take the Danish throne, and due to lack of finance was forced to begrudgingly declare peace with him in 1064 CE. Now recognising that he would never reclaim the Danish throne as his own, Hardrada shifted his attentions towards another rich and historic land: England.

England had been controlled by Cnut the Great's son Harthacnut until 1042, when he died childless. As such, Edward the Confessor had crowned himself king in his absence and proceeded to rule the island nation for over 20 years. When Hardrada heard in early 1066 CE that Edward had died on 5 January, he immediately decided to launch one more glorious Viking conquest. Now 50, Hardrada must have knew that his time on Earth was coming to an end and, before he passed on to the afterlife to meet his hallowed ancestors, he needed to succumb once more to the call of his blood.

For the native English who witnessed the approach of 300 longships and 15,000 men on 8 September 1066 CE in north-east England, it must have felt like observing the coming of the apocalypse. The force was one of the greatest Viking armies ever to be assembled, and if unopposed would bring the nation to its knees. Stepping forth on English soil, Hardrada could taste the coming war, and after just 12 days he was not to be disappointed, with a 5,000-strong subsidiary English force crushed at the Battle of Fulford - see the 'Three ruthless victories' boxout for more information. Striding through the English dead, finally back in his element after years of inactivity and luxury, little did Hardrada know that this was to be his last victory.

Just five days later, his army was surprised by the fierce force of the new English king Harold Godwinson, who marched his men over 180 miles in four days to meet with the Viking warlord at the Battle of Stamford Bridge. It was a battle that would end Hardrada - for a step-by-step account of the battle, please see the 'Hardrada's last hurrah' boxout - and, as history shows, have a profound effect on the course of England and Europe going forward.

Mere weeks after defeating Hardrada at Stamford Bridge, Godwinson himself would too be defeated by the Norman duke William, in large part due to troop exhaustion from the combat and the enforced marching to and from York h had imposed on his army. As such, William became William the Conqueror, and instigated a centuries-long period of Norman rule over England, radically transforming its economy, language, architecture, law and education. Indeed, by the time the Norman presence in England had dissipated, the medieval age had long since transformed into the Renaissance, and its new, intoxicating culture, religion and science had swept away or transformed much of Europe's once-strong Viking presence.

When Harald Hardrada fell on the battlefield in England, it was more than just the flame of one great life being extinguished; it would prove to be the death of the last Viking warrior king.

LEFT Hardrada's last battle was the stuff of Viking legend: a berserker at bay, finally struck down by massed troops

> Hardrada's English victory was short-lived: in less than a week his troops were outflanked by Anglo-Saxon forces

Hardrada's lineage

Great great grandfather
HARALD FAIRHAIR
850 – 932 CE

Noted by many historians to be the first King of Norway, Fairhair became a legendary figure during the Viking Age, with his deeds relayed in numerous epic sagas. He supposedly won many battles against Norwegian opponents on his way to becoming the country's ruler, and famously had anywhere between 11 to 20 sons.

Great grandfather/grandfather
HALFDAN SIGURDSSON OF HADAFYLKE
935 – 995 CE

Little is known about Hardrada's grandfather, other than that he was supposedly Halfdan Sigurdsson, the alleged son of King Sigurd Hrise of Norway, Hardrada's great grandfather. Both Hrise's and Halfdan's lineage is unconfirmed, with only information as passed down from Icelandic sagas mentioning their link to Harald.

Father
SIGURD SYR
970 – 1018 CE

According to Icelandic sagas, Syr was a prudent and modest man who was known for hands-on approach to the management of his lands and properties. Records also indicate that he was a wealthy man, and that in 998 CE, chose to be baptised with his wife into the Christian faith.

Nephew
MAGNUS OLAFSSON
1024 CE – 1047 CE

At times both King of Norway and King of Denmark, Hardrada's nephew Magnus garnered the nickname 'Magnus the Good'. He was crowned King of Norway at 11 and King of Denmark at 18, ruling both lands until his mysterious death aged 23. Upon his death the kingdoms were split, with Hardrada taking the Norwegian crown, and Sweyn Estridsson the Danish..

William the Conqueror

Discover how incredible battlefield courage and brutal treatment of his enemies led the bastard of Normandy to become king of England

> The Bayeux Tapestry, which depicts William's conquest of England, is 50 centimetres tall and almost 70 metres long

On 5 January 1066, King Edward the Confessor of England passed away without a true heir. Upon his deathbed, the dying ruler had bequeathed his throne to the most powerful man in the kingdom, Harold Godwinson, Earl of Wessex. The day after the king's death, Harold received the acceptance of the English magnates in London and was crowned. When word travelled across the Channel to the mainland and reached one of the most powerful nobles of northern France, he flew into a rage. William, Duke of Normandy, believed he was next in the line of succession to the English throne. Harold had stolen what did not belong to him, so as the rightful heir, the duke would do whatever it took to claim what was his; thus, he would become William the Conqueror.

40 years earlier in 1026, Count Robert of the Hiémois, William's father, looked out the window of his room at Falaise Castle to see a young woman below walking alongside the River Ante. Struck by her beauty, the count ordered his servants to bring the maiden to his bedroom that night. Her name was Herleva, the daughter of a lower-class tanner. Even if the stories were true that the count fell deeply in love with her, Herleva never became more than a concubine to Robert.

However, their relationship became much more complicated the following year on 5 August when Duke Richard III of Normandy suddenly became ill and died. As Richard's younger brother, Robert acted quickly to seize the duchy. With the support of several powerful Norman magnates, it did not take long before he became Duke Robert I. Around the same time, Herleva found out she was with child. By the end of 1028, William, the bastard son of the new duke, was born. Since Herleva was a commoner, Robert could not marry his mistress. Therefore, the duke did not immediately recognise his son, so William spent his first years at his mother's home in Guibray. Although still unwilling to make Herleva his wife, Robert eventually gave her proper respect by arranging her marriage to minor noble Herluin de Conteville. She was given even more honour when her son was proclaimed as the duke's legitimate heir; yet, this also meant that William was separated from his mother at a very young age and brought to live with his father at the castle of Falaise.

At the age of seven, William endured another traumatic experience when his father died while on a pilgrimage to Jerusalem in 1035. Luckily for William, Robert cleverly took the precaution to have his nobles accept his son as the ducal heir to Normandy before he left on his journey. Yet the latest duke was still deprived of his parents for the most part, with little contact with his mother, which would have left a major impression upon his childhood. Robert also appointed several close relatives, trusted advisors and loyal companions to take care of William and run the kingdom in his absence. These men, such as William's great uncle Robert, the Archbishop of Rouen, gladly fulfilled

William the Conqueror

"Harold had stolen what did not belong to him, so as the rightful heir, the duke would do whatever it took to claim what was his"

The Battle of Hastings

1 Solid English phalanx
The front lines of the English infantry were formed into an impressive shield wall upon Senlac Ridge. The steep incline of the hill helped the tight phalanx withstand a full frontal assault from the Norman infantry and cavalry.

2 William killed?
The stalemate ended when panic rapidly spread throughout the Norman ranks because they believed William had been slain. The left flank broke in response so the Duke rode to the front with his helmet raised to rally the troops.

3 Unplanned feigned flight
The English who pursued the fleeing Normans soon found themselves cut off and were easily picked off by the more mobile Norman cavalry. Witnessing its effectiveness, William continued to utilise the tactic several more times throughout the battle.

4 Death of Harold
The battle raged on for most of the day. As the English casualties increased, the shield wall gradually diminished, allowing the Normans to attack the exposed English flanks. Even when badly injured, Harold fought until he was finally cut down.

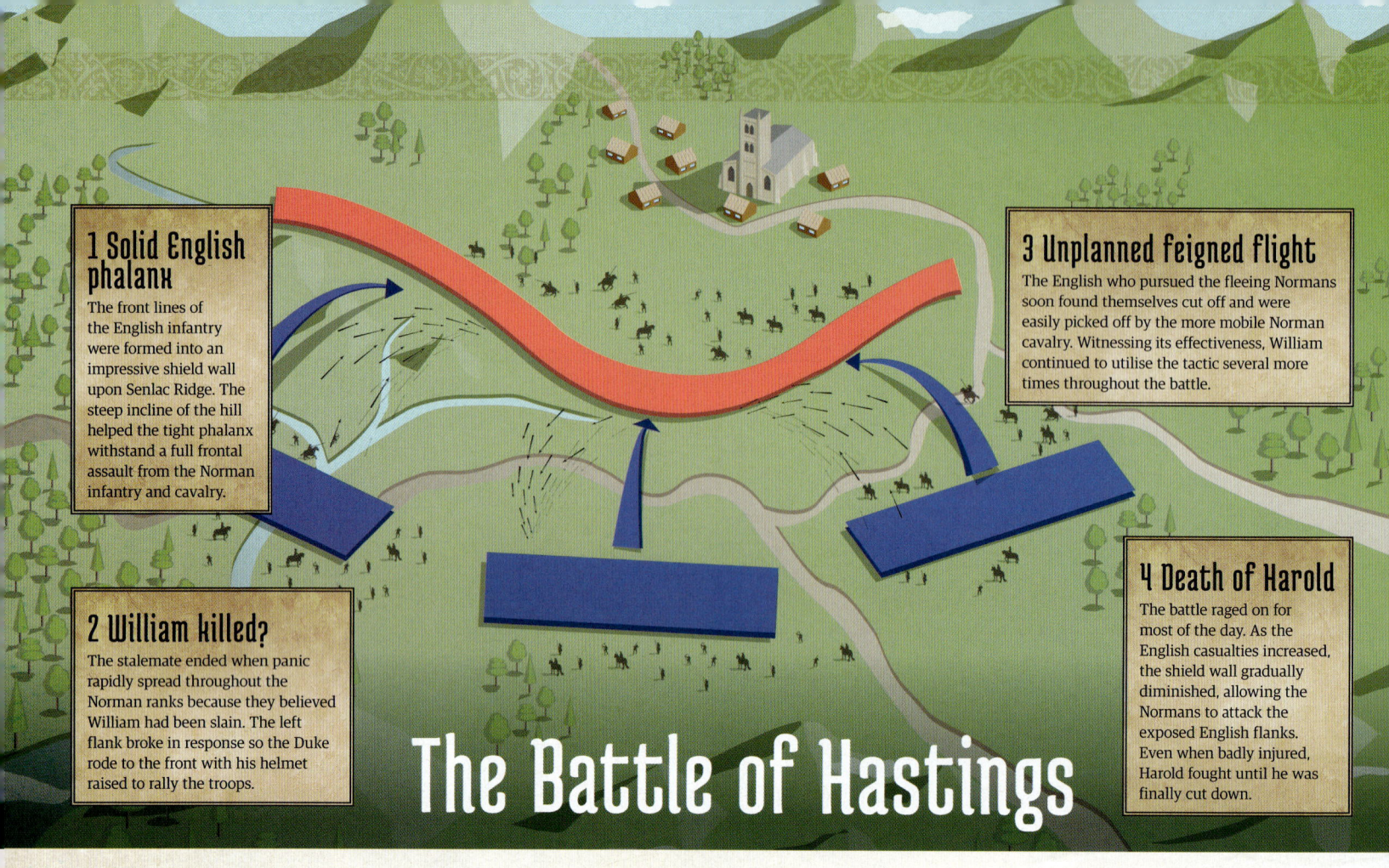

their roles and when it became clear that Duke Robert was never going to return, they continued to do so until William came of age.

Yet it was surprising that Duke William survived his adolescence. Archbishop Robert managed to effectively rule the dukedom until his death in 1037. Afterward, Normandy devolved into anarchy as the aristocracy exploited the minority of the duke to carry out blood feuds with rival families, increase their lands or even plot to remove William to claim the duchy as their own. Many of the latter group were members of the duke's own family, known as Richardides for their descent from the Norman Duke Richard I. Because of this ancestry, several of the Richardides believed their claim to the ducal throne was much greater than that of 'William the Bastard'.

As William matured, he was surrounded by violence as several of his guardians were murdered. In late May 1042, the duke slept in the castle of Vaudreuil. To protect him, William's steward, Osbern, lay beside him. Neither woke as an assassin crept into the room and stood over their bed. William woke to find the throat of his guardian slit open. As the young duke grew accustomed to the deaths of those closest to him, he managed to survive unharmed.

In 1046 and 1047, William faced the greatest threat to his life yet as the Richardides carried out a full-blown rebellion. However, the young duke acted quickly and effectively. William not only gathered his loyal vassals, but also reached out to his lord, King Henry I of France, and appealed for his help. Before long, William and Henry gathered a large enough force to confront the rebel army. At the Battle of Val-ès-Dunes in 1047, the King of France crushed the Norman dissidents, but William would continue to suppress minor revolts for the next three years.

By the early-1050s, William was in his twenties and had not required the supervision of a regent for some time. Free to act with full ducal authority, William quelled rebellions throughout Normandy and then began to look outward. This brought him into conflict not only with the formidable count of Anjou, Geoffrey II Martel, but also with King Henry, who began to fear the growing power of the young duke. Throughout the violent clashes William participated in at home and abroad, the duke quickly began to build a reputation as a fierce warrior capable of leading rapid assaults and laying effective sieges. Tales of the brutality inflicted on those who crossed him spread terror among his enemies.

The prisoner
When William demands Count Guy hand over Harold into his custody, the count obeys him and delivers the English noble to Castle Eu

One of the most horrific instances of William's vengeance took place at Alençon in 1052. After his failed surprise assault on the town, the defenders on the wall yelled down insults about his illegitimate birth and beat animal skins with sticks to mock the fact his grandfather was a tanner. Once he managed to break into the town, William captured 36 of the men and punished them by ordering for all of their feet and hands to be severed. For the rest of his reign, William continued to order similar mutilations carried out on his worst enemies, however, his favoured punishment was imprisonment for several years; many times even for life.

Although nothing can excuse the terrible actions of the duke, his bravery in war and deep devotion to his close friends and family allowed him to attract numerous loyal followers. When his younger half-brothers, the sons of his mother, reached the proper age, William gave them land and prestigious titles. Odo became the bishop of Bayeux, while Robert was made the count of Mortain. Both men became staunch supporters of William and, together with other trustworthy lieutenants like Roger II of Montgomery and William FitzOsbern, they formed a tight-knit group around the duke who helped him greatly to achieve his goals. Yet the most important relationship of the duke was with his wife Matilda, daughter of Count Baldwin V of Flanders. At first,

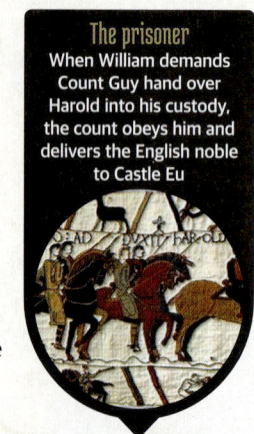

William the Conqueror

LEFT
A depiction of William the Conqueror arriving in England in 1066

Contenders for the throne

Harold Godwinson
Earl of Wessex
Harold was a powerful English magnate. He was present while Edward lay on his deathbed and bequeathed his throne to Harold. The Witan of Anglo-Saxon nobles accepted his coronation.

William
Duke of Normandy
Before Edward the Confessor became king in 1042, he lived in exile at the court of the dukes of Normandy. To show his appreciation, he supposedly promised to leave the throne to Duke William.

Harald Hardrada
King of Norway
The Norwegian king had the weakest claim to the throne and was merely attempting to exploit a great opportunity to further his wealth and prestige through the conquest of rich and prosperous England.

BELOW
The Battle of Hastings proved pivotal for William the Conqueror

Brothers in arms William leaves Normandy to carry out a campaign against Duke Conan II of Brittany and forces Harold to accompany him

The oath Back in Normandy, Harold swears an oath to uphold William's claim to the English throne over holy relics in Bayeux, most likely under duress

111

6 ways William changed Europe

1 The conquest of England strengthened the bond between the British Isles and the European mainland considerably, especially in religious institutions.

2 The effectiveness of knights at the Battle of Hastings and the domination by Norman armies led to an increased use of cavalry in warfare in England.

3 William introduced the English to the advanced continental castle fortifications by constructing many of his own to help his army occupy the country.

4 William's gradual but effective purge of nearly all Anglo-Saxon secular and lay magnates led to an almost entirely Norman aristocracy in England.

5 The Norman process of rebuilding the religious structures of England created a unique Anglo-Norman style for most local churches.

6 In one of his many tense conflicts with the papacy, William successfully defended the rights of Norman dukes to select their own bishops.

the union was a mere strategic alliance with one of the most powerful magnates of northern France. However, over time the couple fell deeply in love with one another. William remained completely devoted to her for the rest of his life and even trusted her with some of the most important positions in his lands.

The increasing power of Duke William led to the joint invasion of Normandy by his two major rivals, Count Geoffrey and King Henry, in 1053. Divided in two, the invasion forces failed utterly as one army was defeated at Mortemer and the other retreated in response. The rivals made another attempt in 1057, but William crushed the allied army at the Battle of Varaville. Within a few years the campaigns ceased, for both Henry and Geoffrey died. With his main adversaries gone and stability finally reached within his duchy, William was no longer forced to defend his lands and was free to go on the offensive.

Shortly after the death of Count Herbert II of Maine on 9 March 1062, William led his first major conquest over the deceased magnate's territory. The duke claimed that Herbert had named him as his heir to the county so from that justification, William claimed the land of a vassal of his enemy, the count of Anjou, by 1064. Two years later, the duke made similar statements to justify the conquest of a much greater prize than the county of Maine.

In either 1064 or 1065, Harold Godwinson, Earl of Wessex, crossed the English Channel and accidentally landed in the territory of Count Guy of Ponthieu. Guy ordered his men to capture the wealthy Anglo-Saxon noble and imprisoned him, along with his retinue, in the castle of Beaurain. Once word reached William of Harold's condition, the duke immediately seized the opportunity. William forced his vassal, Guy, to release Harold and bring the English earl to him. Once in his custody, William did all he could to manipulate Harold into helping him attain his most ambitious prize, the throne of England.

As a child, the king of England, Edward the Confessor, was forced to flee his country and live as an exile in the Norman court of his uncle, Duke Richard II. Danish King Cnut invaded England in 1016 and eventually claimed the English crown, removing Edward's family from the succession. Then in 1042, Edward was allowed to return home and regain his birthright, the throne of England. A major reason for the king's return was the support given to him by the powerful Godwin family of Wessex. In gratitude, the new king bestowed lands and titles upon Harold and his brother; this alliance was then strengthened considerably in January 1045, when Edward married Harold's sister Edith, thus making the two men brothers-in-law. Since Edward had family connections and owed huge debts to both William and Harold, both men believed they should be the primary heirs of the old king who had no heir. With Harold held hostage, William attempted to use a combination of flattery and threats to get the English magnate to not only accept his claim, but also help him attain the English throne upon the death of the ageing Edward. Therefore, Harold accompanied William on his invasion of Brittany in 1064, and when they returned to Normandy, Harold swore an oath of fealty to William. Certain he had achieved his goal, William let the Earl of Wessex return to his island.

Upon Edward's death, it became clear that Harold made his oath to William under duress and thus considered it completely invalid. He also quickly cemented his claim to the throne with the support of several witnesses to Edward naming Harold as his heir, along with earning the election of the Witan, a council of English nobles.

Harold is crowned
On 6 January 1066, Harold ascends to the throne of England after the funeral ceremony of the deceased King Edward the Confessor

The English may have accepted King Harold II, but William did not. William was certain that he had promised the throne to him; he would not forget that fact, nor would he let the English.

The situation looked bleak for Harold later in 1066. While William gathered a large invasion force and enormous fleet of 700 ships, King Harald Hardrada of Norway decided to exploit the vulnerability of England and invade as well. However, Harold and his Anglo-Saxon

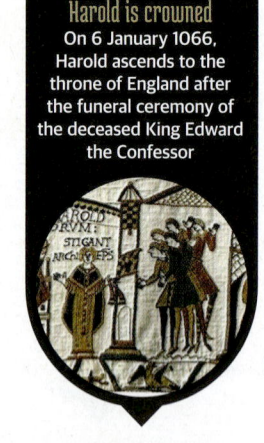

William the Conqueror

LEFT
Some accounts claim William's forces pillaged the English countryside after his invasion

RIGHT
Built in 1068, Warwick Castle still stands tall today

French continental rivals

Henry I
King of France
After helping William keep control over his duchy at the Battle of Val-ès-Dunes in 1047, Henry soon became threatened by the new duke's growing power. The king led two unsuccessful invasions of Normandy in 1053-4 and 1057 to try and subdue his rival.

Fulk IV le Réchin
Count of Anjou
Once he seized the county from his brother, Geoffrey III, in 1068, Count Fulk of Anjou secured an alliance with King Philip against William. Beginning in the early-1070s, he attempted to reclaim Maine on several occasions, but failed.

Philip I
King of France
Threatened by his vassal as king of England, Philip made alliances with Anjou and Flanders to counter the strength of Normandy. Philip's insult infuriated William so much that his enthusiasm to seek vengeance at Mantes led to his death.

The crossing
William leads his army to the coast where the soldiers embark on 700 ships to cross the Channel

ABOVE
An artwork depicting Harold II swearing fealty to William of Normandy

113

Inside a Norman Castle

The castles William introduced were designed to be impenetrable

Main tower
The castle's main tower is the last strong haven in its defence. A potent symbol of power, taking custody of it was very important

Chapel
Was usually located under the armoury and above the ladies' bedrooms and the provisions storage. It welcomed religious affairs

Bakery
The internal supply of bread was essential during any long sieges, so it was essential for the keep to bake its own

Drinkable water
The rainwater cistern, channelled from the wall, guaranteed automatic storage even during droughts and hard times like sieges

Blacksmith
The forging of metals for arms and armour was carried out here by the blacksmiths. The carpenters worked around and nearby them

The Battle of Hastings
The Norman knights charge uphill to reach Senlac Ridge where they attempt to break through the solid shield wall of the Anglo-Saxon infantry

Treasure hall
The lower part of the main tower, under the principals' kitchen and bedrooms, was used to store the castle owner's wealth

Throne hall
The centre of the castle's authority, in this impressive hall orders were dictated and guests were received

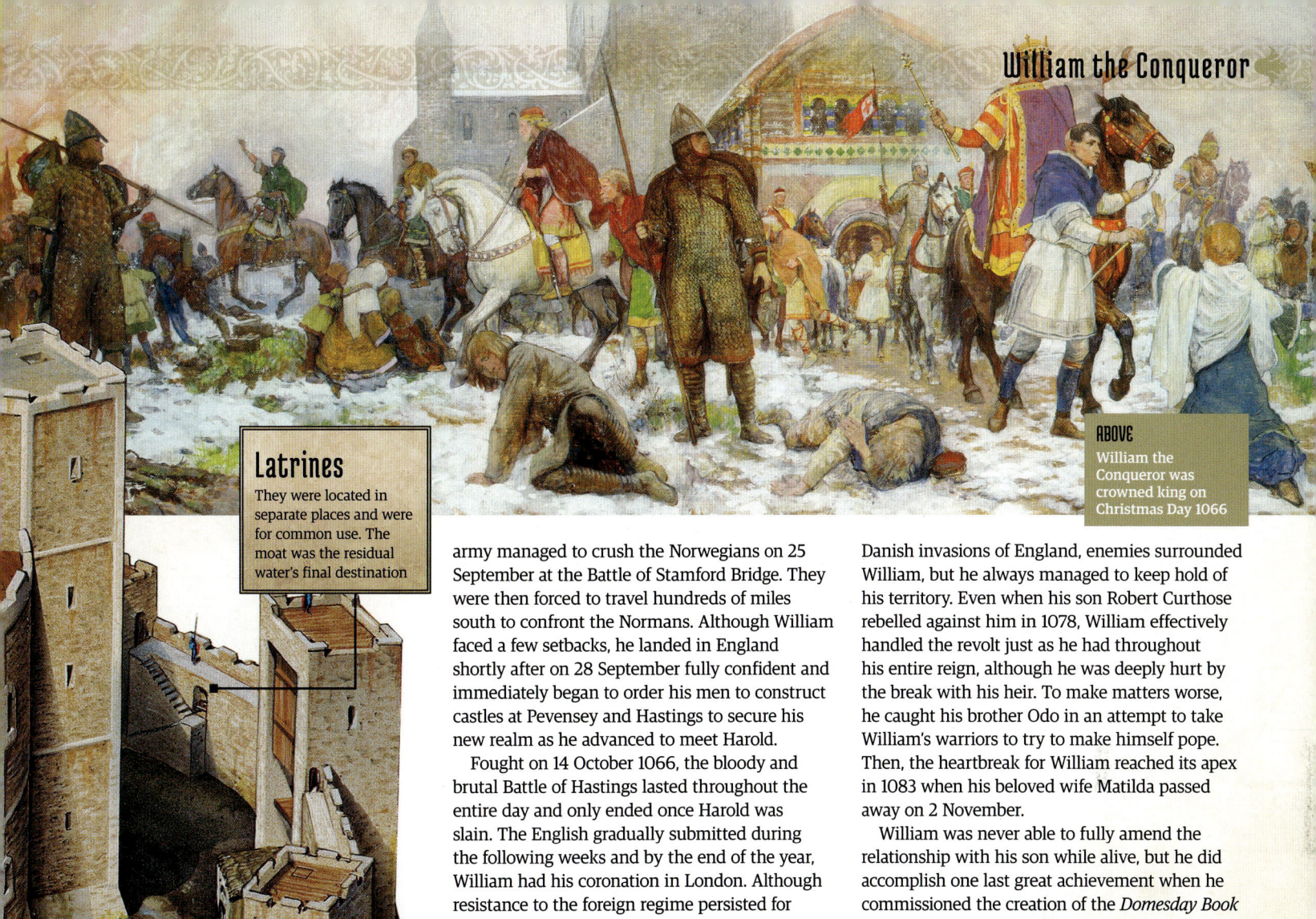

William the Conqueror

ABOVE William the Conqueror was crowned king on Christmas Day 1066

Latrines
They were located in separate places and were for common use. The moat was the residual water's final destination

Dungeons
The prisoners suffered captivity and torture in these facilities, generally located at the top of a tower or below ground

army managed to crush the Norwegians on 25 September at the Battle of Stamford Bridge. They were then forced to travel hundreds of miles south to confront the Normans. Although William faced a few setbacks, he landed in England shortly after on 28 September fully confident and immediately began to order his men to construct castles at Pevensey and Hastings to secure his new realm as he advanced to meet Harold.

Fought on 14 October 1066, the bloody and brutal Battle of Hastings lasted throughout the entire day and only ended once Harold was slain. The English gradually submitted during the following weeks and by the end of the year, William had his coronation in London. Although resistance to the foreign regime persisted for several years, the English never again formed a united front. To quell the revolts, William initiated a process of extreme fortification building and slowly removed the English from positions of power to be replaced by Norman men of his choice, like his trusted friends Roger II of Montgomery and William FitzOsbern.

When those methods did not work to subdue the north, the new king was once again forced to use his last resort; horrific violence. In 1070, King William reached his breaking point trying to put down rebellions in the region, so he decided to turn it into a wasteland. Many people were slaughtered, churches were ransacked, crops were destroyed and livestock killed. In the end, those that survived succumbed to starvation, leaving very little of the population who could ably revolt.

For the last two decades of his life, William's days as a conqueror were over. With the Scots supporting the remaining English rebels, the re-emergence of Anjou and the kingdom of France, as well as the continual threats of Danish invasions of England, enemies surrounded William, but he always managed to keep hold of his territory. Even when his son Robert Curthose rebelled against him in 1078, William effectively handled the revolt just as he had throughout his entire reign, although he was deeply hurt by the break with his heir. To make matters worse, he caught his brother Odo in an attempt to take William's warriors to try to make himself pope. Then, the heartbreak for William reached its apex in 1083 when his beloved wife Matilda passed away on 2 November.

William was never able to fully amend the relationship with his son while alive, but he did accomplish one last great achievement when he commissioned the creation of the *Domesday Book* in 1085. To take stock of his kingdom William had the most comprehensive survey of any preindustrial civilisation in the world created, giving a priceless, incredibly in-depth view of 11th-century England. Shortly after this grand act, William attempted to once again prove his martial prowess through the conquest of the Vexin. Old age had taken its toll, leading King Philip I to insult William with a remark equating him to a pregnant woman because of his increasing corpulence. Sent into his typical rage, William stormed Mantes in retaliation. But as his men burned the town, William's enthusiasm led his horse to rear up and slam the pommel of his saddle into his stomach.

On 9 September, King William succumbed to the intense internal bleeding caused by the injury. In one final act of reconciliation, his son Robert was still allowed to succeed him as Duke of Normandy. However, the conquests he fought so hard to attain were divided as the Kingdom of England went to his younger son, William Rufus. Therefore, the short-lived Empire of Normandy died with the formidable ruler who created it.

Harold Godwinson is killed
Once Harold is slain the Anglo-Saxon resistance ceases and the English army flees from the battlefield with the Normans in pursuit

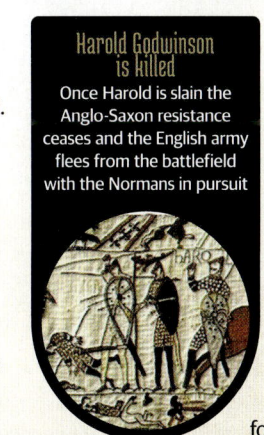

115

Clash of Crowns 1066

When three kings rose to claim Edward the Confessor's crown, England's fate would be decided with steel and blood

Harold Godwinson's army was exhausted. Just weeks ago they had claimed victory against a Nordic invasion in a long, brutal battle at Stamford Bridge. They had marched approximately 400 kilometres with their weapons, gear and armour. It was during this march that Harold had received news of William of Normandy's landing on the shore of Pevensey. With a great deal of his men still in the north, Harold had no choice but to push onwards to meet the infamous Norman Bastard in combat. As Harold stood on the hill overlooking what is today the town of Battle, near Hastings, with his banners wafting in the morning breeze, he observed his army – they were wearied, sick, and still nursing wounds from Stamford. But there was nothing he could do, these were the men with whom England's fate rested, for William was coming for his crown whether he was ready or not.

Edward the Confessor (so called for his piety) had reigned for 23 years, fairly long for an Anglo-Saxon monarch, but he had not borne any heirs. In fact, Edward had turned this to his advantage. With so many ambitious nobles jostling for position, he used the inheritance of his kingdom as a diplomatic tool, and one that, he was likely aware, he would not personally feel the repercussions of. However, this was all fated to come to a head: towards the end of 1065, Edward became severely ill and fell into a coma. He briefly regained consciousness long enough to place his widow and his kingdom under the protection of his brother-in-law, Harold Godwinson, before passing away.

There is much debate over what exactly Edward meant by 'protection', and whether he was actually bestowing Harold his kingdom or just employing him to help the next man who would rule it. However, these arguments are, on the whole, irrelevant. Although he was free to nominate a man of his choosing, it wasn't an Anglo-Saxon king's right to decide who would be his successor; that responsibility instead fell to the Witenaġemot, the king's council of advisers. The Witenaġemot had already begun to debate who would be the right man for the job before Edward's death. They decreed that he needed to be English, of good character and of royal blood – and luckily for Harold, he ticked all these boxes.

Despite a tumultuous family history, Harold had steadfastly and loyally served Edward for years,

> Harold Godwinson and William both had claims to the English throne; Harald Hardrada was an opportunist

Clash of crowns: 1066

117

ABOVE
The Battle Of Hastings by Frank Wilkin shows William being offered the crown of England from Harold's body

Harold Godwinson's sister was the wife of Edward the Confessor, and his family were one of England's most powerful

eventually becoming a trusted adviser. As Earl of Wessex, he was already one of the most powerful men in the country, and he had proved himself multiple times in battle. Edward had also married Harold's sister and his family had ties with Cnut the Great. Perhaps most importantly, Harold held esteem with the elite of English society – he was well liked and reliable (his father was also the richest man in England). In fact, Harold's worthiness was so unanimously agreed by the Witenaġemot that no other names were even suggested. William and other contenders would later claim that Harold had stolen the throne, even that he had murdered Edward to do it, but Harold didn't 'grab' the kingdom, he was gifted it.

Harold seemed to be the perfect king: he was tall, eloquent and a skilled soldier, however, his reign would be one of the most turbulent and infamous in English history. Someone else had his gaze fixed on Edward's throne, and when Harold was crowned, William, duke of Normandy, was furious. William fervently believed England was his by birthright as he and Edward were distant cousins. He also claimed that some years earlier Edward had stated that he was his successor, and this message had been carried to him by none other than Harold Godwinson himself.

The legitimacy of this story is in some dispute; certainly Edward likely promised the kingdom to a host of nobles throughout his reign, but William did not seem to understand that England was not Edward's to give. No other action in Edward's reign indicates that he had chosen William to be his heir. The duke, however, was convinced that the kingdom was his, and set his sights on usurping the ambitious upstart, Harold Godwinson. He immediately made plans to invade England, building a fleet of around 700 ships to carry his army across the English Channel.

Initially William struggled to gain support for his invasion, but when he revealed that Harold had apparently sworn upon sacred relics that he would support William's claim, the church became involved. The finances and nobles provided by the church swelled William's pockets and his army. Harold, well aware of the fiery duke's intentions, assembled his army on the Isle of Wight. However, William did not come. Unfavourable winds halted the would-be conqueror's ships and, with his provisions running low, Harold disbanded his army and returned to London.

Harold probably knew that William would be coming sooner rather than later, however, he had another issue to deal with – sibling rivalry. On the same day as Harold's return to London, Harald Hardrada of Norway, also known as the last great Viking king, landed his fleet of longships on the mouth of the Tyne and joined up with Tostig Godwinson, Harold's younger brother.

Tostig had previously ruled the kingdom of Northumbria, an earldom stretching from the Humber to the Tweed, but his brutal and heavy-handed tendencies had caused him to grow increasingly unpopular with his subjects. In 1065, the thegns of York occupied the city, killed Tostig's officials and outlawed the man himself. The rebels were so furious with Tostig that they demanded Edward exile him, however, it wasn't the king who met with them, but his loyal advisor Harold. Using his strong influence, Harold had Tostig officially outlawed. But the younger brother was not one to take things lying down, and at a meeting of the king and his council, he intervened and publicly accused Harold of conspiring against him. Harold, already aware of the dire state of England at the time, and the imminent threat of William, exiled his own brother. It is likely that Harold took the action he did against his own kin to ensure peace and loyalty in the north – an impossibility with Tostig in charge. However, his younger brother resented him for it. As he fled England and took refuge in Flanders, Tostig let fantasies of vengeance consume him and began to plot his return. Tostig knew he didn't have enough power alone to topple his older brother, so he set about making powerful alliances; he even sought an alliance with William before finally striking gold with King Harald III of Norway.

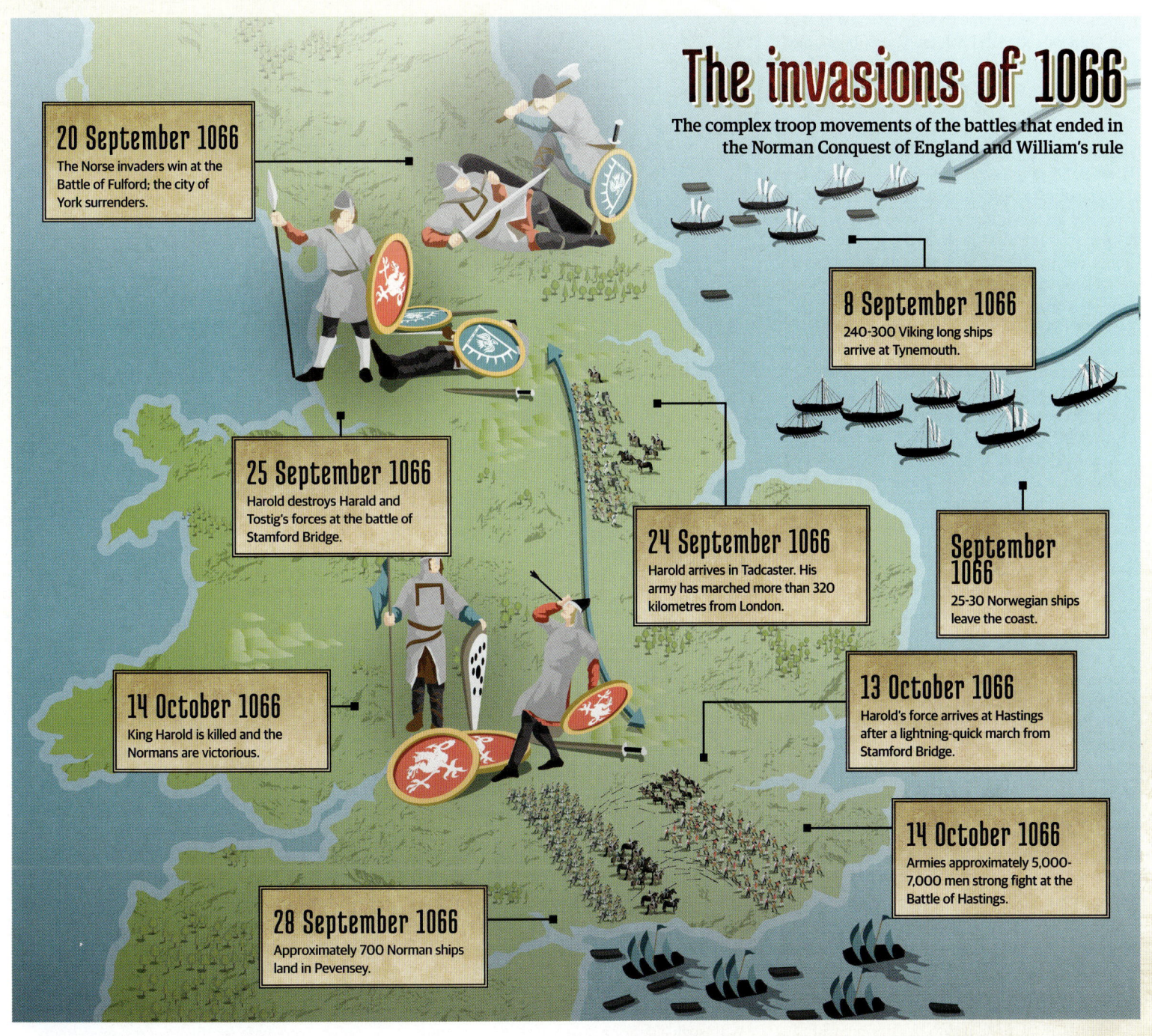

Clash of crowns: 1066

The invasions of 1066
The complex troop movements of the battles that ended in the Norman Conquest of England and William's rule

20 September 1066
The Norse invaders win at the Battle of Fulford; the city of York surrenders.

8 September 1066
240-300 Viking long ships arrive at Tynemouth.

25 September 1066
Harold destroys Harald and Tostig's forces at the battle of Stamford Bridge.

24 September 1066
Harold arrives in Tadcaster. His army has marched more than 320 kilometres from London.

September 1066
25-30 Norwegian ships leave the coast.

14 October 1066
King Harold is killed and the Normans are victorious.

13 October 1066
Harold's force arrives at Hastings after a lightning-quick march from Stamford Bridge.

14 October 1066
Armies approximately 5,000-7,000 men strong fight at the Battle of Hastings.

28 September 1066
Approximately 700 Norman ships land in Pevensey.

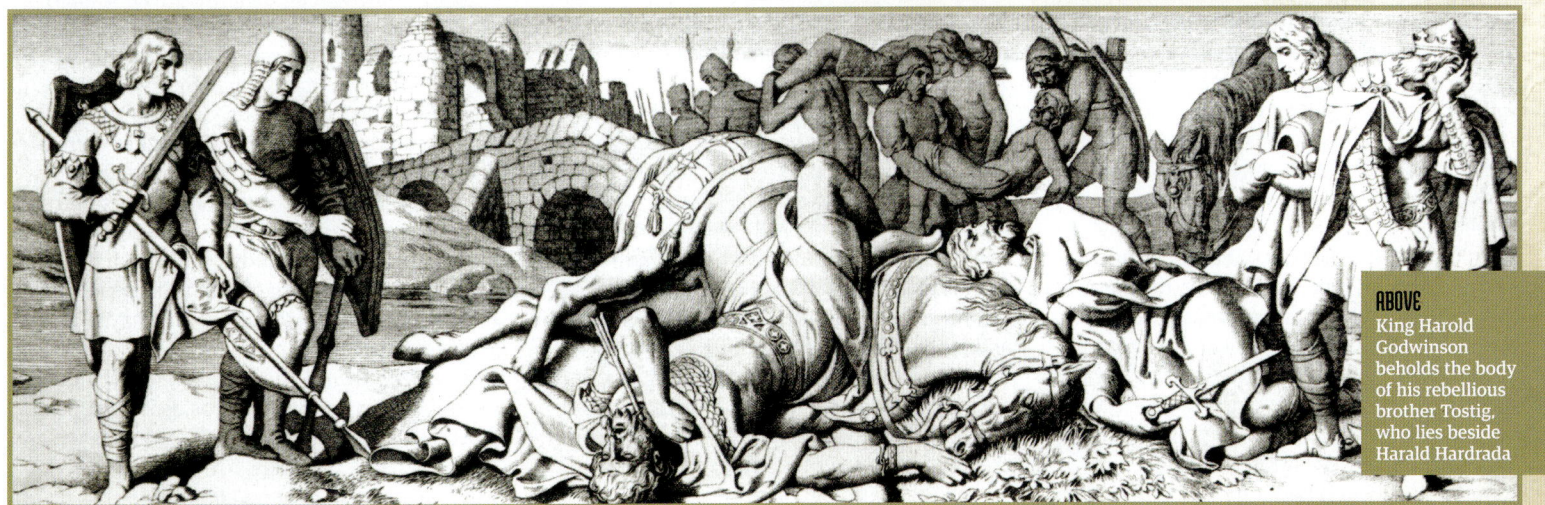

ABOVE
King Harold Godwinson beholds the body of his rebellious brother Tostig, who lies beside Harald Hardrada

119

Hardrada's claim to the throne was even looser than William's. England had previously been ruled by the king of Denmark, Harthacnut, who made an agreement with Magnus, the king of Norway, that if one of them died without an heir, the other would inherit his throne. Harthacnut died childless, so Magnus took the crown of Denmark. However, Edward the Confessor was crowned king of England in his absence. Harald was Magnus's uncle and his co-king, so believed England belonged to him. The idea that his kingdom was being ruled by the son of one of Edward's advisers was outrageous for the Nordic king, and he set his sights on expanding his kingdom.

Whether Hardrada made an agreement with Tostig before setting sail or not is unknown, but either way Hardrada departed in August and met up with Tostig on 8 September. It was clear that Tostig needed Hardrada's help with the invasion, he had a mere 12 ships to Hardrada's 240 minimum. Hardrada spent some time sacking and burning coastal villages, but he then set his sights on York, Tostig's old stomping ground. Hardrada had the men and Tostig knew the lay of the land better than anyone, so together they made an alarming foe to be reckoned with.

The two men who would have to face this united force were Edwin and Morcar, the ealdormen of Mercia and Northumbria. They knew of Tostig and Hardrada's advances through their lands and had already gathered their forces, approximately 5,000 strong, to take down the invaders in what they expected to be a straightforward battle. The armies finally met at Fulford, on the outskirts of York.

The scene of the clash was wet and sodden marshland. The English positioned themselves with the River Ouse on their right flank and the swampy area on their left, a tactic that relied on both flanks holding their own against the invaders. Hardrada, meanwhile, had to think quickly – the English army had confronted him before he could assemble all his men, and many of them were hours away, so he had to be cunning with his deployment. He placed his less experienced troops to the right and kept his best troops with him on the riverbank. The English had caught wind of Harald's delays and so struck quickly. They charged forward against the Norwegian line and, immediately overwhelmed, the Nordics were pushed all the way back to the marshlands.

Hardrada then saw his chance. As the English advanced, he sent the bulk of his troops to sweep around them in a pincer movement, trapping them against the ditch and separating them from the other English flank. As more Norwegians arrived, they opened up a third front against the Anglo-Saxons. The combat in the marshland was brutal and ferocious, with both armies fighting frantically through the thick, sludgy mud. However, the English were now outnumbered by the Norse men, many of them were unable to escape the ditch and those that managed to climb out fled for their lives. Eventually there were so many English bodies strewn across the ground that the invaders could advance without getting their feet wet.

With such a definite defeat, York was promptly surrendered to Hardrada and Tostig with the promise that they would not force entry. This was accepted, perhaps because the duo did not wish to subject their new capital to looting. Instead they arranged that various hostages would be handed over at Stamford Bridge, some 11 kilometres away, which is where the two men chose to retire. The battle at Fulford would not only be Hardrada's last victory, but it would be the last time a largely Scandinavian army would defeat the English.

Little did the victorious invaders know, Harold and his men had been marching day and night from London. Despite the imminent threat of an invasion by William, Harold was so determined to repel the invaders that he and his army achieved the astounding feat of travelling almost 300 kilometres in just four days. Tostig and Hardrada were likely expecting Harold's eventual rebuttal but neither of them had any comprehension of the monumental journey that the king and his army had embarked on, and neither of them suspected a thing as they headed to Stamford Bridge to collect their additional hostages.

Spirits were high for the invaders' men; many of them had even left their armour behind on their ships, and some were simply relaxing in the meadows or out hunting when they spied Harold's men. From the south streamed a horde of Anglo-Saxons fully armed and ready for battle. There is no doubt that the English would have been exhausted, but the Norse were completely and utterly unprepared. According to one account, a brave man rode up to Hardrada and Tostig before the battle began, offering the rebellious brother his earldom if he would turn on the Nordic king. Tostig then asked the rider what Hardrada would get, to which the rider replied, "Six feet of ground… or as much more as he needs, as he is taller than most men." Impressed by the rider, Hardrada asked Tostig for his name; Tostig revealed that it was none other than Harold himself.

RIGHT
Harold was the last Anglo-Saxon king of England

Harald Hardrada believed that his fiscal relationship with the Norwegian throne gave him a right to England's crown

Clash of crowns: 1066

The Battle of Fulford

Often forgotten or ignored, this was a pivotal point in the invasions of 1066 and, ultimately, in deciding England's fate

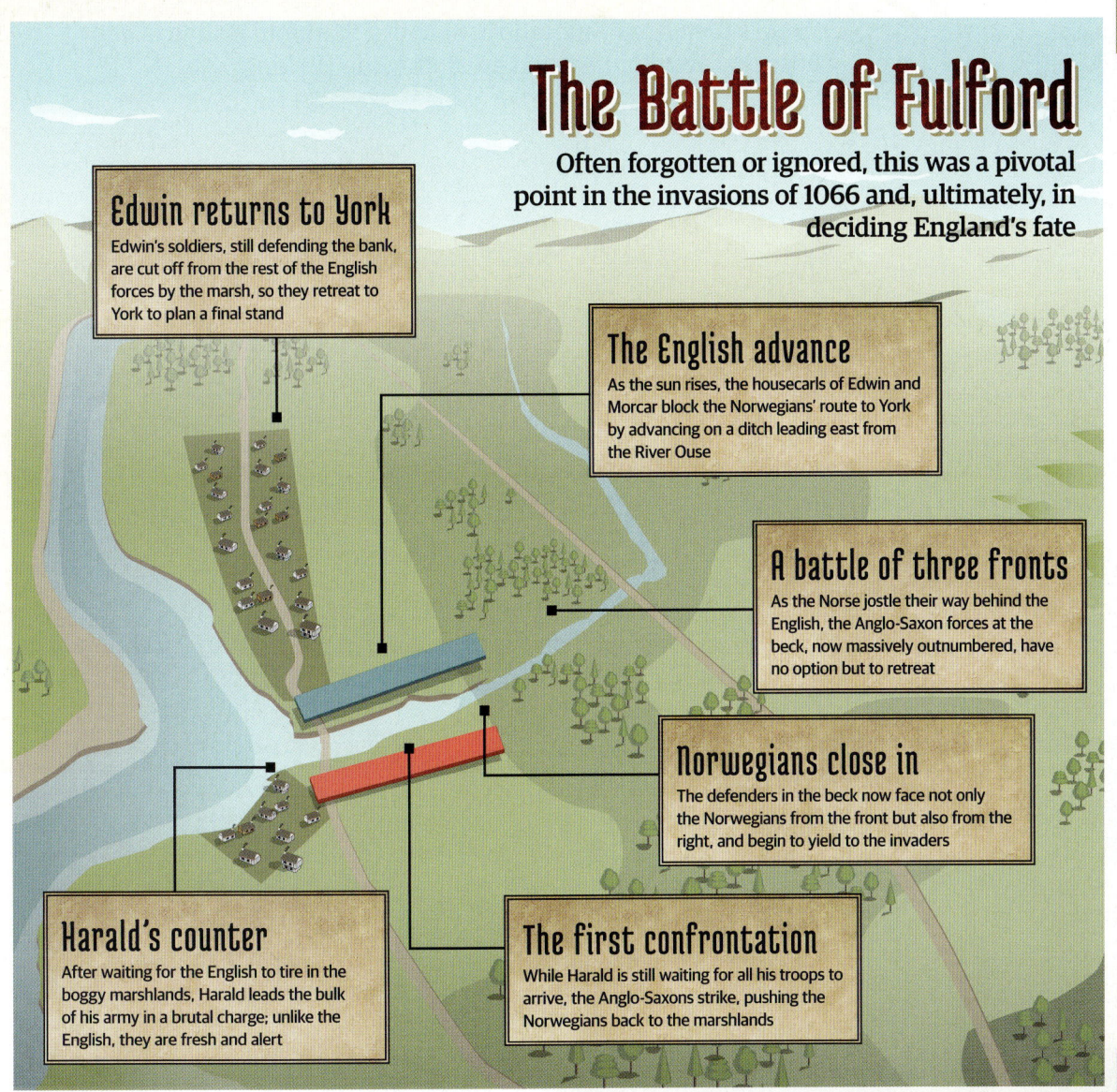

Edwin returns to York
Edwin's soldiers, still defending the bank, are cut off from the rest of the English forces by the marsh, so they retreat to York to plan a final stand

The English advance
As the sun rises, the housecarls of Edwin and Morcar block the Norwegians' route to York by advancing on a ditch leading east from the River Ouse

A battle of three fronts
As the Norse jostle their way behind the English, the Anglo-Saxon forces at the beck, now massively outnumbered, have no option but to retreat

Norwegians close in
The defenders in the beck now face not only the Norwegians from the front but also from the right, and begin to yield to the invaders

Harald's counter
After waiting for the English to tire in the boggy marshlands, Harald leads the bulk of his army in a brutal charge; unlike the English, they are fresh and alert

The first confrontation
While Harald is still waiting for all his troops to arrive, the Anglo-Saxons strike, pushing the Norwegians back to the marshlands

NORWEGIANS

COMMANDERS: Harald Hardrada, Tostig Godwinson
TROOPS: Approx 10,000, of which 6,000 were deployed
KEY UNIT: Experienced warriors positioned on the firm ground near the riverbank
STRENGTHS: Strong starting position, which gave Harald the higher ground, and sheer force of numbers
WEAKNESSES: None
CASUALTIES AND LOSSES: Approximately 750

VS

SAXONS

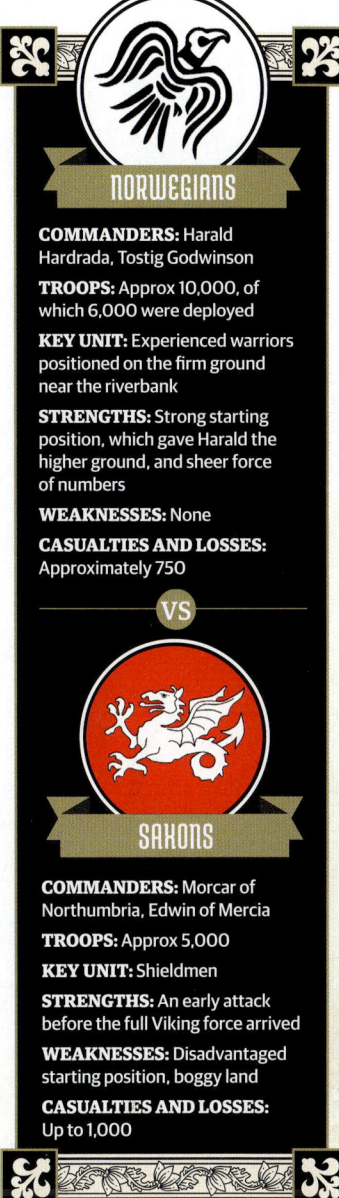

COMMANDERS: Morcar of Northumbria, Edwin of Mercia
TROOPS: Approx 5,000
KEY UNIT: Shieldmen
STRENGTHS: An early attack before the full Viking force arrived
WEAKNESSES: Disadvantaged starting position, boggy land
CASUALTIES AND LOSSES: Up to 1,000

Whether this account is true or not, neither party was in the mood for deals or truces, this was to be decided once and for all the old fashioned way. Once the scrambled Nordic forces gathered together, they deployed in a defensive position. The English cut through the invaders on the west side of the River Derwent with ease, however, the bridge itself presented them with problems. They would have to pass through the vulnerable chokehold to continue their advance, and according to the *Anglo-Saxon Chronicle*, one man stood in their way. A huge Norse axe-man guarded the narrow crossing of the bridge alone, holding back the entire English army. He brutally cut down anyone who approached, until eventually he was defeated by an English soldier who floated downstream in a barrel and thrust his spear up through the bridge.

This delay gave the Nordics time to assemble a triangular shield wall, and this was where the real battle began. The tired but determined Anglo-Saxons clashed repeatedly against the Nordic shields, hammering them over and over again. The fighting lasted for hours, with the advantage

RIGHT
The battle devolved into a brutal clash against the Norse shield wall

The Battle of Stamford Bridge

Harold's men finally met the invaders at Stamford Bridge in a battle that would make and break the English king

Surprise attack
After agreements were made to hand over hostages to Hardrada at Stamford Bridge, Harold's troops take the Norwegians totally by surprise by streaming in from the south

The shield wall goes up
Rushing to put on their fighting gear, the invaders hastily put up a defensive shield wall on the west side of the bridge

The shield wall breaks
Overwhelmed by the sheer number of English, the Norwegian shield wall is broken; survivors flee across the bridge

The Anglo-Saxon wave
The Norwegians have time to put up a shield wall but as the English pour across the bridge, brutal fighting wages. Ultimately, the shield wall falls and Tostig and Hardrada join the fallen

The chokehold
According to the Anglo-Saxon Chronicle, a lone axe-man stays behind to block the narrow crossing of the bridge, killing 40 Englishmen until he is finally wounded

Delayed reinforcements
Norwegian reinforcements, led by Orre, arrive. They briefly cause considerable damage to the English flank, but the Anglo-Saxons regroup and defeat them. Survivors drown in the rivers as they rush to escape

NORWEGIANS vs SAXONS

COMMANDERS: Harald Hardrada, Tostig Godwinson
TROOPS: Approx 9,000, 3,000 of which arrived late
KEY UNIT: Axe-men
STRENGTHS: An almost impenetrable shield wall
WEAKNESSES: Unprepared, many men were without armour
CASUALTIES AND LOSSES: Approx 6,000

COMMANDER: Harold Godwinson
TROOPS: Approx 15,000, significantly more than the norwegian force
KEY UNIT: The professional housecarls
STRENGTHS: The element of surprise
WEAKNESSES: Forced to cross the narrow choke-point of the bridge
CASUALTIES AND LOSSES: Approx 5,000

changing hands many times throughout. However, the Nordics' lack of armour cost them dearly and the ranks began to fall. Hardrada -a giant of a man and the last Viking king - was slain by an arrow to his windpipe and Tostig too met his end in the land he had fought for his entire adult life. Even reinforcements led by Eystein Orre, who had rushed all the way from Riccall, were not enough to quash the Anglo-Saxon army. This force, known as Orre's storm, was so fatigued that it is said many collapsed and died of exhaustion as they reached the field. Although they were able to briefly hold back the defenders, they too fell

Clash of crowns: 1066

> The victory at Stamford Bridge gave Harold's forces a morale boost, but ultimately sapped their strength for Hastings

ABOVE
The name 'Hardrada' was actually a nickname Harald earned meaning 'Hard Ruler'

BELOW
A silver penny showing a contemporary, if rather faded, depiction of Harold Godwinson

victim to Harold's determination, and then they fled for their lives.

For Harold, Stamford Bridge was an epic victory and cemented his position as a strong and reliable English king. However, it would also forever be intrinsically linked to his downfall. Just three days after Harold's success, another would-be king landed on his shores. William had finally arrived.

Harold feared William for good reason; the Duke of Normandy had a fearsome reputation, and this was not all bravado. William had been born to his father's mistress, and his illegitimate status had plagued him throughout his life. Commonly referred to as 'The Bastard' by his enemies, William was a man who, from the age of seven or eight, had faced constant criticism and challenge because of who he was. Throughout his life he had to fight for everything he had. William had grown up in a land gripped by war and chaos, he had been jostled between ambitious nobles who wished to use him for power, and from his earliest years of rule he had to squash constant rebellions. In spite of this, through sheer determination and a clever marriage to Matilda of Flanders, William 'The Bastard' had managed to consolidate power in Normandy against all odds.

This whole experience had made the duke hard, tough and fiercely determined to succeed - there wasn't much in life that could hold William back, and Harold claiming the throne that was rightfully his was not something he could just stand by and accept. The two men were no strangers - William had saved Harold when he was held hostage and the two men proceeded to fight side by side. Harold was even recorded as having rescued two of William's soldiers from quicksand. Together the two defeated William's enemy, Conan II, and William thanked Harold for his services with a knighthood. If William's claim was true, and Harold did swear an oath to the duke, then it is easy to understand why this hot-blooded warrior was furious at Harold's betrayal. Once a friend, he was now an enemy, and William knew only one way to deal with enemies: war was in his blood, he was moulded by it.

William's timing was disastrous for Harold but hugely beneficial to himself. The duke had enough time to build a wooden castle at Hastings, raid the surrounding area and thoroughly prepare his force for the oncoming storm. Harold, meanwhile, was anything but prepared. The English king had left a great number of his forces in the north, and the men he did bring had to march south from London in approximately a week. By the time they reached Senlac Hill, near Hastings, the troops were absolutely exhausted.

Harold knew his surprise tactics would not work here, so he set up his army in a defensive position atop the hill. Each of his flanks was protected by marshy land that would make an enemy advance difficult. He positioned his strongest fighters, the housecarls, at the front of his shield wall. At 9am, the trumpets rang out and the Normans moved. The archers attacked first, sending arrows raining over the English men. However, Harold's position on the hill, and his soldiers' sturdy shields, prevented much damage.

William decided that if the archers couldn't do it then he would have to act quickly. He sent his army forward in three groups, with himself riding through the middle, the papal banner billowing above his head. The attackers rode hard, but they were still unable to break the Anglo-Saxon shield wall, and they retreated once more. Harold's men, excited by what seemed like another victory, gave chase to the fleeing Normans. It was at this point that a rumour began to circulate that William had been killed. Sensing a lull in morale, the duke pushed back his helmet and rode among his men, commanding them to attack the English who had broken away from the hill. With a revitalised Norman force, the English were overwhelmed, and few who descended the hill survived.

At around midday, there was a lull in the battle, with both sides resting and replenishing their strength, it was then that William decided to change tactics. Witnessing the victory of the previous English pursuit, he decided to draw them out again. When the battle resumed, the Norman cavalry thundered forward into the shield wall.

123

The fighting was brutal and desperate, with Harold's own brothers cut down in the melee, but still the shield wall held. As ordered, the Normans retreated and once more Harold's men pursued them down the hill. All at once William's soldiers turned and attacked the English.

The battle raged on until 4pm, and with the English numbers now depleted, the shield wall grew shorter and weaker. William saw his opportunity and sent his whole army up the hill, while the archers continued to shoot, and this time it worked. The shield wall finally broke and the Normans wreaked havoc, cutting down Harold's remaining housecarls and, at some point, the cursed king himself.

It is of some debate if Harold died as a result of an arrow to the eye or was felled with a sword, as the famous Bayeux Tapestry depicts both. What we do know is that his death had a tremendous effect on his men. Leaderless, the Anglo-Saxons began to flee the field into the woods behind. However, Harold's loyal soldiers remained by his body and fought until the end.

Hastings was not an easy-won battle. William too lost a great number of his men, and bodies were still found on the hillside years later. When Harold's mother requested that William return her son's body to him, he refused, stating that Harold should be buried on the shore of the land he sought to guard. Still rumours persisted that Harold had not died at all, but instead had gone into hiding, to one day return and reclaim his land. The people's love for Harold was still strong, and although William may have won the battle, the war to truly become the ruler of England was one that would wage for years to come. William's victory at Hastings was decisive, but it was not the final one: it would take further years of brutal subjugation, changing the land, its language and inhabitants, for the Normans to triumph.

ABOVE This rather anachronistic 13th-century manuscript shows Harold being killed by William at Hastings

What If?
With the clash of three kings, England faced three fates

JANUARY 1066
William prepares for invasion
Believing himself the rightful heir, William gathers an army of noblemen and a fleet of 700 vessels.

SEPTEMBER 1066
Harald Hardrada's forces invade
Also believing the crown to be rightfully his, Norse king Harald Hardrada invades England, sailing up the Ouse to land in Yorkshire.

20 SEPTEMBER 1066
The Anglo-Saxons are defeated at Fulford
Harald is confronted by Harold's earls and they do battle at Fulford. The Saxons are outnumbered and the Norwegians claim York.

25 SEPTEMBER 1066
Anglo-Saxons triumph at Stamford Bridge
After marching his men North, Harold faces the invaders and defeats them at Stamford Bridge, killing Harald Hardrada.

14 OCTOBER 1066
Harold Godwinson defeated at Hastings
After William's fleet crosses the Channel, Harold faces them at the Battle of Hastings. But the English are tired and ultimately lose to the invaders.

25 DECEMBER 1066
William crowned king
William initially faces opposition but after capturing London he is finally crowned king. Rebellions would continue to rock the country for years after.

25 SEPTEMBER 1066
Nordic triumph at Stamford Bridge
Despite being ambushed by the Saxons, the Nordic forces triumph over Harold's men, and Harold himself is killed.

14 OCTOBER 1066
Nordics defeat Normans
Hardrada's forces are amply prepared to face William's, and after a brutal battle, the Norman would-be conqueror is defeated by the Norwegians.

20 SEPTEMBER 1066
The Saxon earls triumph at Fulford
Harald Hardrada and Tostig are defeated at Fulford by the northern earls, Edwin and Morcar.

28 SEPTEMBER 1066
Godwinson's troops march south
Aware that William's ships are incoming, Godwinson marches his army south from London to meet them.

29 SEPTEMBER 1066
Saxons defeat the Normans
With a well-rested army, Harold is able to fight off William and the Norman invaders at Hastings; Harold is celebrated as a hero.

KEY
— REAL TIMELINE
— KING HARDRADA TIMELINE
— KING GODWINSON TIMELINE

Clash of crowns: 1066

The Battle of Hastings
The pivotal clash that would forever alter the destiny of medieval England and cement 1066 as one of the most important dates in English history

Harold sets up his base
Harold's army establishes a position on Senlac Hill, then sets up a fence of sharpened stakes along a ditch. The king orders his men to remain in this position no matter what

Right on target
William's archers fire before and after the assaults and Harold is hit and killed, most commonly believed to be by an arrow to the eye. Leaderless, the English forces flee

The Normans retreat
William's men are met by a barrage of spears and axes, and are forced to retreat. A rumour quickly spreads that William has been killed

The Saxons move
English forces break away from their position and pursue the invaders. William's presence on the field spurs a counterattack and the English are overwhelmed

The battle begins
William orders his archers to shoot into the Saxon shield wall, when this fails his spearmen and cavalry lead an assault

A tactic emerges
William sends his cavalry to the shield wall then draws the Saxons into more pursuits by feigning flights. Still the shield wall does not break

NORMANS vs SAXONS

NORMANS
- **COMMANDER:** William of Normandy
- **TROOPS:** Unknown, approx 7,000-12,000
- **KEY UNIT:** Norman cavalry
- **STRENGTHS:** An experienced leader and rested troops
- **WEAKNESSES:** Weak starting position: the English were positioned on the top of the hill with their flanks protected
- **CASUALTIES AND LOSSES:** Unknown but the figures were heavy. However, not as high as the Saxon losses

SAXONS
- **COMMANDER:** Harold Godwinson
- **TROOPS:** Unknown, approx 5,000-13,000
- **KEY UNIT:** The king's bodyguards, or 'housecarls'
- **STRENGTHS:** The tremendously deadly battle-axes
- **WEAKNESSES:** Significant losses recently endured at the battle of Stamford Bridge, lack of cavalry
- **CASUALTIES AND LOSSES:** Approx 50 per cent of the force

---

10 OCTOBER 1066 — Normandy falls into disarray
Left leaderless, with a king in his infancy, Normandy descends into civil strife that will continue for two decades.

1068 — A kingdom at peace
Through careful negotiation, Harold is able to contain the raids by the Celts and strike a deal with Wales and Scotland, leaving the island divided, but at peace.

1072 — England grows strong
Harold exploits France, claiming many strategic ports without issue. He also forms strong bonds with Scandinavia, making him a powerful figure on the globe.

1200s — The Northern Empire expands
With its strong trade routes, the Northern Empire of Europe steadily expands. This trade network spans all the way from the Americas to the eastern Mediterranean.

1300s — Southern Europe falls
After many wars between the countries of southern Europe, the Northern Empire fully dominates Europe, with Scandinavian culture engulfing the Latin influences.

1069-70 — William strikes back
In response to the Northern rebels, William carries out a series of bloody campaigns known as the Harrying of the North.

1080s — The Tower of London is built
In an effort to secure control over England, William orders the construction of many castles, the most famous being the White Tower of the Tower of London.

1085 — The *Domesday Book* is created
To further secure the land holdings of himself and his vassals, William orders the creation of the *Domesday Book*.

9 September 1087 — Death of William
While on a military campaign, William falls ill and dies. His death begins a war between his two sons for control of his kingdoms of England and Normandy.

1135-54 — Civil war reigns supreme
After the death of William's fourth son, Henry I, a succession crisis sparks a brutal civil war known as the Anarchy.

21 NOVEMBER 1066 — Hardrada is crowned
In a country that has previously been ruled by Scandinavian kings, Hardrada is able to persuade any would-be rebels to accept his rule.

1080s — England gets Norse
Nordic influences take hold of England: the language becomes heavily Nordic, and the battle-axe becomes the primary weapon of choice.

1110 — Norway grows strong
With Norway growing stronger, it faces its enemy France in a bloody war that wages for years. Finally the Nordic forces claim victory and the spoils are divided.

1200 — The Nordic Empire expands
The Nordic Empire becomes one of the most formidable in Europe; this powerful axis crushes the influence of the Catholic Church and its associated nations.

1390 — America is found
Due to the strong British/Norse partnership, the Nordics land in America, claiming the land long before their Spanish rivals. The country is quickly developed.

125

The Norman Conquests

The Normans didn't just conquer England. These ex-Vikings carved out kingdoms and principalities through Europe and beyond

The king, Charles the Simple, lord of the Franks, stood waiting. Before him, the nominated Northman hesitated. What was he waiting for? It was all straightforward. The king had signed a treaty with the Northmen, ceding them the territory north of the River Epte to the coast, in return for their allegiance and conversion to Christianity. He had stood godfather to Rollo, the leader of the Northmen, at his baptism, and received his pledge of loyalty by taking the Northman's hands in his own. Now, to really underline who was in charge, one of the Northmen just had to kiss the king's foot. So why was he hesitating?

But before Charles could turn to his bishops, who had suggested the foot-kissing, to ask about the delay, the Northman, one of Rollo's chief warriors, finally bent down. Put instead of putting his lips to the king's foot, he grasped the foot and raised it, forcefully, up to his face. Taken by surprise, the king toppled over backwards.

This was in 911. Having raided extensively in France and Britain, Rollo and his band of Vikings settled around Rouen in the lower reaches of the River Seine, sea raiders turned land wardens through signing the Treaty of Saint-Clair-sur-Epte. By 933, the Northmen, or Normans, had expanded the territory under their control to encompass almost all of the historic territory of the Duchy of Normandy. The Northmen had quickly abandoned their previous language, Old Norse, learning French, and just as quickly they forswore their old pagan gods, becoming devout and determined Christians instead.

But while the Normans had adopted some key aspects of Frankish civilisation, they retained many characteristics from their days as sea raiders, most notably restlessness and tactical cunning. But this amalgamation of Christian and Viking cultures produced something new: a reckless courage that often enabled them to face and defeat enemies who had apparently overwhelming numerical superiority. For the pagan Vikings, raiding and conquest was a matter of business: unless victory was practically certain they preferred to withdraw and fight again another day. But the Normans, fired by a new faith, really believed that by courage and daring, and with God's aid, they could overcome any odds. So they set out to do so.

In this they were greatly aided by adopting the military practices of the Franks. Once sea raiders, the Normans quickly became the most skilled knights in Europe, training their sons in the art of cavalry warfare from a young age. Having learned to move quickly and strike fast, the Normans adopted and refined the art of castle building, starting with the simple motte and bailey that could be thrown up quickly in newly conquered territory, through to the great stone keeps that enabled them to dominate these territories.

Pilgrimage united the Norman love of adventure, their restlessness and their religious

The Norman Conquests

> The Normans adopted Christianity with gusto, becoming a key force in the Crusades and building iconic churches

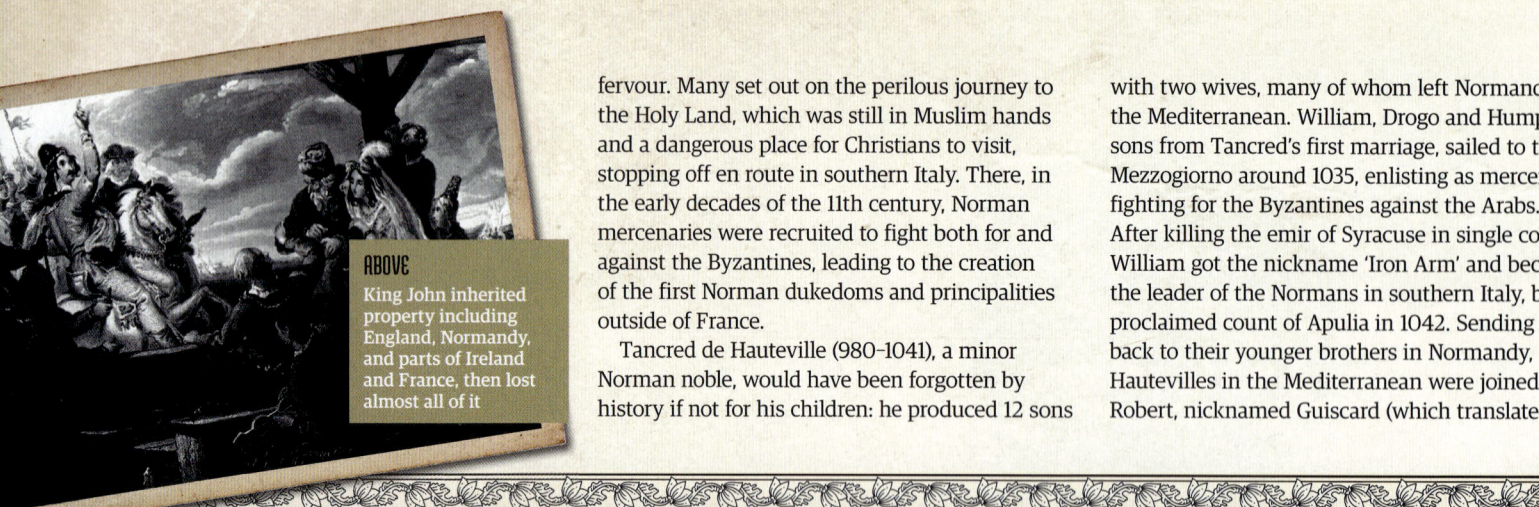

fervour. Many set out on the perilous journey to the Holy Land, which was still in Muslim hands and a dangerous place for Christians to visit, stopping off en route in southern Italy. There, in the early decades of the 11th century, Norman mercenaries were recruited to fight both for and against the Byzantines, leading to the creation of the first Norman dukedoms and principalities outside of France.

Tancred de Hauteville (980-1041), a minor Norman noble, would have been forgotten by history if not for his children: he produced 12 sons with two wives, many of whom left Normandy for the Mediterranean. William, Drogo and Humphrey, sons from Tancred's first marriage, sailed to the Mezzogiorno around 1035, enlisting as mercenaries fighting for the Byzantines against the Arabs. After killing the emir of Syracuse in single combat, William got the nickname 'Iron Arm' and became the leader of the Normans in southern Italy, being proclaimed count of Apulia in 1042. Sending word back to their younger brothers in Normandy, the Hautevilles in the Mediterranean were joined by Robert, nicknamed Guiscard (which translates as

ABOVE
King John inherited property including England, Normandy, and parts of Ireland and France, then lost almost all of it

Abolitionist Normans

Anglo-Saxon England was famous for two exports above everything else: hunting dogs and slaves. Slavery was deeply embedded in Anglo-Saxon society, with at least ten per cent and maybe as much as 30 per cent of the population enslaved. The Anglo-Norman chronicler, William of Malmesbury, noted how slave traders would buy up people throughout England then export them. But William was writing about something that had ceased. By his time, some 60 years after the Conquest, the Norman kings had outlawed slavery. Historians, a sceptical bunch, used to think that the Normans ceased using slaves because rent-paying tenants were more profitable. But while that might have accounted for agricultural slaves, many female slaves were taken and kept as concubines. Moreover, England, with a vibrant economy and currency, continued the practice. It seems that the Normans abandoned slavery because of the moral scruples of their churchmen, who were in the vanguard of a great reform movement in the Church, and their ability to convince the nobility that slave taking and slave trading was wrong. Lanfranc, the Archbishop of Canterbury from 1070 onwards, was vociferous in his condemnation of slavery and William, Lanfranc's pupil as a little boy, complied. The ban was not immediately effective – a Church council condemned slavery in 1102 – but by the time William of Malmesbury wrote in the 1120s, slavery had effectively ceased in England.

ABOVE
Excavated manacles showing the chains Vikings used to restrain people taken to be sold as slaves

Timeline

Defining moment
Treaty of Saint-Clair-sur-Epte 911
Charles the Simple decided to deal with the problem of Viking raiders by giving the raiders who had established a camp on the lower reaches of the Seine title to the land in return for their swearing allegiance to him, converting to Christianity, and their acting as wardens to prevent other Vikings sailing up the Seine to raid Paris. In return, the Vikings, led by their chief, Rollo, received the land between the River Epte and the coast. Rollo, now Count of Rouen, expanded the territory under his control and by 933 the Duchy of Normandy was established.

Defining moment
Sicily 1061
Five years before their duke in Normandy ventured across the English Channel, Robert Guiscard and his younger brother Roger sailed across the Straits of Messina and landed in Sicily, taking the strategically vital city of Messina, which commands the straits, unopposed after Roger took the garrison by surprise. Palermo fell ten years later and by 1085 they had the island under their control. It was an extraordinary achievement that highlighted the particular Norman combination of daring, cunning and determination. But it was their conduct as rulers that marked Robert and, especially, Roger as exceptional: they welded a disparate and often antagonistic population into a brilliant new culture.

1002
● Marrying up
Emma, sister to the Duke of Normandy, married Æthelred, the king of England, bearing him two sons, and fatefully linking the English crown to the Dukes of Normandy.

1017
● Normans head south
The first Norman knights arrived in southern Italy on pilgrimage. They found a fractured political situation that welcomed effective mercenaries, so they stayed and gradually began to establish themselves there.

1066
● The other conquest
The most famous date in English history led to the death of the last Anglo-Saxon king of England, the wholesale replacement of the Anglo-Saxon aristocracy by Normans and their allies, and the devastation and depopulation of much of the north, as William savagely repressed rebellions.

1098
● Crusade
Many Normans answered the pope's call for a crusade to take back the Holy Land. Among the crusaders was Bohemund, great-grandson of Tancred, whose sons had established the kingdom of Sicily. Bohemund became the ruler of the principality of Antioch.

The Norman Conquests

'the resourceful' or the less complimentary 'fox' or 'weasel') in 1047 and their youngest brother, Roger, in 1057. The two younger brothers conquered Calabria by 1060.

In Rome, the attitude of Pope Leo IX had swung from welcoming these potential allies against the Byzantines to fearing them, then to accommodating them at arm's length in the hope that their taste for conquest could be directed elsewhere. And just across the Straits of Messina, in Muslim-controlled Sicily, there was the ideal target. So in 1061, Robert and Roger de Hauteville began the first Norman conquest of a large island. It took them 30 years to gain complete control of Sicily; the fortunes of war did not always run according to plan. But with Sicily taken, the brothers proved wise and skilful rulers. Robert took southern Italy, while Roger became the first Count of Sicily. In Sicily, Roger declared Arabic an official language alongside Latin, Greek and Norman French, and recruited Muslim and Greek administrators to help govern the island. Under Roger and his son, Roger II, a unique Norman-Byzantine-Arab culture developed and flourished, producing architectural masterpieces such as the Cappella Palatina in Palermo and Monreale Cathedral, as well as fostering translations of classical works from Greek into Latin and developing and improving the agricultural techniques brought by the Arabs to Sicily. The island became a byword for good administration and brilliant culture.

From Sicily, the Normans established bases along the coast of north Africa, putting garrisons into major towns from 1146 onwards although their presence there was short-lived, coming to an end in 1180. Normans also served as mercenaries for the emperors of Byzantium, while Bohemund, one of the leaders of the First Crusade (1095-1099), was the great grandson of that minor Norman noble, Tancred de Hauteville, who had sent his sons south fifty years earlier. Bohemund became Prince of Antioch, one of the Crusader states and the most easterly of the Norman conquests.

After their famous conquest of England in 1066, the most obvious direction for the Normans in Britain was west, into Wales. William installed some of his most powerful barons on the borderlands of the Marches, and gifted them great local power and almost complete autonomy. The Marcher lords became a power in their own right, and a threat to the English crown for the next few centuries, with Roger Mortimer even deposing Edward II in 1326 and becoming the ruler of England in all but name for three years. However, the Welsh threw back the initial Norman invasion and retained their independence until Edward I's conquest two centuries later.

Within the British Isles, the greatest area of Norman influence, after England, was Ireland. Norman forces first landed in Ireland in May 1169, called to act as mercenaries for the king of Leinster. More Normans arrived in 1170, most notably Richard de Clare, 'Strongbow'. While the invasion proved militarily successful, bringing Ireland into the Angevin Empire, the Anglo-Normans who arrived in Ireland, after initially settling in ethnic enclaves called 'the Pale' in the east of the country (hence the expression 'beyond the pale'), married and merged into Irish culture, eventually becoming as committed to the country as the native Gaels. Norman influence in Ireland can be traced through the many surnames having Norman roots, including all those with the prefix 'Fitz', Barry, Burke, D'Arcy, Treacy and Lacy. What had started out as a roving group of Viking raiders and pillagers had come a long way, and forever altered the history of Europe and the wider world.

Warrior countess

Among the contending powers in southern Italy were the Lombards. To bring them onside, Robert Guiscard contracted marriage with Sikelgaita, the daughter of the Prince of Salerno, putting aside his previous wife to do so. It proved a splendid match. Sikelgaita was a remarkable woman, who had already studied at the medical school in Salerno, which was pioneering the treatment of illness, and according to the chroniclers she was as remarkable for her size and strength as for her learning. Once married, Sikelgaita took part in military campaigns – Robert trusted her to conduct the siege of Trani – and was one of his most trusted councillors. At the Battle of Dyrrachium in 1081, Sikelgaita took to the field in full armour and rallied the Norman troops when they were retreating, upbraiding them for their cowardice before taking a spear and leading them back to the battle. She bore Robert eight children. Following Robert's death in 1085, Sikelgaita was dowager duchess of their domains until 1090.

Defining moment
Shipwreck 25 November 1120
King Henry I set out from Normandy for England. Among the flotilla of vessels was the White Ship, carrying Henry's only legitimate son, William. Soon after it set sail, the White Ship hit a rock and sank, drowning all but one aboard. With only his daughter, Matilda, left to him, Henry made her his heir and arranged her marriage to Geoffrey Plantagenet, Count of Anjou. But when Henry died in 1135, many of his English barons refused to accept Matilda as their ruler, taking Stephen of Blois, Henry's nephew, as king. This began 20 years of civil war, known as the Anarchy.

Defining moment
Fall of Normandy 1204
From his father, Henry II, and his brother, Richard the Lionheart, King John inherited possessions that included England, Normandy, half of Ireland, Anjou and Aquitaine – a veritable empire. But possessing neither the political flair of his father nor the ferocious military skill of his brother, but with a surfeit of Plantagenet vices, John proceeded to lose almost all of it to King Philip Augustus of France. By 1204, even Normandy was gone.

May 1169 — Invasion of Ireland
The first Norman mercenaries arrived in Ireland to support the deposed king of Leinster. In 1171, Richard de Clare, 'Strongbow', arrived, followed six months later by King Henry II. The long English involvement in Ireland had begun.

1174 — Beauty in stone
In Sicily, King William II commissioned the building of the great cathedral in Monreale. The church blended Norman, Byzantine and Muslim architectural styles into a dazzling synthesis.

1191 — Conquest of Cyprus
Almost by accident, while on his way to the Holy Land as part of the Third Crusade, Richard the Lionheart conquered Cyprus, establishing Anglo-Norman rule on the island that ensured the island remained in Christian hands for centuries afterwards.

1194 — Loss of Sicily
The last Norman ruler of Sicily, William II, died childless, leaving the kingdom to his aunt, Constance, wife of the Holy Roman Emperor Henry VI. A rebellion by other claimants was suppressed and in 1194 the Kingdom of Sicily passed into the rulership of the House of Hohenstaufen.

History of the Dark Ages

Future PLC Quay House, The Ambury, Bath, BA1 1UA

History of the Dark Ages Editorial
Editor **April Madden**
Art Editor **Jon Wells**
Head of Art & Design **Greg Whitaker**
Editorial Director **Jon White**
Managing Director **Grainne McKenna**

All About History Editorial
Editor **Jonathan Gordon**
Art Editor **Thomas Parrett**
Editor in Chief **Tim Williamson**
Senior Art Editor **Duncan Crook**

Contributors
Edoardo Albert, Wayne Bartlett, Charles Ginger, Jack Griffiths, Frances White and Jon Wright

Cover images
Joe Cummings, Adobe Stock (AI), Shutterstock

Photography
All copyrights and trademarks are recognised and respected

Advertising
Media packs are available on request
Commercial Director **Clare Dove**

International
Head of Print Licensing **Rachel Shaw**
licensing@futurenet.com
www.futurecontenthub.com

Circulation
Head of Newstrade **Tim Mathers**

Production
Head of Production **Mark Constance**
Production Project Manager **Matthew Eglinton**
Advertising Production Manager **Joanne Crosby**
Digital Editions Controller **Jason Hudson**
Production Managers **Keely Miller, Nola Cokely, Vivienne Calvert, Fran Twentyman**

Printed in the UK

Distributed by Marketforce – www.marketforce.co.uk
For enquiries, please email: mfcommunications@futurenet.com

History of the Dark Ages First Edition (AHB6978)
© 2024 Future Publishing Limited

We are committed to only using magazine paper which is derived from responsibly managed, certified forestry and chlorine-free manufacture. The paper in this bookazine was sourced and produced from sustainable managed forests, conforming to strict environmental and socioeconomic standards.

All contents © 2024 Future Publishing Limited or published under licence. All rights reserved. No part of this magazine may be used, stored, transmitted or reproduced in any way without the prior written permission of the publisher. Future Publishing Limited (company number 2008885) is registered in England and Wales. Registered office: Quay House, The Ambury, Bath BA1 1UA. All information contained in this publication is for information only and is, as far as we are aware, correct at the time of going to press. Future cannot accept any responsibility for errors or inaccuracies in such information. You are advised to contact manufacturers and retailers directly with regard to the price of products/services referred to in this publication. Apps and websites mentioned in this publication are not under our control. We are not responsible for their contents or any other changes or updates to them. This magazine is fully independent and not affiliated in any way with the companies mentioned herein.

FUTURE Connectors. Creators. Experience Makers.

Future plc is a public company quoted on the London Stock Exchange (symbol: FUTR)
www.futureplc.com

Chief Executive Officer **Jon Steinberg**
Non-Executive Chairman **Richard Huntingford**
Chief Financial Officer **Sharjeel Suleman**

Tel +44 (0)1225 442 244

Part of the

ALL ABOUT HISTORY
bookazine series

Widely Recycled | ipso. Regulated